Meir Today, Gone Tomorrow

The old A50 on Meir bank on a snowy winter's day.
The trees to the right are in front of Meir House, a large house which dominated the landscape.

Nicholas Cartlidge

For Jose Anne,
and Madeleine Ann
and Tim
and Eleanor
and Ben
and Philippa

ACKNOWLEDGEMENTS

A book like *Meir Today, Gone Tomorrow* could not have appeared had it not been for the assistance, interest & determination of many people in its writing.

I would like to thank Eric Clutton, for his eye witness account of life at Meir Aerodrome; Ken Oakley, whose prodigious efforts helped uncover the legends and mysteries of Meir Golf Club and its course. I am obliged to Peter and Jackie Sutherland in Ottawa, Canada and Dr Leslie Sutherland in Sudbury, Canada for their valuable help: Rosie Atherton at the John F Kennedy Library, Boston, Massachusetts, USA; Tony & Gill Swift; Len Wrench, ex-Home Guard for their interest; Mrs JA Webber, headteacher at Longton High School, Meir, Stoke-on-Trent; Dorothy Mear, Philippa Cartlidge; Edna and Tony Murray, Paul Brindley, Richard Talbot; and Irene Ogilvie in Ottawa, Canada for her reminiscences.

I am much indebted to Richard Burgess, Helen Burton, Mal Beech, Brian Peach, Irene Pryce and the late Gerald Burgess plus many former colleagues & friends at Keele University, Staffordshire for their contributions.

Thanks to Professor Geoffrey Boulton FRS, OBE, FRSE; Reverend Trevor Harvey MA; Rev John Foulds; Father J Nowotnik; Tommy Cliff, sadly no longer with us; Maureen Cliff; Terry Atkinson; Doug Brogan; Staff at Meir library and the Hanley Reference Library in the City of Stoke on Trent, especially the diligent Margaret Beard; Jeremy Billington MPS; John Roberts & James Barlow for their invaluable insights. The late Carlo Witasek and former members of the Keyhole Committee; Solicitor Richard Stevens who helped unravel the legal niceties of the Sutherland estate and Florrie Scott for her memories. Joan Bowman's account of life in the Women's Land Army is a treasured recollection of the privations the country suffered during the Second World War; Steve Hill MSc; Cliff & the late Dot Perrin; Alan Key, whose phenomenal recall answered many questions; Scott Wilson & Kirkpatrick of Chesterfield: Gerald Mee for the Reading photographs; The Staffordshire Advertiser; The editor of Sentinel Newspapers; Stuart Robinson; Martin Elliott; the late Dave Follows; The Editor of The Ottawa Citizen and various sources I have been unable to trace.

Statistical data on the 2001 census is reproduced under licence from Her Majesty's Stationery Office.

Lastly to my wife who has helped me in innumerable ways.

CHURNET VALLEY BOOKS
6 Stanley Street, Leek, Staffordshire. ST13 5HG 01538 399033
leekbooks.co.uk
© Nicholas Cartlidge and Churnet Valley Books 2004
ISBN 1 904 546 22 6

CONTENTS

NICHOLAS CARTLIDGE

Born in the Meir in 1942, Nicholas Cartlidge was educated at Longton High School, Sandon Road, Meir under its headmaster Mr MV Gregory.

A professionally qualified chemist, attending the North Staffordshire Polytechnic in Stoke on Trent (later Staffordshire University) he was elected and admitted a Member of the Royal Society of Chemistry in 1973. He retired in December 2002.

He and his wife Jose Anne married in 1966 and have three children.

A Meir Half Century, his first book, appeared in 1996 and is stocked in some Stoke on Trent City libraries as well as the University library at Keele. It is now out of print. The book was well received and as a result, he was invited to talk on Meir's past, together with aspects of its recent history for the BBC. He has contributed several articles for the popular Sentinel publication, *The Way We Were*.

Nicholas has lived in Meir for most of his life and seen many of the changes in the town over a period of forty years and more.

Meir Today, Gone Tomorrow covers 65 years of the life and times in Meir. It completes the story of Meir's development up to 2004, its successes and failures, comparing the town's varied, colourful and surprising past with its uncertain future.

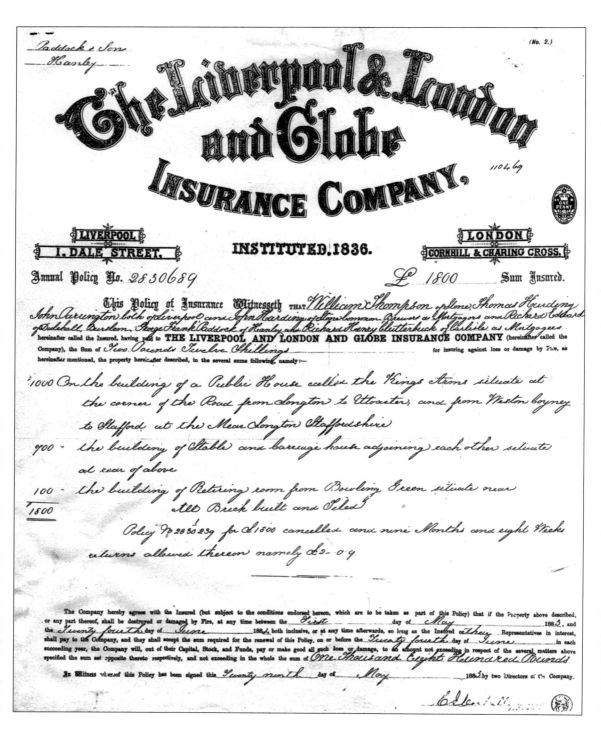

This insurance certificate from the old King's Arms, Meir, dated 1883, is from when the inn was owned by a consortium of business men. The inn was insured for £1000, the outbuildings £700 and the 'retiring room' to the bowling green for £100. *Courtesy Bass Museum, Burton on Trent.*

INTRODUCTION

The majority of a previous book on Meir, *A Meir Half Century*, was compiled from archive material, containing little from personal memory as understandably its time frame 1889 to 1939 was beyond the recall of most human experience. Since *A Meir Half Century* appeared in 1996, an enormous amount of new information has been researched and documented; articles for a local newspaper, the Internet and radio have complemented this.

While archive material has been used again in Meir Today, Gone Tomorrow, a larger proportion of the book is told from personal experience. In defence of undoubted criticism, human memory is subject to distortion. Some recollections may sit awkwardly with the written word. I have not altered any aberrations.

The book falls into two main parts. The first, a chronological account of life and times in the Meir from 1939 to 2004, is set alongside world and national events. Contained at the start is a radio script for those who have not read A Meir Half Century, painting with a broad brush Meir life up to the outset of the Second World War. The saga of the new A50 road scheme signified a turning point in Meir's history, altering the town. The story of those who lived through its construction, is told for the first time. The contributions made to the health of Meir, by just two doctors out of many, Drs Justin McCarthy and Ganapathy will surprise many, while on the ecclesiastical side; the impact of Rev Trevor Harvey MA and Father W.A. Oddie, PhD is considerable. I have brought up to date the entire history of Holy Trinity church, Meir with their present clergy, Rev John Foulds and at St Augustine's with Rev Jan Nowotnik.

The second part contains more detail on specialised aspects of Meir life - what might be thought of as Meir's 'Past Glories': Meir Golf Club, the Aerodrome with its wartime aircraft assembly, and the well-known Broadway Cinema, are some that many will know well. There are also Meir's more memorable 'people'; Amy Johnson, Prince George, Sir Hugh Fraser, Keith Ogilvie DFC, John F. Kennedy, Ernest Albert Egerton VC, Reginald Mitchell, Professor Geoffrey Boulton FRS, OBE, FRSE, an 'old boy' of Longton High school in Sandon Road, Joseph Leese RN, who sailed with Captain Scott to the Antarctic in *Terra Nova*, Florence Dayson the wife of Reginald Mitchell, Stephen Mear, reputedly a millionaire, along with other less famous who touched Meir's life.

But above all it contains personal recollections of those in Meir who recall perhaps happier times. Their cherished memories are I hope the essence of *Meir Today, Gone Tomorrow*.

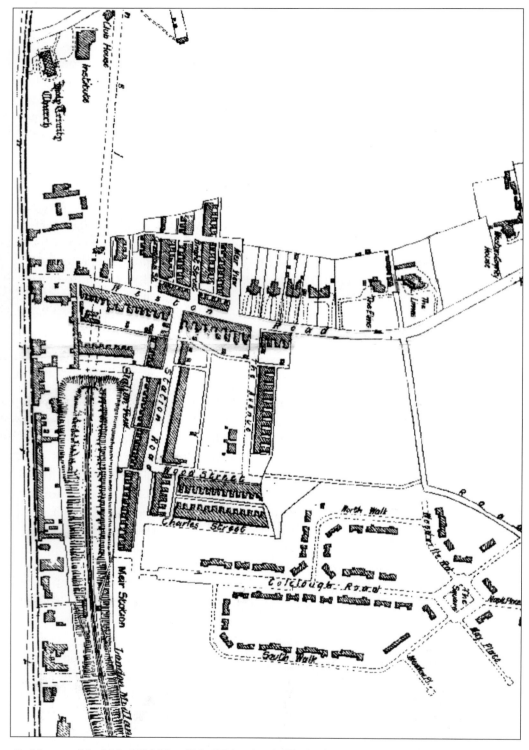

Parish map of the Meir, 1926. Note Holy Trinity church, The Institute and Meir Golf Course Club House.

CHAPTER 1

"Everyone sets out to do something, and everybody does something, but no one does what he sets out to do."   *Gerald Moore 1852-1933*

By the middle of the 1930s, the town of Meir in Staffordshire had come of age. In just three decades the transformation from a small farming community lying at the southern end of Stoke on Trent, to a huge town was remarkable.

Meir Road at the intersection of Bengry Road and Star and Garter Road about 1910. *Lovatt Collection.*

With Meir a cock stride away, the green fields had been a temptation the City council found hard to resist in resettling families from slum clearance areas, especially Longton. Rural ways for those in Meir vanished forever. Just how that mass migration affected The Meir is reflected in the census figures. In the 1890s just under 2800 people were living in this scattered village at the top of Meir bank, by the early 1930s it was around 14,000.

Smoky Longton in the 1930s. Many Meir folk worked in Longton's 'pot banks' during the 1930s.

Meir Residential Estate, Uttoxeter Road was prestigious modern development built by Tompkinson and Bettelley, 1930s. The estate was largely demolished for the new A50. *Hill Collection.*

The Meir Square estate came into existence, losing somewhere along the way the original name of its principal thoroughfare, Aynsley Road - after John Aynsley a former Lord Mayor of Longton - to Leason Road. Building continued but not at a pace that satisfied everyone: *The Bishop of Lichfield has denounced the poor living conditions of the working class population of 239,200 in the City of Stoke on Trent; one out of every five persons is living in housing unfit for human habitation.*

The scale of the problem was immense however there were tangible signs that the City's efforts were beginning to turn the tide. The Staffordshire Advertiser blared:

Writing in an annual report, Dr Alan Wotherspoon, the medical officer for Stoke on Trent said that "infant mortality was now 85 per 1000 compared with 89 in 1933 and an average of 98 per 1000 between 1922 and 1931. The child population of Stoke on Trent from 1 to 5 years of age was estimated at 17,140 and plus the births under 1 year gave an estimated population of 21,250 under 5 years. Deaths of children from 1 to 2 fell from 1219 in 1919-1923 to 469 from 1930 to 1934 while for those 2 to 5 years of age fell from 1,374 to 345 during the same period. There had been a great improvement in the health and vitality of the surviving children.

By 1936, Meir, now a town, along with its main church, was described as:

...an ecclesiastical parish formed from the parish of Caverswall and part of Normacot. It has a station on the London, Midland and Scottish Railway. The church of the Holy Trinity, at a cost of £2,800, is a building in the late Gothic style built on a site given by the 4th Duke of Sutherland KG. It consists of a chancel, nave and temporary vestry. The living, a perpetual curacy (without residence) net yearly value £350 is in the gift of the Bishop of Lichfield.

With its new migrants, Meir was broadly-based spanning the whole spectrum of social classes from the not so well off to the very well to do. And with its expansion followed a deserved commercial prosperity. The vast number of people living within a short distance of the town easily supported a thriving, broadly based shopping centre, which like Topsy, just grew and grew. The list below illustrates the diversity of 1930s Meir:

Barlow, Jas, The Elms, Weston Road.
Mear, Stephen, Weston Coyney House, Weston Road.
Burslem & District Industrial Co-operative Society, Weston Road.
Chadwick, Elizabeth Ann Mrs, Grocer, 32 Weston Road.
Adderley, Frank, Chemist, 41, Weston Road.
Aldridge, Mary Alice, Milliner, 65 Weston Road.
Parks Pharmacy, 66 Weston Road.
Cappers Limited, Grocers, 69 Weston Road.
Bennett, Luke B. Watch and Clock Repairer, 71 Weston Road.
Massey Arthur, Farmer, Uttoxeter Road.
Nixon John, Farmer, Uttoxeter Road.
North Staffs Aero Club (Leslie Irving Hon Sec), Uttoxeter Road, Longton.

In addition, Meir boasted a smattering of medical men too.

Griffith, Michael Joseph MB; B.Ch; BAO physician/surgeon at 106 Weston Road.
Heath, William BA MRCS LRCP physician and surgeon, The Beeches, Uttoxeter Road.
Ferguson, William Lawrence, Dental Surgeon, Highfield House, 717 Uttoxeter Road.

And the first landlord of Joule's newly opened public house, in 1935, in Weston Road:

Johnson, Robert Arthur, King's Arms Public House, Meir.

The dawning of 1936 had seen the death of George V, while across the Channel, Hitler, who had been swept into power on a wave of euphoria, became even more threatening. Mass unemployment and currency devaluation galvanised the German people and the ominous signs of an increasing momentum would soon be revealed to a suspicious world.

Locally the Rev. William R Bell became Meir's new parish priest, his 10 year ministry lasting throughout the Second World War at a period in its history when the town frequently resembled an armed camp. December in the same year also saw the opening of the Broadway cinema at Meir crossroads. Its Art Deco styling and, for the time, state of the art equipment was admired by all who queued and paid their admission money in the foyer. Throughout the 1930s, Meir, was a rapidly growing 'bedroom suburb', as the programme at the opening of the Broadway put it.

A programme recorded for the BBC at the studios of Radio Stoke in Hanley on a snowy day in December 1997 gives an overall impression of life in Meir in those pre-war years. Entitled *A Pre War Meir Christmas* it aptly went out on Christmas Eve. It drew on the Christmas season throughout the 1930s, and portrayed the life and times of those in Meir with something of a broad brush.

Many will know Meir had its own airport, one which had seen the arrival of the famous and well known. Didn't the Prime Minister of Australia land there in 1935 to open a bazaar at St Gregory's Roman Catholic church in Longton? And of

TISER, SATURDAY, MAY 25, 1935

PRIME MINISTER OF AUSTRALIA

Flying Visit to Stoke-on-Trent

course the visit of Prince George was a never-to-be-forgotten moment.

There were tragedies too. Just before Christmas in 1935, Dorothy Clive piloting her Miles Hawk aircraft came to grief avoiding some trees on her final approach during a snowstorm. Her cousin, who was the only passenger, also died in the crash.

But for the children there was a just one very special person they all

NORTH STAFFS. STORM TRAGEDY
Plane Crashes at Meir Airport

The Wrecked Aeroplane. Inset: Miss Clive, the pilot

wanted to see touch down on Meir's main runway in November. The newspapers trailed the event for weeks, gradually building up the excitement as the moment got nearer:

Father Christmas comes by air to Lewis's on Saturday November the FIFTH.
He arrives at Meir aerodrome by aeroplane at 10.20 AM.

It went on, *Everyone is invited to see Father Christmas in his aeroplane from Iceland. After greeting all the boys and girls, he will proceed in his gaily decorated coach....*

From the aerodrome, his journey took him out on to Uttoxeter Road, a road the Romans had made centuries before.

It's difficult today to appreciate physically what a closely-knit community Meir was in those days. Small shops, some in terraced houses either side of Leese's garage, bordered the road before the King's Arms. With Duncan Ross, Chemists, across the way in a parade of shops which disappeared round the corner into Sandon Road past the King's Arms, and to the right, more in Weston Road. This was the Meir.

And there was a smattering of farms, which almost nudged into the town centre, where Weston and Sandon Roads met Uttoxeter Road at the roundabout. Diagonally opposite the King's Arms, stood the newly opened Broadway cinema, the brain child of Herbert Clewlow, who along with Harold Knight, both directors of Knight and Sons, Hanley, had given Meir one of its most endearing meeting places. Apart from the wireless and newspapers, many kept abreast of events worldwide through the Pathe or British Movietone Newsreels, then part of most cinema programmes. At the end of the thirties when this country had a television audience numbered only in hundreds, the Broadway cinema played a large part in many Meir peoples' lives. Of course the cinema was also known for another 'special feature'. Hands up, how many remember, the double seats at the Broadway? Well, we'll gloss over that. Hands down!

Almost in the same week as the doors of the Broadway first opened in December

Sandon Road, Meir, after the Duncan Ross shops were built in the 1930s. The open land to the left was used for the Meir Library and Meir Health Centre in the 1960s.

Weston Road, Meir during the 1930s/1940s. Note the 'Meir Villas' stone high on the building, extreme right.

1936, this country was in crisis. With the death of George V, the Duke of Windsor, the 'man who would-be-king', dithered for a year between Mrs Simpson and his duty to the throne. However, there is no evidence whatsoever to suggest the Duke ever sat in the Broadway. Well not in the 'cheap seats' anyway!

With Santa scarcely out of sight on his way to Hanley via Longton, Fenton and Stoke, the children would already be writing out lists of toys to post up the chimney, as most houses had open fire grates. But how would the people in the Meir spend a typical family Christmas?

For dad, at least, it would be a chance to put his feet up and take it easy. Towards the end of the 1930s, the pottery industry, in which many Meir people worked, enjoyed something of a boom, as the threat of unemployment had receded. And anyway, what the heck, it would soon be Christmas, and the prospects of a few days off would have put a spring in the old man's step as he set out to walk to work down Meir bank, on a cold and frosty winter's morning.

For mum, a respite from the daily routine was slim. In those days, it was rare for women to go out to work. So, at this time of year, in addition to her daily round, she would have the awesome task of conjuring up a feast fit for a king, on a kitchen range, which, were it around today, many would have great difficulty even warming up a tin of baked beans.

However there was plenty to do for the more active in Meir and what's more you didn't need a car. As the 1930's unfolded, Meir found itself in a very fortunate position. So much so, that by 1939, the town could be said to be almost self contained. It had numerous shops, a bowling green, tennis courts, a golf course, a cinema, airport and railway station, three churches and four, at least four, public houses.

John Joule and Sons, the Stone Brewers, had rebuilt the King's Arms in 1935 on the site of the earlier pub and provided a convenient place for those who liked a quiet pint. At dusk, lights from the public bar and lounge would spill on to the pavement, illuminating the faces of the shoppers in Weston Road. But if you had a spare a moment for a 'swift half', you might have bumped into Joseph Leese, who, home from the sea, now lived at the Holy Trinity Church Institute, in Box Lane. After all, it was he who had sailed in *Terra Nova*, under Captain Scott's command to the Antarctic in 1910 in an attempt to be the first at the South Pole. Three years later the ship returned along with Able Seaman Leese, leaving the bodies of the gallant Captain and his four companions buried in the ice. What a tale he could tell, as the logs crackled in the big grate in the saloon bar. Dentist Lawrence Ferguson, another regular, lived at Highfield House. His home, overlooking the lawns of Holy Trinity church, still stands there, proudly today.

One man out and about, was Holy Trinity church's parish priest. At Christmas, he had the daunting task of putting in simple terms the mystery of why the Son of God should come amongst us as a child to save men's souls. Christmas was not as commercialised as it is today and had not been way laid by the merchants and moneychangers. The American humorist, Ogden Nash, would plead for 'a few more angels and a few less angles' when trying to recapture these innocent times.

After the schools in Uttoxeter Road, Colclough Road and St Augustine's had performed their nativity plays, held their Christmas parties and said 'goodbyes', a waterfall

The 'untidy' roundabout at Meir crossroads contrasts with the style of John Joule's hostelry, the King's Arms.

of babbling children spilled into the streets, their high pitched voices filled with glee. Gloria, Gloria, Gloria! It was Christmas!

Christmas day was like no other. For the children hours whizzed by like minutes. John played with his blue and red racing car with a clockwork spring you wound up with a key, AND his box of lead soldiers, neat and in rows, while Joan patiently dressed and undressed her new doll a thousand times in its clothes. And there was more; some sweets, an orange, perhaps, and a colouring book, maybe. But grown-ups had their pleasures too! For those devoted to the game of golf, with a seasonal gift of new clubs to try out, there was the Meir Golf course, started in 1895 and patronised equally by the well-to-do and those of more humble origins. O joy, to stride out on Meir's fairways for some fresh air. And following a quick nine holes, a snifter - or two - in the clubhouse.

George V started broadcasting to the nation in the 1920s at the Wembley exhibition. By the 1930s, the King's Christmas speech had become traditional. With no wall to wall Disney as a distraction, his majesty had centre stage and was listened to with great respect, especially by those at the Territorial Army drill hall in Uttoxeter Road next to the Broadway.

More than a few in The Meir would work off the excesses of a sumptuous meal and Auntie Elsie's mince pies, by heading for the Victoria ground, 3 miles away, to 'root' for the 'Potters'. Very few had cars, so you either caught the 'bus or went by Shanks' pony. At that time of course, the team had an up and coming star in its ranks, none other than the young Stanley Matthews. During the Christmas holidays in 1936, Stoke played twice. In the Christmas day match against Chelsea, Stoke won 2-0 before a crowd of 25,000 - and on Boxing Day (a Saturday), they took on Liverpool, holding them to a 1-1 draw before a

HALL & SONS, Station Garage and Chaplin Rd. Garage, **LONGTON**
Telephone 339 (Day and Night).   Telegrams: "Hall & Sons, Longton."

Motor Char-a-Bancs and Taxi Landaulettes for Hire.   Excursions arranged.   Estimates given.

Local transport in the 1920s and 1930s.

A detailed engineering drawing of the road scheme which straightened the A50 at the Meir during the early 1930s. Note the major buildings and farms close to the town centre.

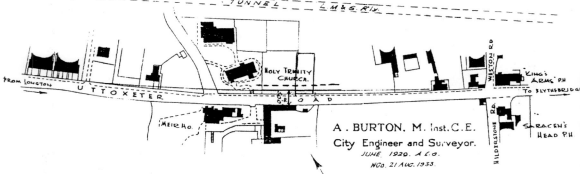

massive 39,000 crowd. Of an incident in the match, a sports reporter wrote:

Then we saw the real Matthews. Again and again he ran past 2 or 3 men at good speed, with the ball at his toes, leaving these would-be tacklers behind, one after the other. It was sheer sleight-of-foot, and the openings he made for his colleagues on his left, ought to have produced a crop of goals.

The plight of the poor at Christmas is specially pitiful. Many didn't even stretch as far as a few essentials. To that end, several charities had been started in Meir by far-seeing and compassionate men. One was named after its founder, Henry Hill JP, in the 1930s, had been running for many years, doling out cash to those financially bereft during the festive season. On one occasion, 164 people received 4 shillings each. Elderly people had help from another charity, begun by a former Lord Mayor of Longton. The John Aynsley Gift had invested £500, which at 4% yielded twenty pounds in a good year. For those unable to attend, the 5 shillings was sent plus a meat pie, by post. I only hope there weren't too many hungry postmen around! One year the prize for the 'eldest lady' was won by someone aged 100, whilst a man from Uttoxeter Road received the 'Gents prize', 5 shillings.

And throughout Christmas day, the tolling, tuneless bell at Holy Trinity church would summon the faithful, frequently between 150 to 200 communicants, to worship at one of five services held to celebrate Christ's birth. Of the many occasions and celebrations that would change in Meir in the future, for many, the season of Christmas would somehow, always be the same. Gloria, Gloria, Gloria.

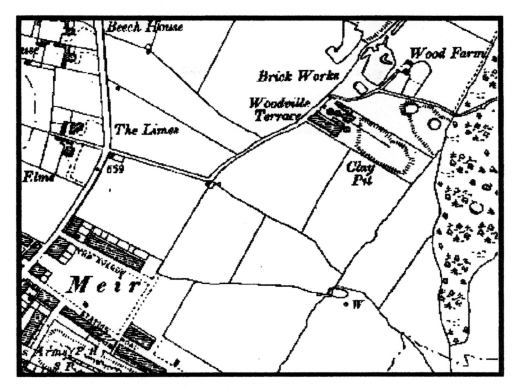

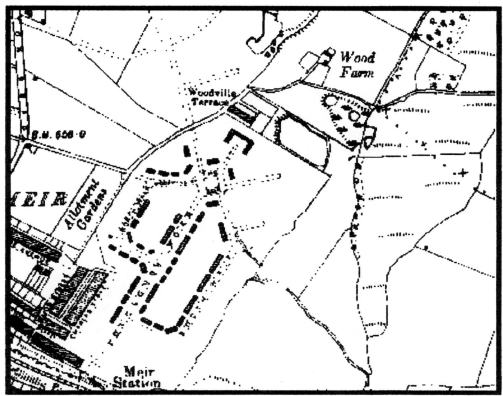

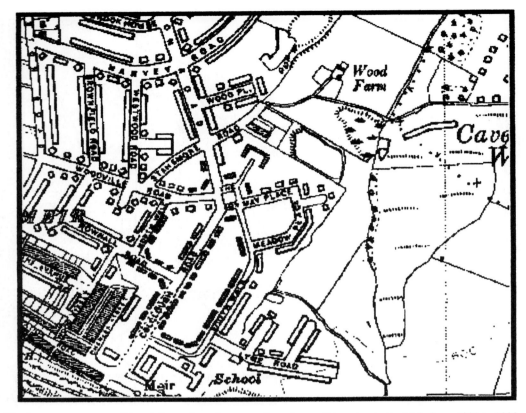

The three maps on page 15 and above show the expansion of council housing in the Meir from 1901 to 1938.

Workers' cottages at Wood Farm, Meir, in Woodville Terrace, built for employees of the brickworks.

Meir Road perhaps about 1910. In spite of the passage of time and the loss of the trees much of the terraced housing in Meir Road is still there.

Meir in the 1920s. The new A50 now disappears under the tunnel at this point. The farm, left, in Uttoxeter Road (now approx site of Kwik save) had the Golf course running behind it. The Saracen's Head, in the centre, was demolished in the 1930s and rebuilt further up Sandon Road. The land on the right was the site of the Broadway cinema from 1936 until 1973. The road running into the distance, later the busy A50, now disappears under the town centre in a tunnel. *Bennett collection.*

William Blake photo of Meir crossroads taken in the late 1920s. The old Kings Arms is left of the main road where Weston Road runs off towards Leek. The Saracen's Head is opposite on the right.

Old Weston Road, Meir, before the Second World War. Note 'Meir Villas' on the building far right. This plaque was partly filled in to foil any German paratroopers who might have landed. Most of the houses are still there, a welcome touch of mellow Victoriana in Meir's present architecture.

Looking across the old A50 to the old Saracen's Head on the corner of Sandon Road, probably 1920s. The Saracen's Head public house is seen from the upper storey of Arthur Bennett's house opposite. Later this inn was the site of livestock sales in what was then a farming community. *Bennett Collection.*

Looking down Uttoxeter Road in the 1920s. The tree-lined thoroughfare is long gone and now covered by the new A50. Some big houses remain on the right, overwhelmed by an enormous footbridge.

The past rurality of Meir can be seen in this old photograph. Looking down what is now
Sandon Road into Weston Road, the old King's Arms, centre picture, with the
Saracen's Head to the right, stand on opposite side of the present day A50.

Weston Road, Meir, looking towards the crossroads in the 1920s/1930s.
Parts of the town here are essentially unchanged today.

The Toll Cottage left and Saracen's Head, right, frame Lewis's Lane, later Sandon Road in this evocative early panorama of Meir. *Bennett Collection.*

Seen from another perspective, Sandon Road runs into the distance in this amazing view of a Meir long gone. The Toll Cottage, right and Saracen's Head pub just squeezing on at the left hand side complete the scene. Uttoxeter Road is running left to right, Blythe Bridge to Longton. The Toll Cottage was the site of the Broadway cinema 1936 to 1973. *Bennett Collection.*

With a farm next door, left, Arthur Bennett's home stood at the crossroads of the A50 and A520, Uttoxeter Road and Weston Road. Road-widening later claimed this cottage - a portent of things to come.

From a field in Sandon Road, Meir. The Saracen's Head, far right, by telegraph pole, the King's Arms, white in centre, the Toll Cottage, centre, Arthur Bennett's house and the beginnings of Bracegirdle's farm, far left. Sleepy Meir in the late 1920s. The Broadway cinema was built close to the site of the tree. *Bennett Collection.*

A tram trundles up Uttoxeter Road in the early 20th century past what was Ewie Hollison's shop. Note the mature trees, now no more. It can be seen to better effect on p 24.

These terraced houses in Uttoxeter Road, below Hollinson's Corner were all demolished for the new A50. Was the new road an excuse for housing clearance?

The stone laying ceremony at Normacot Methodist church, Meir Road in 1910.
The town saw a tremendous burst of church building in the late 19th and 20th century.

Normacot Methodist church, Meir Road, Meir December 1993.
With the new A50 the access from Meir Road was lost.

CHAPTER 2

*"The difficult is what takes a little time; the impossible is what takes a
little longer."*   *Fritdjof Nansen, Norwegian explorer 1861-1930*

Although life in Meir appeared to continue at a leisurely pace, for those who chose to look,
ominous signs that all was not well, began to seep into the newspapers. The word that the
manufacture of gas masks was about to start was received with a certain unease especially
by those who recalled the use of mustard gas during the First World War. John Singer
Sargeant's graphic painting of soldiers affected by gas, each holding on to the one in front,
left nothing to the imagination.

But when duty called and the time came, gas masks were given out in double quick
time. From the Victorian school in the village of Caverswall hundreds were distributed in
a matter of days. Everyone was catered for, even babies, who had a larger variety of mask
into which they could be placed entirely in the event of an enemy gas attack. Many recall
with mixed feelings those cumbersome claustrophobic devices which always smelled of
rubber whatever was used to cover it up.

A local demonstration of how to wear gas masks prior to WW2.

The year 1937 was almost at an end. As well as the Coronation, the planned annual
expenditure for Staffordshire County Council was set to exceed £3 million for the first time.
Gigli the Italian singer sang in the Victoria Hall and trade nationally was on the up and up, the
local pottery industry commemorating the royal occasion with a whole range of mugs, plates
and loving cups. *'The pottery industry in 1937 experienced one of the best trading periods
since the post-war boom and at the moment there is a distinctly cheerful note as to its future.'*

Housing too was going up with alacrity, and several new developments
complemented Meir Residential Estate and the burgeoning Council estates. Messrs Tipping
the builders were at work on the Hillside Estate in Grosvenor Road. Compared with today's
prices the typical price of a detached house, 1 Harcourt Avenue, at around £475 looks

Ordnance Survey 1938. The expansion of the town with new housing around Wood Farm and the Meir Golf Course at Gibson Place, Oak Place and Poplar Grove clearly visible.

minuscule but against wages and prices at the time, most of the few who could afford to buy needed assistance from a building society to help pay for it.

In 1938 cheerful news came aplenty, a year that saw the appearance of two giants of the musical world in the local arena:

'Sir Thomas Beecham and the London Philharmonic Orchestra are to appear at the Victoria Hall, Hanley on the 17th January. Prices are 7/6d Centre Balcony, or Arena 3/6d or on the platform (limited accommodation) for 2/-'

The second, a renowned composer and a world class performer par excellence captivated the audience with his skill, dexterity and faultless technique. His visit to Hanley was a never to be repeated experience for musical devotees and concert goers. Described as 'six and a half feet of majestic indifference' he appeared at the Victoria Hall on the 17th March. The prices of the seats were Balcony, 10/6d to 8/-, Gallery, 5/6d to 3/6d. The Evening Sentinel music critic (F.B.) could not praise him highly enough although he did have a moan about the attendance.

'It would have been nice to see all the Arena seats occupied on so memorable occasion, but Rachmaninoff can never have played to a more exemplary audience. Genius was listened to with rapt attention.'

Following his death in March 1943, his Second Piano Concerto was used by Noel Coward in *Brief Encounter* and enjoyed even greater popularity when it was made into a film starring Trevor Howard and Celia Johnson as the ill fated lovers.

If local trade was improving the weather was not and this time it was not just the vicarage tea party that was under threat:

'Bad weather conditions which caused cancellations of displays in several parts of the country, curtailed the Empire Air Day programme arranged on Saturday by the North Staffs Aero Club at Meir Aerodrome. Of the 30 RAF machines expected, only 16, including the 46 (Fighter) Squadron (Gloster Gauntlets) from Digby Lincolnshire were able to reach Stoke-on-Trent, but the large crowd was rewarded with some spectacular flying. An Avro Anson coastal reconnaissance machine, an Airspeed Oxford trainer and a Hawker Fury were open for inspection and were a continual source of interest. In connection with the display, a demonstration was given by members of the City ARP (Air Raid Precautions) under Mr G Totty. Major HM Powell commanded a contingent of the 41st Anti-Aircraft Battalion Royal Engineers, which also gave a display. The RAF personnel were entertained to a luncheon with the Deputy Lord Mayor (Alderman AJ Dale), who extended a civic welcome to the visitors.' 4th June, 1938

Knowing that the City had recently thought little of Meir aerodrome, it was an amazing 'about face' by the City's civic deputy. Although the sabre-rattling of Empire Day would become in time a pleasant if soggy memory, the underlying need for a more purposeful well equipped Air Force was only too apparent:

'The RAF Volunteer Reserve Training School which has been established at the Stoke-on-Trent Corporation Aerodrome at Meir was opened on Monday and the instruction will shortly commence of the first batch of 25 volunteers. In much the same style as the T.A.,instruction will be given by qualified RAF instructors in the evenings and at the weekends. The school will have a complement of 25 training planes for use in the

instruction of that number of volunteers-to be drawn from the Stoke-on-Trent area-at a time and the full course will extend over three months. In this way the school will be able to turn out 100 qualified pilots each year. In connexion with the Air Ministry scheme for the training of the Civil Air Guard, the North Staffs Aero Club which also operates from Meir, have received nearly 300 applications to join, many of them from women and they have completed arrangements for the commencement of training on September 1st.'   6th August 1938

On the civil front too, preparations for war went on. As if to allay the public fears, especially those resident in Meir and Stoke on Trent, newspapers declared that the *'Air Raid Precautions (ARP) are going full steam in Stoke-on-Trent and the scheme was as far advanced as any.'* The Great British Public could now leave on their 'hols' happy *'everything was under control on the defence front',* but still with a nagging doubt whether they'd locked the back door at home before leaving for the train station:

'NORTH STAFFS EXODUS: Throughout Saturday, the stream of travellers continued by road and rail with special trains on Sunday to take people to the Welsh Coast and Lancashire.' Whilst adding almost as an afterthought: *'In the early hours of Sunday morning, the 41st (5th North Staffordshire Anti-Aircraft Battalion RE (TA)) left by road for Lincolnshire for their first camp since conversion to their present status.'*

As war threatened, Caverswall Castle, a victim of the English Civil War in the 17th century crept back into the papers with the sale of a piece of its history in September 1938.

'A portrait of Matthew Cradock, a member of Parliament for Stafford from 1644-1655 has been sold for 105 guineas; Matthew Cradock owned Caverswall Castle in the Commonwealth period, 1649-1660, when it was garrisoned for Parliamentary troops.'

Christmas was approaching fast. Even if the City council didn't think much of Meir's aerodrome, Santa Claus was definitely not of the same persuasion, his ride through the streets again raising the expectations of wide-eyed children watching his journey through Meir.

The degenerating political situation cast a sombre shadow over the celebrations as the New Year 1939 was welcomed in. The Air Ministry had always had its critics but no-one could censure them now for their actions in the first days of January. Hitler's ranting was becoming increasingly bellicose and a state of readiness was in force at Training Centres in this country. The RAF Volunteer Reserve (RAFVR) stationed at Meir Aerodrome, using Tiger Moths and Hawker Harts since 1938, had operated as No 28 Elementary and Reserve Flying Training School. It was the subject of an address to members of the Stoke-on-Trent Rotary Club by Colonel P.Y. Birch. Hopefully there were no spies among his listeners:

'The total establishment of the school at Meir would be about 213 and present requirements were for another 70 pilots, 37 observers and 75 wireless operators. Recruiting for the ground section had not yet begun. He dealt with the training of entrants and said after each satisfactory year of service, a pilot received a training fee of £25; in other sections the fee was £20. Recruits, he said, were being drawn from Cheshire, Staffordshire and Shropshire. In the event of war, recruits would NOT be sent to fight at once. They would be assessed and sent as occasion demanded to advanced service training schools.'

18th Feb 1939

The former Longton High School built in the 1930s, now Sandon High School Business and Enterprise College. The cladding seen here was applied during the 1990s.

Civilian preparations continued. Ration cards appeared in the coming months together with an abortive examination of the defences which in March 1939 *'poor weather made aerial observation difficult'*.

Throughout June and July, the news of the German armies on the move in Europe became ever more depressing. The 'Empire Display' at Meir aerodrome would never be more significant than now, marking the 'coming of age' of the Royal Air Force and in many ways the only chance of salvation from Hitler's tyranny:

'The admission to the Empire Air Day Display on May 20th 1939 will be 1s. for adults and 3d for children. They will be held at 78 aerodromes in the UK, including 63 RAF stations, 11 civil aerodromes, where personnel are being trained by the Royal Air Force, the Auxiliary Air Force and the Royal Air Force Volunteer Reserve. The remaining four are purely civil aerodromes. Stations will be open from 2pm until 7pm. The public will be afforded the opportunity of witnessing the performance of the latest types of monoplane fighter.'

But optimism continued unabated. In the last month of peace for nearly six years a simple ceremony held near Rough Close Common signified that whatever the outcome of the conflict, belief in the future and a brighter tomorrow was undimmed. Right would prevail:

'The foundation stone of St Francis's church at Rough Close was laid by the Bishop of Lichfield last week. Those present applauded warmly as Dr Woods ceremonially began the construction of the new building in these trying times'.

5th August 1939

Issued by the Ministry of Information *in co-operation with the War Office and the Ministry of Home Security*

Beating the INVADER

A MESSAGE FROM THE PRIME MINISTER

IF invasion comes, everyone—young or old, men and women—will be eager to play their part worthily. By far the greater part of the country will not be immediately involved. Even along our coasts, the greater part will remain unaffected. But where the enemy lands, or tries to land, there will be most violent fighting. Not only will there be the battles when the enemy tries to come ashore, but afterwards there will fall upon his lodgments very heavy British counter-attacks, and all the time the lodgments will be under the heaviest attack by British bombers. The fewer civilians or non-combatants in these areas, the better—apart from essential workers who must remain. So if you are advised by the authorities to leave the place where you live, it is your duty to go elsewhere when you are told to leave. When the attack begins, it will be too late to go ; and, unless you receive definite instructions to move, your duty then will be to stay where you are. You will have to get into the safest place you can find, and stay there until the battle is over. For all of you then the order and the duty will be : " STAND FIRM ".

This also applies to people inland if any considerable number of parachutists or air-borne troops are landed in their neighbourhood. Above all, they must not cumber the roads. Like their fellow-countrymen on the coasts, they must " STAND FIRM ". The Home Guard, supported by strong mobile columns wherever the enemy's numbers require it, will immediately come to grips with the invaders, and there is little doubt will soon destroy them.

Throughout the rest of the country where there is no fighting going on and no close cannon fire or rifle fire can be heard, everyone will govern his conduct by the second great order and duty, namely, " CARRY ON ". It may easily be some weeks before the invader has been totally destroyed, that is to say, killed or captured to the last man who has landed on our shores. Meanwhile, all work must be continued to the utmost, and no time lost.

The following notes have been prepared to tell everyone in rather more detail what to do, and they should be carefully studied. Each man and woman should think out a clear plan of personal action in accordance with the general scheme.

Winston S. Churchill

STAND FIRM

1. What do I do if fighting breaks out in my neighbourhood ?

Keep indoors or in your shelter until the battle is over. If you can have a trench ready in your garden or field, so much the better. You may want to use it for protection if your house is damaged. But if you are at work, or if you have special orders, carry on as long as possible and only take cover when danger approaches. If you are on your way to work, finish your journey if you can.

If you see an enemy tank, or a few enemy soldiers, do not assume that the enemy are in control of the area. What you have seen may be a party sent on in advance, or stragglers from the main body who can easily be rounded up.

CARRY ON

2. What do I do in areas which are some way from the fighting ?

Stay in your district and carry on. Go to work whether in shop, field, factory or office. Do your shopping, send your children to school until you are told not to. Do not try to go and live somewhere else. Do not use the roads for any unnecessary journey ; they must be left free for troop movements even a long way from the district where actual fighting is taking place.

3. Will certain roads and railways be reserved for the use of the Military, even in areas far from the scene of action ?

Yes, certain roads will have to be reserved for important troop movements ; but such reservations should be only temporary. As far as possible, bus companies and railways will try to maintain essential public services, though it may be necessary to cut these down. Bicyclists and pedestrians may use the roads for journeys to work, unless instructed not to do so.

ADVICE AND ORDERS

4. Whom shall I ask for advice ?

The police and A.R.P. wardens.

5. From whom shall I take orders ?

In most cases from the police and A.R.P. wardens. But there may be times when you will have to take orders from the military and the Home Guard in uniform.

6. Is there any means by which I can tell that an order is a true order and not faked ?

You will generally know your policeman and your A.R.P. wardens by sight, and can trust them. With a bit of common sense you can tell if a soldier is really British or only pretending to be so. If in doubt ask a policeman, or ask a soldier whom you know personally.

CHAPTER 3

'Let us therefore brace ourselves to our duty and so bear ourselves that if the British Empire and its Commonwealth lasts for a thousand years men will still say "This was their finest hour".'   Winston Churchill June 1940 Hansard.

The inexorable slide into war during the summer of 1939 was marked by an increasing number of uniforms on the broad tree-lined streets of Meir. The aerodrome, now in the hands of the military, bristled with men from the Royal Air Force Volunteer Reserve. Some time before hostilities began, training had continued, not just at the TA centre in Meir, but elsewhere in the Potteries. Flight Lieutenant V.J. Reynolds RAFVR (T) recalls:

'The RAF Volunteer Reserve Centre on the A34 at Trentham had about 20 pilots 50 wireless operators/ air gunners and 70 ground staff under training in August 1939. The work at Trentham was linked with flying at the old Meir aerodrome which the RAF used as an elementary flying school. Some of the pilots joined Fighter Command in time to take part in the Battle of Britain in 1940.'

Units of the Territorial Army, billeted at the Drill Hall in the centre of the town were a common sight leaving no one in any doubt what was coming. In what might have been regarded as 'last minute tuition' before the curtain finally fell, a bizarre flying accident during the first week in August, not too far from the King's Arms, had the locals scratching their heads wondering if this was it. Had the balloon gone up already?

'An aeroplane belonging to the North Staffs Aero Club which made a forced landing in a field at Cookshill,near Caverswall on Tuesday evening, struck and broke a high tension cable with the result that the district's electricity supplies were cut for a short time. The occupants of the 'plane were Mr Peter Massey, an instructor from the Aero Club, Meir and Mr Seekings a pupil. Mr Seekings was receiving instruction in forced landings when the incident occurred. Neither pilot nor passenger was hurt and the 'plane suffered only slight damage, being able to return to Meir Aerodrome after a short delay.'

Sunday September 3rd was a time the country caught its breath. The tremulous voice of Neville Chamberlain announced the dreaded news with solemnity. Later, newspapers filled in more detail. Over garden walls, on street corners and outside the pub, knots of people gathered to discuss its implications. They accepted it with a quiet resignation. Many recalled with horror the First World War and the terrible loss of life. What did fate have in store for them? Would they survive? Comedian Robb Wilton later parodied the occasion with his catch phrase 'The Day War Broke Out!' at the start of his music hall act. However just then, it was understandable that no one felt much like laughing

Behind all this bluff and bluster, plans were already in train should the unthinkable happen. Two days earlier, on Friday 1st September, the mass evacuation of children left this country's largest cities as devoid of childish patter as any Pied Piper could have made them, so that by the first Sunday evening of the war almost 1.5 million had been removed to a 'place of safety' out of London. Among these youngsters were people like Michael Aspel, Jonathan Miller and the 'Brylcreemed' soccer star, Johnny Haynes. The evacuation

Evacuees arriving for Caverswall at the beginning of the War, still at the railway station
- and still in good spirits despite the upheaval.

was patchy and not all children were relocated. In London, less than 50%, in Manchester 40% and in Sheffield, 85% actually stayed put. But while, for some, parting from parents and home caused heartache, for others it was a welcome escape from the grimy existence of the city.

'I thank God I was evacuated, not because I avoided danger but because it changed my way of thinking. It made me love the country. I would never live in town again. I found a refuge, quiet and peaceful, after an unhappy home life. I found another family who I really loved-and still do.'

Were there any local families who had evacuees billeted with them? Caverswall received dozens from Manchester and according to Mrs Evelyn Cooke a long-term resident of Gravelly Bank, Lightwood, Stoke-on-Trent evacuees were billeted in Kingsmead Road, Meir. But how did they feel about being away from home?

The Bishop of Lichfield caught the mood of the moment, *'Work must go on.'* Just what this meant for Lichfield Cathedral, was soon apparent. *'Seven of the windows are Flemish in the Lady Chapel and are being removed by Messrs J.H. Bridgeman & Son, Lichfield'* to be carefully replaced with plain glass. The figures of Bishop Ryder and the Sleeping Children by Sir Francis Chantrey, one of England's greatest sculptors, were also removed from the line of fire and thickly encased in sand bags for protection.

Almost immediately, ingenious ways to assist the 'War Effort' ushered in the era of 'Backs to the Wall' and saw this island race at its most resolute. Action on the 'home front' was vital, growing potatoes and vegetables on spare available land was one example of keeping the kitchens of the nation filled. In Longton Dr F.R. Oliver opened the Longton Drubbery Allotment Association.

From now on there would be no restraining the culinary inventiveness of the more ingenious cooks as they conjured up such delights as Woolton pie. *Delightful and Interesting Dishes to Cook With Carrots* would lead digestive systems into a bewildering cul de sac of instantly forgettable and inedible delicacies, which might do more damage to the human frame than all the bombs that Hitler could muster. With inevitable rationing, it took real creativity to eke out the meagre weekly supplies of 12 ozs of sugar, 4 ozs of bacon and 4 oz of butter. There were very severe penalties for failure to obey an uncompromising code of conduct in this hour of need; those who erred were dealt with harshly. *'Father Alphonsus Power was castigated for having a quantity of butter that had arrived in Britain from Eire and for failing to place it at the disposal of the Minister of Food. He was fined £20.'*

At the cinema many sought oblivion. The Broadway, a favoured venue for the forces stationed in Meir, had double seats which were much in demand. In the soporific warmth

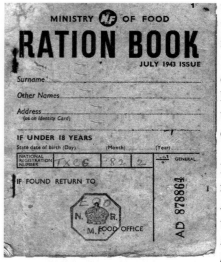

tainted by the faintly clinical aroma of carbolic soap, it was easy to put aside what Dame Fortune might have in store.

Those venturing farther afield to Hanley had a wider choice. The Odeon showed *Wuthering Heights* with Laurence Oliver and Merle Oberon, although, even at a time like this, there was still opposition to Sunday cinema by the Free Church Council, God bless 'em!

Throughout this mayhem, two much beloved charities, like dinosaurs from gentler days, helped elderly residents acquire one or two 'little extras': *'The Henry Hill and John Aynsley Charities were distributed last week. 200 old people, many over 80 and 90 years old, received a welcome addition to their slender means besides gifts of tea and sugar.'* Could these two benevolent men but see their old town now, what would they have thought? But time was of the essence. 1939 was drawing to a close. Many would die before peace would bring the promise of a better tomorrow. And for Meir too, was this the end of its 'golden age'?

New Year 1940, began with a great snowstorm on January 27th and 28th, news kept out of the papers. Just how the censor suppressed news of something so widespread is difficult to imagine - but it was wartime. In 1940 William Lawrence Ferguson, dentist, lived at Highfield House, Uttoxeter Road, while the address of the Rev. Harry Christie Sheldon BA was given as Mayfield, Uttoxeter Road. Had Meir's parish priest, Rev Bell, moved from The Vicarage in Weston Road, in 1936, to new quarters because of the war? Playing a full role in the war, the vicar of Holy Trinity Church, Rev R.W. 'Bobbie' Bell and his curate Rev D.A.J. Stevens, held services for parishioners and military personnel alike. Many RAF parade services took place at Meir aerodrome, and those held on August 11 at 9 am, and Holy Communion at 7am on September 8, at the height of the Battle of Britain, were typical.

Food was on everyone's mind. Whatever could be done to alleviate the pressing problem of food production was welcomed. An advert of April 1940 caught the public mood. *'Ploughing up the fields.'* If it still left empty stomachs, it gave an impression the whole country was pulling together.

In the same month, locally born composer, Havergal Brian was awarded £140 in recognition of his services to music despite it being said of him, *'...a critic for the Staffordshire Sentinel, he trod too hard on too many toes to please the gentle people of the Potteries.'* Born in Dresden, Stoke-on-Trent, he counted Sir Edward Elgar amongst his friends but Brian's philandering ways strained their relationship, forcing Elgar, a religious man, to break off their association. The piece of music that, unfairly, symbolises Brian's work, his Gothic Symphony, is a gargantuan musical work requiring the services of hundreds of choristers, musicians and a large auditorium. Such were its demands on the rare occasions it was heard, performers invariably outnumbered the audience two to one.

In April 1940, the Bishop of Lichfield, Archbishop Woods, ceremonial trowel in hand,

The beginning of the War portrayed in a contemporary magazine.

laid the foundation stone of a new church in Edensor, Longton. This reassuring belief in a future was heartening. Later in the summer, the Bishop dedicated St Francis' church, Meir Heath. Costing £10,000, incredibly £3,000 of this had come from children. It was decided that *'it was better to put up the building now rather that later, otherwise it might never see the light of day.'* The former vicar of Holy Trinity church, Meir, Rev H.C. Sheldon (now at Silverdale) his successor, Rev R.W. Bell, Holy Trinity Church, along with his curate Rev D. Stevens and Rev Edward Fenton Woodward (vicar of SS Mary & Chad) were present.

During that perfect summer, the Staffs Advertiser proclaimed *'the harvest was the easiest since 1927',* silencing the perpetual whining by the farming fraternity. The Battle of Britain raged across the skies of these islands. Hitler, viewing the white cliffs of the English coast from Cap Blanc Nez in Northern France, assumed, wrongly, that it would be a formality, just

A local harvest.

a matter of time before German troops stood victorious on England's 'green and pleasant land'.

Mercifully the Royal Air Force and its allies were triumphant. Daily throughout the summer of 1940, the Luftwaffe was repulsed. Hundreds of men and machines perished as the enemy threw everything into the fray. Dog fights between the Royal Air Force and Luftwaffe were a common sight as they duelled against the backdrop of a cobalt blue sky over southern England. William Shakespeare could never have foreseen such a momentous occasion as that which was unfolding when he wrote:

This royal throne of kings, this sceptred isle, This earth of majesty, this seat of Mars,....
....This happy breed of men, this little world, This precious stone set in the silver sea......
....This earth this realm, This England.   Richard II Act 2 sc 1.

By September, the Royal Air Force had inflicted such a heavy defeat on the Luftwaffe that the plans to invade the British Isles were postponed indefinitely. Playing a major role in the Battle of Britain alongside Sydney Camm's Hurricane, was Reginald Mitchell's elegant Spitfire. Its speed, fire power and manoeuvrability made it a feared adversary by pilots of the Luftwaffe. The throaty roar of its Rolls Royce Merlin engine was unique. It is always guaranteed to make those, old enough to remember, think just how close the country came to defeat. Sadly, its designer, Reginald Mitchell did not see the victory; he died from cancer in 1937. Of 20,334 Spitfires built, 47 still survived in 1998.

In late summer, news filtered back about those 'nearest and dearest' in the forces abroad. Captain Fred Hewitt of the Royal Artillery was reported a prisoner of war (POW) in Germany in August 1940. Married to a Meir girl, Margaret Cattanach, just before he left for France, Captain Hewitt was safe for the time being. His relatives could breathe again.

With so many men abroad, women took over their roles in various branches of industry. 'On the buses' they were employed as conductresses but was it a concession to their femininity that a regulation *'no bus would leave the depot after 10 pm'* was drafted? What would feminists think of that today?

Men yet to be called up, and those medically unfit, too old or in a 'reserved occupation', played their part in the defence of the realm in many ways. The Home Guard - immortalised through *Dad's Army* - was one. With the defeat in France, the government looked to the home front as invasion by Germany looked possible. Anthony Eden, Secretary of State for War, announced on the BBC Home Service on May 14, 1940 that *the government was setting up a new force named the Local Defence Volunteers.'* He said: *'We are going to ask you to help in a manner which I know will be welcome to thousands of you. The government has received inquiries from all over the Kingdom from men who want to do something for the defence of the country. We want large numbers of such men between the ages of 17 and 65 to come forward and offer their services. In order to volunteer what you have to do is to give in your name at the local police station.'*

Within a week, there was a quarter of a million names. Locally, new volunteers attended their first meeting at The Weston Inn, Weston Coyney, becoming members of the LDVF, Stone Battalion, Sub Group E, A Company. Platoons were also set up at the Meir and Blythe Bridge while the area HQ was at the Windmill, Meir Heath. Winston Churchill, finding the name Local Defence Volunteers uninspiring, changed it to the more familiar Home Guard. Training was given in fieldcraft, observations and use of weapons, some of which was put into operation at Meir aerodrome where firing practice was arranged. Mr L Plumpton, manager of the Broadway cinema in Meir and combatant during the Great War, was appointed Captain of the Home Guard unit. Caverswall vicarage became an emergency communications centre where the parish priest played his part - when the vicar, Rev. V Gower-Jones, later enlisted as an army chaplain, his duties were performed by Rev E. Banks of Shelton.

Another civil defence organisation was the National Fire Service (NFS), whose purpose was to back up the regular Fire Service. In the NFS was Tommy Cliff, who lived in Meir:

'As a tradesman I was in a what was known as a reserved occupation until I was 21. I was based in Meir and being in this reserved occupation I attended night school classes in Tunstall during the war. Following my journey back home from night school I had to report directly to the National Fire Service Depot in Uttoxeter Road, Meir, by Meir Methodist Church. If I was needed for duty that night, I would sleep over behind the Tommy Cliff in his National Fire Service uniform in WW2.

'C' Company Home Guard, The Meir, 1940-1944, 3rd Staffs Battalion photographed close to Holy Trinity church. *Courtesy Len Wrench.*

Men of the Auxiliary Fire Service, later the National Fire Service, at their post in Uttoxeter Road, Meir. Bill Bloor is third left. Many of the firemen were sent to Liverpool and Coventry during the Blitz.
Courtesy of Dennis Bloor.

The former National Fire Service station during the World War 2, now a garage, Swedish Car Parts. Terry Atkinson on the right.

brick-built fire station under an old army blanket which itched like hell. There were two other NFS depots in the area available if we needed them. One was at Weston Coyney, where another trailer-mounted water pump was kept in an old garage, and another at Longton, but with Meir aerodrome close by our depot, there was always the chance of attack from German aircraft or one of our own aircraft crashing.'

Although the Meir NFS depot did not have a regular fire engine, Tommy Cliff recalls: *'We did have access to a few portable pumps of our own, mounted on their own trailers, which we pulled along using cars. I remember one of these 'tow-cars' was a big open-topped Chrysler motor car. But there was another vehicle in Meir we sometimes had at our disposal. We nicknamed it the 'Red Shadow.' Basically this vehicle was a truck with a cab behind, to which a frame and a cross bar had been attached. A ladder was then strapped to this with a piece of rope and the other end of the ladder secured at the tail end of the truck. And that was it - this was all we had.'* Still better than nothing at all.

Meir Golf Course had closed, but with its golfers gone, George Bartlam maintained the fairways in *'in an odd moment'* away from his daily round on the farm.

THE   MEIR   SCOUT   HOUSE.   THE   FIREPLACE.

The Meir scout house in Chatsworth Place was opened in 1941.
Below: Commemorative brochure celebrates 50 years of scouting at Kibblestone, 3 miles from Meir.

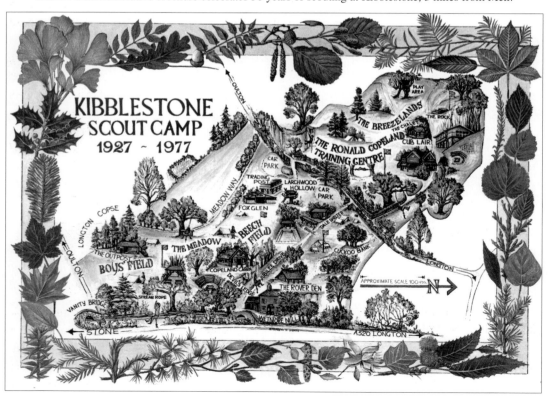

CHAPTER 4

'We will fight them on the beaches. We will never surrender'

Winston Churchill

1941 began grimly. The evacuation of Dunkirk, successful as it was in rescuing Allied servicemen from French beaches - including Stanley Bowman from Meir - was one amongst many setbacks. A campaign to bolster morale was required at home and abroad, that the Allies could overcome the enemy. Newspapers assured its readers that the 'bulldog spirit' would prevail, come what may, although no one was sure WHEN.

The mobilisation of the country's workforce into producing much needed military materials began. Industrial factories that before 1939 had produced motor cars now manufactured aircraft, engines, tanks and guns. But with increased bombing by the Luftwaffe of factory areas, plans to manufacture armaments using 'shadow factories' were put in train.

The idea was a simple one. A duplicate or 'shadow' factory would carry on industrial war production if enemy action put the original site out of action. Lord Nuffield and Wilfred Joseph were pioneers in advocating this scheme across the country. One local *'shadow factory'*, managed by Rootes Securities Limited, and covering over 500,000 sq feet, was located at Meir and Blythe Bridge. Here, at the eastern end of Meir, bombers, night fighters, coastal and torpedo aircraft all rolled off the production lines. Once finished they were trundled across Grindley Lane to Meir Aerodrome for testing for airworthiness before ferry pilots flew them to their ultimate destination.

The resolve of young men and women hardened. The time was rapidly approaching when they would be called to arms. *'Ours not to reason why, Ours but to do or die.'* Some local schools persuaded them to join in effect a junior branch of the Royal Air Force. As encouragement early in March 1941 a very distinguished airman paid them a courtesy visit:

'There was an inspection of 2 out of 5 Air Training Corps (ATC) squadrons by Sir William Mitchell KCB, KBE, DSO, AFC, MC, Inspector General of the RAF. He inspected the Longton High School 239 Squadron and was received by Mr M.V. Gregory, the headmaster and acting officer commanding the squadron of four flights; one was entirely composed of boys from the school, while the others were of former scholars and ex-elementary boys.'

Throughout 1940 and 1941 Nazi bombing inflicted enormous damage on major cities. The landscape changed over-night. Churches were not immune, with many damaged and destroyed. Coventry Cathedral was virtually obliterated when Coventry was set on fire by German incendiaries in 1941.

But war or not, the 50th anniversary of the dedication of Holy Trinity church took place on June 8, 1941, Rev. Bernard Paton Jones officiating at 6.30 pm. On the surface a happy occasion given the circumstances, but other more sombre services intruded into the fabric of Meir's everyday life. A requiem service at Holy Trinity in 1941 for Pilot Officer GC Blunt and Leading Aircraftman A. Ashley brought home the human cost of war that many only perceived as distant. The Bishop of Lichfield visited to lend his physical and moral support presiding at an RAF and Homeguard Service Parade in the Meir TA Drill Hall on June 20, 1941.

CHIEF SCOUT IN THE POTTERIES

Meir Youth Centre Opened

Lord Somers, K.C.M.G., D.S.O., M.C., paid his first visit to Staffordshire since succeeding the late Lord Baden-Powell as Chief Scout, when on Saturday afternoon he formally opened the Scout House which has been built by the City of Stoke-on-Trent and District Boy Scouts' Association at Chatsworth Place, Meir.

War throws up many contradictions and it must have puzzled many in Meir that now, at such a critical moment in the war, May 1941 should see the opening of a long sought after, but hardly essential facility in Meir. Lord Somers visiting the city for the first time since succeeding the late General Baden-Powell as Chief Scout, opened the Scout House in Chatsworth Place:

'Its construction was due to a collaboration between the City of Stoke on Trent council and the District Boy Scouts Association. The war has caused the abandonment of a

THE MEIR SCOUT HOUSE.   THE DORMITORY.

scheme for the erection of a new community centre in Meir which was the largest of the city's housing estates. Mr Ronald Copeland has given £200 and along with a grant from the Imperial Scout Headquarters in London, the fund quickly totalled £500. It is the only centre of its type in the Midlands and features a troop room, a Rover den, patrol rooms, kitchen, shower, bath, changing room and accommodation for a workshop. In addition to providing a centre for social events, lectures and meetings for boys in the district, it provides an important extension of scouting activities and youthful exuberance in war-time Meir.'

The financial cost of the war, in human and financial terms, was enormous. Many schemes began during the war's early stages. The sale of War Bonds and War Savings campaigns were common here and later in the United States. Post War Credits too, another extra form of taxation, was paid by non-military personnel working during the war for which certificates were issued. The government promised to repay in peacetime the principal loaned plus interest, but in truth most savers reached retirement before this happened. Since one Spitfire cost around £5,000 a determined and sustained effort was required to raise more money for all those shot down. The public in many towns, like Stafford and Leek, saved what money they could and sponsored their own named aircraft whose fortunes in combat were avidly documented.

A growing awareness emerged that these loan schemes alone would be insufficient to raise enough money. The burgeoning cost of the war would mean increasing the government's income through greater taxation. With this in view, Sir Kingsley Wood, Chancellor of the Exchequer raised the rate of income tax by 1s.6d to 10 shillings in the pound. In April the previous year, income tax had already been set at 7s 6d in the pound, along with an extra 3d on tobacco, 1d on a pint of beer and 1s 9^1/2d on a bottle of whisky.

The following tables in pounds (£), shillings (s), and pence (d) were introduced in 1941-42. 12d. = 1s. 20s = £1. One shilling was equivalent to 5 pence of modern currency.

INCOME TAX TABLE FOR A SINGLE MAN FOR THE YEAR 1941-1942

Total Annual Income(£)	Old charge (£.s.d) Annual	New charge (£.s.d.) Annual	Post War Credits (£.s.)
120	---	7.10. 0	7.10
150	6. 5. 0	17.17. 0	9.15
200	16.13.0	32.10. 0	10.16
300	37.10.0	66. 2. 0	17. 7
400	70. 5. 0	111. 2. 0	23. 6
500	105.14.0	156. 2. 0	26.13
600	141. 2.0	201. 2. 0	30. 0
800	211.19.0	291. 2. 0	36.13
1000	282.15.0	381. 2. 0	43. 6
1250	371. 6.0	493.12. 0	56.13
1500	459.17.0	606. 2. 0	60. 0

The government would in 1942 double the income tax of an 18 year old miner with a weekly wage of £3-8-0d plus overtime, indicating the seriousness of the country's plight.

With less disposable income life's little extras were trimmed back. Visits to the pub and cinema would be fewer with more nights stopping in. The main source of entertainment was the radio, many favourites drawing live audiences - and large Forces' audiences. There was *Much-Binding-in-the-Marsh* (everyday events at an imaginary RAF station) with Kenneth Horne, Richard Murdoch and Sam Costa; *ITMA* (*It's That Man Again*) with the irrepressible Tommy Handley, Arthur Askey and Jack Train's 'Colonel Chinstrap' ('*I don't mind if I do*') and Mrs Mopps ('*Can I do yer now sir?*'), and of course Vera Lynn. The BBC broadcast *Workers' Playtime* to wartime factories like Meir and Swynnerton using the 'Tannoy' public address system, helping people get through the day.

By October, news of a promotion relieved the gloom and was received with great pride by those who knew the family living in Meir: 'Mr Harry Charles Walters, 22, has been made a Squadron leader in the RAF. The son of Captain J.B. Walters M.C. and Mrs S.Walters of Lynwood, Weston Road, Meir, Squadron Leader Walters joined the Royal Air Force Volunteer Reserve (RAFVR) in 1939 at the outbreak of hostilities.'

On the battlefield, at sea or in the air, the Grim Reaper was never far from the combatant but to meet one's demise in a domestic environment was to say the least, unfortunate and unexpected. But no matter how it came death wore the same face: 'Harold Maskery (43) foreman bricklayer, of 58, Broadway, Meir died when he was hit by a lorry whilst walking to work.'

While an attempt to provoke the United States by sinking the *USS Reuben James* with the loss of 115 US sailors had failed, the attack on the US Pacific fleet by the Japanese in Hawaii, in late 1941, succeeded in *'awakening the sleeping giant.'* For British and Empire forces the entry of the United States in to the war was an event they and Winston Churchill had been seeking for some time:

'December 7, 1941 a day that will live in infamy, the United States was deliberately and violently attacked by the naval and air forces of the Empire of Japan.' President Franklin Delano Roosevelt (FDR) proclaimed addressing US Congress in the wake of the attack on Pearl Harbor, leaving in its wake over 3000 US Navy personnel and civilian deaths.

During the previous year, FDR and Britain's wartime leader of the coalition government, Winston Churchill, had signed the Lend Lease Arrangement, loaning $8 billion of US military equipment to the UK. 50% of the entire American war production was earmarked for the UK, without which, this 'Sceptred Isle' might have been overwhelmed. But there were strings attached to the agreement. For its part, the United Kingdom handed over millions of pounds in gold bullion, gave the USA access to British dependencies and waived patents to cutting edge technology in scientific and industrial research. But these were desperate times and desperate times required desperate measures.

Across Europe, people were on the move, if not escaping Hitler's armies then avoiding Allied bombing. This country, as in the First World War, accepted and sheltered many fleeing the fray during that cold winter of early 1942: 'There was a reunion held at Stoke Catholic Church for Belgian refugees after a solemn mass. 85 guests were entertained to a tea by Sister Winifred at St Dominic's High School.'

Britain's colliers were an essential ingredient of the war effort and a much-respected churchman, Rev. E.S. Woods, saw it as his duty to promote their cause. Following his descent at Mossfield Colliery, Longton, accompanied by the Rector of Hanley in late March, the Bishop of Lichfield only had a short time to wash his hands and face, don a clean shirt and return in early April to perform a duty in Longton:

'The new church of St. Paul the Apostle, Edensor was consecrated by the Bishop of Lichfield on Saturday, 28th March'. The nave only was consecrated - the chancel, lady chapel and tower were to be erected after the war.

Whether it was the fear of German invasion or merely a public safety matter, in June 1942 proposals were announced to immobilise all cars for the duration of the war. Owners were urged to drain the fuel tank, remove the carburettor and pack it in a box. Labelled, bearing the owner's name and address, they were to be handed in at the nearest police station. Was this really necessary? Fears were voiced that petrol soaked carburettors stored in some back room at the local 'nick' actually constituted a greater risk to the guardians of the law than had things been left alone.

Tragically in October three Meir lads, paying the price for a few minutes inattention, died whilst on fire watching duty at the Co-op store in Gravelly Bank. Leslie Goodwin (16) of 24 South Walk, Thomas Joseph Reynolds (15) and Jack Fallows of 30 South Walk, Meir, all perished. It was thought a kettle on a gas ring, boiled over putting out the flame, asphyxiating them all. Six months earlier, on April 1st, 1942 Tom Amos Hall, a platelayer who lived two doors away from one of the lads at 34 South Walk, Meir died at work in the Foley sidings. Death it seemed was everywhere.

The Co-op store at the junction of Gravelly Bank and Sandon Road, Meir.

My own birth, 6 weeks after the battle of El Alamein, was part of a sequence of events typical of the war. In early December an approach to the Commanding Officer of my father's Royal Marine's detachment allowed him compassionate leave to be present at my birth. He left his unit and returned to Meir, the friends with whom he had trained during summer 1942 sailing without him. Convoy ONS 154 left Port Glasgow, just after Christmas 1942, to join the Eastern Fleet in Indo China. One ship in the convoy, a re-registered French merchant man of 2,455 tons renamed *HMS Fidelity*, carried just four 4 inch guns, four torpedo tubes, two Kingfisher seaplanes and a motor torpedo boat, to defend itself and my father's Royal Marine company on board.

Sergeant John Cartlidge Royal Marines 1942.

A few days out, the convoy came under a sustained attack from a German U boat wolfpack during which, of fifteen ships torpedoed, 14 sank. *HMS Fidelity,* after picking up survivors from the stricken *Empire Shackleton,* was itself torpedoed by U435 under its Commander Lt. Cdr. Strelow, sinking on December 30, 1942. 324 Royal Marines and one woman perished. By the merest of great good fortune my father had side-stepped death to live and fight another day.

1942 saw a dramatic change in the Allied cause. Often said that 'before El Alamein we hadn't won a battle, and after it, we never lost one', in the new year of 1942 the 'blood, tears, toil and sweat' of Winston Churchill began to tilt the war in favour of the Allies.

Having left Blighty in January 1943, my father was involved in the invasion of Italy and waded ashore with the Royal Marines in Sicily. Unscathed at the end save for a bout of sandfly fever, he afterwards spoke little of it, save for odd snippets of friends who had fallen along the way.

While the draft continued, those at home carried on. Many women found employment in armaments and factories, while others joined the Women's Land Army. With over 80,000 farmworkers in the services, labour was short on the land. One girl who opted to work on the land was Joan Bowman from Meir. With husband Stanley on active service, she joined 'the Land Army to help the war effort':

'It was a bright and breezy morning, when, having said my farewells to various members of the family, I set off for Stoke station feeling very self-conscious in my uniform and slightly tight shoes. I didn't realise when sending my shoe size, to allow for the thicker socks! Still, away I went holding a suitcase of my father's in one hand and a packet of sandwiches in the other. I handed my ticket to the collector, "Not another one!" he said. I realised what he meant when I passed through the barrier; green and brown uniforms everywhere!

I moved to the far end of the platform and as I stood there, a worried looking lady came up to me. "Excuse me," she said, "but are you going to Henley in Arden?" I nodded. "Oh in that case, can my daughter Margaret join you?" Margaret and I looked at each other and smiled. "Of course!" I said. "Why not?" Little did I realise then the length of time we would be together. The train arrived and we climbed into a carriage, four more girls came in after us and before we knew it we were making friends and deciding to try and keep together. The journey seemed endless. Finally we arrived at our destination. Stiff and tired we got out of the train to be met by a member of the Land Army who led us to a large truck. We were bumped and jostled along country lanes until the truck pulled up in a driveway of a large isolated house, surrounded by a big garden then just fields, apart from one farmhouse and a church.'

Before the war Joan had spent time working in the fields and orchards in Kent and Sussex and with this experience of living in the countryside and its quietness, she settled into her new role quickly, but with some of the girls coming from busy towns, the silence and lack of houses really made their spirits drop.

Girls and women, from every walk of life, many of whom had never seen a cow, tractor or chicken, quickly buckled down to life on the farm. It was hard tiring work, with long hours but the camaraderie of those desperate days helped make life worthwhile. They all had working and dress Land Army uniforms, a greatcoat, hat, green sweater, brown breeches, working shirts, a tie, knee socks, boots, an oilskin and a drill jacket.

'As I had chosen market gardening, which was fairly light work, I was going to work in the garden with three other girls. At 6.30 am we were woken up by a bell and banging on the bedroom door. It was a cool sunny morning, the birds were singing and far off a dog barked. It was scene of complete tranquillity. Given a hoe we busied ourselves with the weeds in the vegetable garden. At the day's end we all had a hot bath - but in 2 inches of water this wasn't easy. Those who came late, didn't even get hot water!

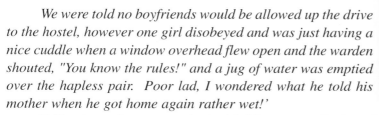

Joan Bowman

Stanley Bowman

We were told no boyfriends would be allowed up the drive to the hostel, however one girl disobeyed and was just having a nice cuddle when a window overhead flew open and the warden shouted, "You know the rules!" and a jug of water was emptied over the hapless pair. Poor lad, I wondered what he told his mother when he got home again rather wet!'

Following a *'wrong posting'* with Margaret to Bedworth, Joan and her friend were billeted next at Atherstone, Warwickshire in a low wooden L-shaped building alongside an old Roman road, Watling Street:

'The warden was tall, stern looking, and though quite strict at times, was very fair with you. The meals were well cooked and plentiful. Miss Hazard was her name, called 'Haphazard' behind her back, her pride and joy was her dog called Phoebe - woe betide any girl heard calling her 'Flea-be'.

Before I go any farther I had better say that our hours of work mostly were 8.00am to 5.30pm unless it was hay-making, harvesting or threshing, when with threshing you often had to work till 5pm on Saturdays instead of one o'clock. At the end of the week you received the princely sum of £2.50, a little extra if you'd been threshing - you really felt well off then.'

Generally there was a little left from this pay after all the expenses had been paid, for make up and outings.

'We had two leaves a year, one week at Christmas, the other during a lull in haymaking and harvesting. The Land Army did issue you with a chit for a rail ticket at these times, any other time you paid your own fare.

After work there wasn't much amusement except the local cinema and because of a 10pm curfew the girls did not see the end of many of the films. They got a late pass on Saturday night to go dancing. Given wartime restrictions, we twisted hair round pipe cleaners and make up was sparingly applied. Those who had perfume were very lucky.'

Although she enjoyed greenhouse work, tending to thousands of outdoor tomato plants, orders now stated that those employed in nurseries would in future be billeted in private houses. Joan didn't want to leave the hostel, so regretfully she had to leave the nursery and take farmwork. This did though have its moments.

'One morning while cleaning out the cowshed, which was really old with a cobble-stone floor, and giving my rendering of Silver Wings in the Moonlight, my feet shot from under me and down I sat in all the water and manure. What a mess! I went to the farm door, knocked on it and asked the farmer if I could pop back to the hostel. "Why?" grunted my happy boss. I turned round. "Alright" he growled "but hurry up!" I had to stand up on the pedals of my bike, no way could I sit on the saddle. I don't know what the people at the laundry thought when they got my smelly overalls!'

There were occasions when some of the Land Girls were injured, some quite badly, working in amongst what was then primitive farm machinery.

''I was once again loading a cart one day with hay, stretching out my hands to clasp a bundle off another girl's pitchfork, when one of the prongs entered my hand between my thumb and forefinger. There was quite a hole. The Warden looked at my swollen hand that night and said it was nothing to make a fuss about, and it was off to work again next day. For a week I had to use the pitchfork across my wrist, the farmer's wife dressing my hand each morning. At the end of the week, the Warden looked at it and I got told off for letting her do it!'

After a year at Atherstone, Joan was moved back to Stratford, leaving her friend Margaret to return to Bedworth. The Stratford Hostel, a large wooden building in rolling countryside did not match up to the quality of the food there 'which was dreadful' so much so, that Joan spent some of her wages in cafes. Breakfast was soggy slices of fatty bread, whilst evening meals started with soup often with maggots floating in it!

'When we had salad we used to have bets over who had the most greenfly! Packed lunches were invariably cheese sandwiches with a bun; you gave a cheer when you found a currant. If we could, we exchanged our cheese for jam sandwiches when the ladies from the village came to help in the fields. When working with Italian prisoners of war they would offer us slices of Lyons cream roll. We felt rather guilty accepting cake but we were heartily sick of buns.'

But life in Stratford did have its compensations: *'I used to salute William Shakespeare on his monument most mornings as I cycled to work over Clopton Bridge, you could imagine how dreamy a town it must have been in his day, the River Avon, lined with weeping willows. Then the graceful swans had their peace disturbed at the weekends when rowing boats were still for hire in the summer.'*

Joan was moved again, this time to Temple Grafton and a large house, some of which was still occupied. Fourteen Land Girls were billeted here: *'I was in a top floor with five beds in it. To my surprise I found I was in the next bed to my friend Margaret - we hadn't seen each other for months as she had been in the Bedworth hostel. So with two other friends, Jean and Mary who came from Leeds, we four spent nearly all our weekends together in Stratford.*

Some of the 'powers that be' suddenly realised that the WLA did exist and sent a few entertainers to the village hall. This was hilarious as the hall was small, but well-built, however the curtains often got stuck so you only saw parts of the performers. There were only oil lamps for lighting and these would gradually go dim and so had to be lowered down on chains and vigorously pumped up again. Even that treat finished one morning. While I was working near to the village there was a tremendous bang. We thought it was a bomb but it was a plane that had crashed, the crew baling out. The plane just missed the village school, partly demolishing the village hall and landing in a field. No one saw a cat or dog for days afterwards!'

After a year at Temple Grafton, Joan had had enough of the poor food and general discomfort. When an opportunity arose to go into private billets in the village with another girl, she jumped at the chance and stayed on one farm. Although domestic conditions were better, the work was at times very hard, like harvesting sugar beet and sprout picking and sorting potatoes by hand on the edge of the open fields with a cold wind blowing. But even here there were compensations.

'One of the labourers was very good at catching rabbits. I took one back to my landlady and the other girl was given milk and eggs, so we helped out our rations. We also had a good big piece of cheese as we were land workers.'

Offered a job on a fruit farm, where she stayed until the end of the war, it was far from dull. With no public conveniences near their work, a 'call of nature' could sometimes lead to embarrassing situations.

'I had to go fruit picking at a farm with a girl I was billeted with, working in the cowsheds. I never thought to ask her where the toilet was so I was hunting around when I spied a small brick building. Going inside there was a kind of pipe going into a hole in the floor and a convenient

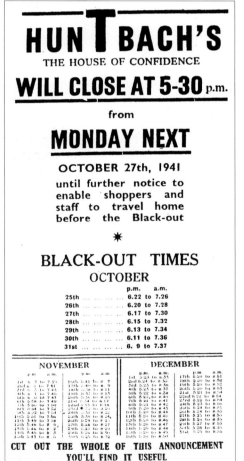

bucket which I used, tipping the contents down the hole. When I told my friend about it that night she said, 'The toilet is in the house!' Evidently the hole was the well that provided *water to the house. They'd have some strong tea that night!'*

She was injured again this time by a wayward horse who trod on her foot causing it to swell. A farm labourer quickly took her to a cold rain water butt, removed her boot and sock and plunged her foot in, to reduce the swelling. Even so she still couldn't walk properly for a week afterwards.

'Fruit picking was a lovely job unless it rained, in which case the water would run up your sleeves. I found apple trees safe enough as the branches were very pliable, but damson tree branches would crack under your weight which was quite frightening when you were high up on a ladder.'

Cycling into Stratford one June evening, Joan looked up to see huge planes towing equally large gliders across the sky. Next morning a farm labourer told them *'our troops are once more on French soil.'* The D-Day invasion had begun. It took until May 8th 1945 before the war in Europe was declared over. *'We were given two days holiday which we spent in Stratford, all food and drinks in the canteen were free. For one day happiness was everywhere even though the Japanese held out until August.'*

With the war over Joan said goodbye to her friends and returned home. Her husband Stanley had survived the war and they were re united. But whatever the future held in store for them both, Joan remembered with great affection Margaret, Jean and Mary, her fellow Land Girls, who had cheered her up when she was depressed and with whom she'd had lots of laughs even when things went terribly wrong.

While mayhem and murder was afoot and on horseback, it may seem odd that the social welfare of the great British public should be thought important. The Beveridge report, a milestone in welfare, appeared, and indicated failings in the social fabric of the country. Local churchmen encompassed a similar opinion, after all, they were at the cutting edge of it, with experience of deprivation within their parishes. And Stoke-on-Trent had plenty. The Venerable Percy Harthill writing in the Stoke Parish Magazine praised the report as a 'real landmark' in social progress, urging its acceptance in principle.

'WINGS for VICTORY' MAY 8th to 15th

OUR AIM —

10 LANCASTERS   10 HURRICANES

10 SPITFIRES

The sense that the corner had been turned and victory was within the grasp of the Allies did not for one moment slacken the pace of fund-raising activities. A 'Wings for Victory' campaign the previous year in Stoke-on-Trent raised an enormous £1.8 million. But a great many had died. Airmen lost from 1939 to 1st Jan 1943 topped 38,000 pilots and crew with another 10,000 missing. 10,000 aircraft had been lost whilst the Royal Navy had lost 41,000 out of 133,000. Many more would lose their life in securing the peace.

Operation 'Market Garden', the Battle of Arnhem, was a disaster in 1944. Allied forces held a much superior German army at bay before being overwhelmed. Amongst so many who paid the price was Lance-sergeant John Baskeyfield, a local choirboy from Stoke-on-Trent, ultimately awarded the Victoria Cross posthumously.

And the war threw up the unusual. One such incident, early in March 1944 and involving a Meir naval officer, was to elevate him into the annals of naval jurisprudence. It began innocuously on the afternoon of March 13, 1944. Cruising on the surface a lookout on the U boat, U 852, 500 miles north of Ascension Island and 700 miles south of Freetown, reported a vessel off the starboard bow. The ship, the Greek registered freighter, *SS Peleus* had left Freetown, W. Africa 5 days earlier, bound for South America and the River Plate, chartered to the British War Transportation Ministry. The U boat captain ordered his ship ahead of *Peleus*, a chase that lasted two and a half hours. By now it was dark. In a deafening moment, two torpedoes hit the *Peleus* in number 2 and 3 holds. It sank in minutes. Nobody knew how many crew had abandoned ship, jumping into the open sea before *Peleus* sank. Those who escaped now clung to the flotsam of hatch covers and rafts. U 852 surfaced asking the survivors about their destination and cargo. Now in a moment of unspeakable cruelty, the U boat commander, seeking to remove any evidence of the attack, ordered his crew to first machine gun the rafts to sink them along with the bodies of the *Peleus'* crew, and then in a gruesome attempt to eradicate all traces of the *Peleus,* throw hand grenades into the waterlogged rafts. U 852 slipped under the waves.

Two and half weeks later, off the west coast of Africa, U 852 now on a course for the Cape of Good Hope was located with direction finders from its radio transmission concerning the Peleus' sinking on March 15. The U boat escaped but on April 30, British radio intelligence found the submarine again off the southern tip of Aden. In early May, caught on the surface by RAF Wellingtons, U 852 was hit by depth charges and raking gunfire. Damaged, Kapitanleutnant Heinz Wilhelm Eck submerged his boat but chlorine gas from spilt battery acid caused him to re-surface, beaching off the Somaliland coast at Ras Hafun. In the ensuing exchange many of the U852's crew died and Eck was taken prisoner.

The fate of many of the deadly U-boats, including U852, towards the end of the war.

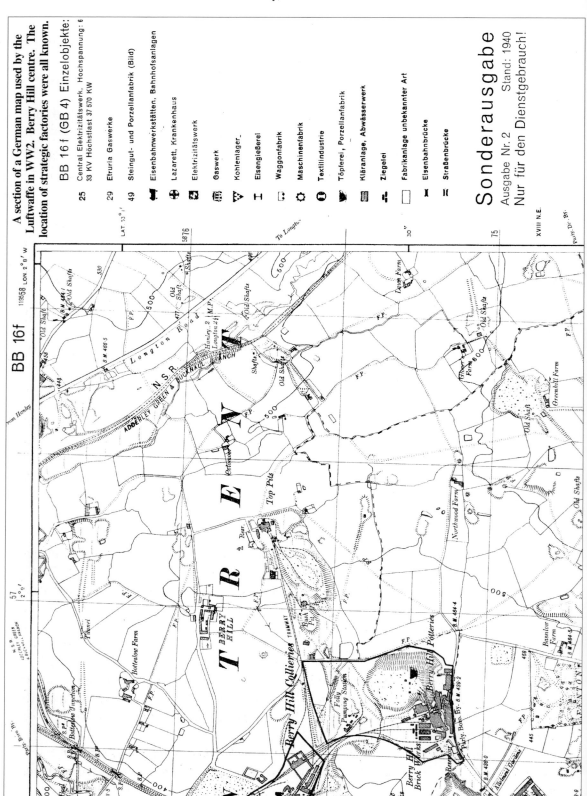

A section of a German map used by the Luftwaffe in WW2. Berry Hill centre. The location of strategic factories were all known.

BB 16 f (GB 4) Einzelobjekte:

25 Central Elektrizitätswerk, Hochspannung: 6 33 KV Höchstlast 37 570 KW

29 Etruria Gaswerke

49 Steingut- und Porzellanfabrik (Bild)

Eisenbahnwerkstätten, Bahnhofsanlagen

Lazarett, Krankenhaus

Elektrizitätswerk

Gaswerk

Kohlenlager

Eisengießerei

Waggonfabrik

Maschinenfabrik

Textilindustrie

Töpferei, Porzellanfabrik

Kläranlage, Abwässerwerk

Ziegelei

Fabrikanlage unbekannter Art

Eisenbahnbrücke

Straßenbrücke

Sonderausgabe
Ausgabe Nr. 2   Stand: 1940
Nur für den Dienstgebrauch!

CHAPTER 5

'If anything can go wrong, it will!'   Murphy's Law

Despite the submariners attempts to destroy their logbooks, a British boarding party encountered a wealth of information including the boat's Kriegstagebuch (KTB) or war log. Although unaware of the significance of the entire incident at the time, for one British Naval Officer in the boarding party, the entire episode would ensure him of a place in naval history.

The ordeal of three members of the SS Peleus' crew, adrift for 35 days in a tiny life raft, was over. By a miracle on April 20, 1944 they were spotted by a keen-eyed hand on the Portuguese registered Steamer, *SS Alexandre Silva,* bound for Angola. Lifted aboard, Chief Officer Liossis, greaser Rocco Said and seaman Dimitrios Argiros slowly recovered their faculties. When the freighter docked a week later they recounted their harrowing story to British Intelligence Officers. Immediately classified as Top Secret, the survivors' testimonies led to the indictment of Lt Eck and four officers on October 6, 1945.

Heinz Wilhelm Eck's joined the Reichsmarine in April 1934. Commissioned in April 1937 he took command of U 852 in June 1943. Now two years later, he was facing the daunting prospect of a War Crimes trial. Instrumental in the capture of Lt Eck 18 months earlier was a young local Royal Navy lieutenant. The Evening Sentinel announced proudly:

'A local naval officer Lieutenant Kennedy-Gordon aged 33, of Myrtle Villa, Uttoxeter Road, Meir, was responsible for the capture of the German U-boat commander, Captain Heinz Eck, who with four other members of the crew are facing trial at Hamburg. The trial opened yesterday, the five being charged with committing war crimes in that they, in the Atlantic in March 1944 when captain and members of a U boat, sank the Greek ship, Peleus in violation of the laws and usages of war, and were concerned in killing seven British merchant seaman by firing hand grenades at them.'

Lieutenant Gordon in an interview with the Sentinel told this graphic story:

'After the sinking of the Greek ship, our intelligence service kept track of the U boat and our sloop HMS Falmouth came up with her in the Gulf of Aden when we were escorting the French sloop, D'Entrecasteau. The U boat which was identified as U 852 reputed to be of 2,700 tons, had been attacked and somewhat damaged by our aircraft. We too attacked. In an attempt to escape our radar beam the submarine went in close to shore finally going aground. Vain attempts were made by the crew to get her afloat again. A boarding party in charge of myself then left in the ship's motor boat with orders to capture the submarine crew who were still under fire from the guns of the sloop. When we were one and a half miles away, the submarine blew up, the crew of 70 having first abandoned their ship. About 30 managed to reach the shore, the remainder were either drowned or had fallen victim to our guns. We had kept the boat under fire in the hope of preventing the crew abandoning and scuttling her.

We captured the survivors and I personally had the pleasure of taking Captain Heinz Eck as my prisoner. Able Seaman Bailey of Porthill was also a member of our boarding party.'   18th October, 1945

In the spring of 1945, facing the inevitable collapse of the Third Reich, on May 1, 1945, Hitler promoted one of his most trusted officers as his heir before committing suicide. German Radio solemnly announced, *'On the 30th April the Führer nominated Grand Admiral Dönitz to be his successor.'* Karl Dönitz was Führer for seven days then captured at Flensburg before surrendering the German Armed Forces to the Allies in May 1945.

It was Dönitz's U boat 'Wolf Pack' strategy that had devastated Allied shipping early in the war and forced the United Kingdom to the brink of defeat. Now in the autumn of 1945, with victory in Europe and the Far East secured, the War Crimes Tribunals began in Nuremberg and lasted 11 months. The two cases of Grand Admiral Karl Donitz and Lt. Eck were amongst the many heard before the Judge Advocate, Mr Melford Stevenson KC.

At the trial of Lt Eck, the testimonies of Chief Officer Antonios Liossis, greaser Rocco Said and seaman Dimitrios Argiros of the *SS Peleus* condemned Eck along with four of the officers of U 852. But before sentence could be carried out, 'Leutnant Eck the German U boat Commander who was captured by a Meir Naval Officer, Lieutenant K. Gordon, is to be a witness at the Nuremburg trial. The execution of Lt Eck has been postponed and his evidence is being taken by a Commission.' Nov 1945

Testimony from Lt Eck was then given in court in the trial of Admiral Dönitz. A crucial principle of Dönitz's defence related to the actions of Lt Eck and his crew over the sinking and subsequent actions against the *SS Peleus,* that Eck's actions 'were not in pursuance of an order from him'. By doing so, Dönitz was divesting himself of any involvement in the incident. He must have realised by this act, he was condemning Lt Eck to death. Both Dönitz and Eck were found guilty. Whilst Dönitz was imprisoned to be released in 1956, Leutnant Eck was shot on Luneburg Heath.

Kapitanleutnant Heinz-Wilhelm Eck remains the only U boat captain ever to be tried, convicted and executed for war crimes during the Second World War - a saga in which Lieutenant Kennedy Gordon from Meir played a large part.

Meir aerodrome at the end of 1945 was winding down as the necessity for its aircraft and services diminished. Eric Clutton recalls the scene:

'In 1945 things happened fast after I had left Meir. So much so three months later when I came back on leave, the airfield was DEAD. When I left the Flight Sheds at Meir Aerodrome in December '45 to join the RAF, the 'Mustang' contract and 'Liberator' contract had ended. Just a few dozen Harvards were left. In its heyday, the whole top end of the airfield along Grindley Lane and Sandon Road, was choc-a-bloc with row after row of Harvards and Mustangs. I was used to taxiing P51 Mustangs but not Harvards. There was a very good reason for this. There were 'Standing Orders' that no Harvard should be started unless someone was standing by with a fire extinguisher because they caught fire easily, mainly due to the starting process requiring three hands! The Mustangs were much more civilised.

The Harvards and Mustangs were towed across Grindley Lane from the factory, although one or two Mustangs were driven across. A few guys were employed whose job it was to taxi the aircraft about as required, and by devious means I managed to take their place on a few occasions taxiing Mustangs at 16 years old. I had done a fair bit of flying with the Air Training Corps (ATC) so had as much idea as the regular guys anyway. The

Beaufighters, an important British plane in WW2, were made in Meir.

five bombers in the official photographs are indeed Liberators-the last of the contract. They flew in from RAF Coastal Command and we removed the turrets etc and converted them to freighters. The first one made three attempts to land, all on different days, but it was empty of course and eventually landed uphill with no problems. All landings were made up hill - the slope of the airfield making downhill a bit dodgy as the pilot of a Lockheed P38 Lightning discovered. The pilot, an American, had decided to visit his girlfriend in Stoke. He ran off the end of the runway and had to deliberately 'ground loop' it, collapsing the undercarriage. In the event he crashed through the perimeter fence ending up with a wing tip hanging over into Uttoxeter Road. After his disaster, unscathed and non-plussed, he caught a bus and continued his journey! We had a few similar incidents a Meir.

The first Liberator to arrive at Meir airfield was interesting to say the least. It landed in a very short distance (uphill), it proceeded to taxi up the hill to the Flight Sheds on the two inboard engines, with Mr Schultz driving and a guy under each wing tip. The 'Lib' has a 100 ft wingspan and the 2 flight sheds were 120 feet apart, so it was a tight squeeze! We all downed tools and stood around to watch the fun. One wing tip guy must have been a bit dozy because the 'Lib' converged on one of the Sheds and the wing tip impacted the huge open doors (2 feet thick and full of concrete at the bottom). Schultz never felt the impact so he just kept going, shunting this door into the next one and the next one and so on. We just took one look and fled! The doors hit the opposite end of the hangar with an enormous crash, followed by a rain of dust and bird droppings from the roof. Fortunately the doors stayed on their tracks but I saw the wing of the 'Lib' bend like a bow before it straightened out with a BOING! and the whole four-engined bomber gave two hops sideways! I can see it now. We just replaced the wing tip!

When I worked at Meir, cameras were very much 'verboten' although I met up with Mr Schultz (our chief test pilot) after the war, when he was headmaster of a small country school near Rugeley. His office was full of photos taken at Meir! I wonder what ever happened to them?'

Throughout the later stages of the war 'DIMMING TIME' notices still operated, typically 5.31pm to 8.55am but ended on the Monday following April 19, 1945. With peace, life returned to near normality. Windows were not curtained any more and street lights could be lit, except for a strip around the coast. Double British Summer Time ran from Easter Monday April 2, 1945 to July 15, 1945. During WW2, Double Summer Time - 2 hours in advance of Greenwich Mean Time (GMT) - was used for the period when ordinary Summer Time would normally have been in force, while in the winter clocks were kept just ONE hour in advance of GMT. Its main use was in saving electricity by creating longer hours of daylight in the evenings.

At the Broadway, *The Purple Heart* starring Dana Andrews and Richard Conte had patrons pouring through its Art Deco doors, while for the second part of the week, the fare included John Wayne in *Fighting See Bees*. After so much death an odd choice, but with 26 local cinemas, devotees had a feast of films within a short distance of their front door.

With the peace, the coalition government that had weathered the good and bad times between 1939 and 1945 was dissolved. The quest for a new prospective parliamentary candidate kicked off in early summer. In Meir - then in the Stone constituency - it was a three horse race. One rowdy election meeting at the Broadway Cinema at which Major Hugh Fraser, the prospective Conservative candidate, addressed a volatile audience of miners, would make history.

On the sporting side, Stoke City's Stan Matthews and Frank Soo represented the RAF against Coventry on January 20. In February Matthews, Soo, along with Neil Franklin all played for England against the 'auld enemy', Scotland at Villa Park. As well as local pride in this Stoke City trio playing at international level, many at the Victoria Ground would have warmed to the news that former Stoke City player, Driver Harry Davies, had been awarded the Military Medal for his contribution to the victory.

It was not the club's only war-time connection. Another came in the unlikely shape of an armed trawler. Named *Stoke City*, its crew gave monetary gifts to the Lord Mayor (Alderman Kemp), even collecting £10 to be distributed between City sailors' orphans.

Notwithstanding, Stoke-on-Trent and Meir had avoided heavy bombing, much of the city's housing stock was in a poor state of repair. A new building programme was started, given the obvious constraints of cash and labour. At a Housing Committee City Council meeting with local builders and building trades representatives, the Lord Mayor, Alderman Kemp declared alarmingly *'The city needed 25,000 houses'*. Coming at the end of the war, the chances of achievement were slim. The number actually built in Stoke on Trent between 1945 and 1958 was under 20,000.

But there were opportunities, for some anyway. Leading Aircraftman Frank Boden RAF, and a former pupil of 239 Squadron ATC, gained a commission as a Pilot Officer, following training in Canada; his proud parents living at 94 Weston Road. Another ex 239 Squadron ATC graduate Sergeant Granville Edwards, Royal Air Force Volunteer Reserve (RAFVR) received 'a wing' as a wireless operator/air gunner.

For others the future was clouded by sadness. For a moment Clara Walklate and daughter Pat, the announcement that Sergeant William Henry Walklate, husband and father had been killed in action would supersede everything else. Their front door at 6 Meir View would remain closed to keep the world at arm's length and contain their grief, while at 44

Everyone had to have an identity card and coupons were issued to limit the purchase of many items like food and clothing.

Grosvenor Road the family life of the relatives of Lance Corporal HG Wright, aged 32, killed on active service in Germany, lay in ruins.

Throughout the war the clergy ministered to the faithful and those not so sure, come hell or high water. Many, the Rev Gower Jones of Caverswall was one, saw it as his duty to be 'under fire' with the rest of the men, joining the Forces as chaplains. Father Reginald Joseph Moore won the Military Cross in Italy in 1945, while others worked assiduously on the home front, raising funds for numerous good causes. The Bishop of Lichfield said:

'The quality of the work of the rank and file of the parochial clergy, toilsome, self-sacrificing and inconspicuous is not always understood or appreciated by the public. Those who are 'in the know', realise to the full what the clergy are always giving of service to the church and the community.'

The Military Cross

Was this a clever recruitment drive, following news in January that 'There was a shortage of clergy with no curates coming forward?' But in Normacot, parishioners welcomed the Rev. C.R. Ollier M.A. from Boothen, Stoke, succeeding Rev.W.E. Mountford in February 1946.

January 1946, the coldest for 5 years(21.5F on January 26), pushed up the price of coal by 3s 6d a ton. The food supply too, unreliable and volatile, was epitomised by an advertisement for MacFarlane Lang biscuits in the local press; 'There wouldn't be any biscuits for some little time!' Oh lackaday! Nor would there be any sweets either as Old Betty Plant, the sweet manufacturer, caught fire.

The first summer in peacetime for 6 years saw 450 child evacuees from 'homes' in North Staffordshire return to Greater London. How many evacuees were billeted in Meir for the duration, one wonders? Were you one?

Stan in the famous 1953 Cup Final.

Most working people, especially women, were still employed in pottery manufacture.

CHAPTER 6

'This island is made mainly of coal and surrounded by fish. Only an organizing genius could produce a shortage of coal and fish at the same time.'
Aneurin Bevan 1897-1960

In 1946, with few pleasures and little money for 'treats' in post-war Britain, the BBC shouldered the burden of how the great mass of the population learned of news, world events and sporting occasions. What then must have been the reaction to a newspaper story that *'Wireless licences would soon to cost £1 a year'*? Was nothing sacred?

Many in the Meir were football supporters, religiously following Stoke City, the 'Potters', and the progress of their favourite player, Stanley Matthews. Returning after war time service with the RAF, Matthews was awarded his 44th cap in 1946 in the England vs Belgium match. Stan now held the record number of appearances for England pipping previous holder Arsenal's Ernie Hapgood. Matthews, one of the finest footballers of his generation and probably of all time, never reaped the huge monetary rewards of future soccer stars. However Stan, a modest man, undoubtedly was thrilled and probably embarrassed at the public recognition of his talents. The local paper noted, 'Stanley Matthews has been awarded £100 of savings certificates by the Council of the Football Association.'

Stoke City Football Club directors also made an application to give Stanley Matthews a gift themselves. At the presentation Sir Ernest Johnson summed up what many felt about this 'Son of the Potteries': *'There was no one who had helped more put Stoke on the map than Stanley Matthews, whose modesty and general character was that of a gentleman. They could never repay what he had done for sport in North Staffs. Well done, Stan!'*

A month later he returned in his best suit wearing a clean shirt and with Sunday shoes polished for another accolade. This time, Stoke City Council presented him with an illuminated address commemorating his record number of appearances playing for England. It read, *'To Stanley Matthews, We, the Lord Mayor, Aldermen, Councillors and Citizens of Stoke-on-Trent desire to express our deep affection of the honour you have brought to the city by setting up a record of international appearances for England in football matches, a feat which will probably remain for all time. We are gratified that you have proved to the world that Stoke-on-Trent has a son of which we are justly proud.'*

Stanley Matthews replied that he was delighted he had been able to render some service for the city by his football activities; this was the proudest moment of his life. That was Stan all over though wasn't it, modest to the end!

Unhappily between the two presentations, tragedy overtook luckless spectators at Stoke City's FA cup match at Burnden Park, Bolton. At the match refereed by Fenton-born Mr Dutton, many were crushed to death. Perhaps it was fate; footballers are overly superstitious, many following absurd rituals before going on to the field of play. Incredibly in November 1946 when Stoke City Football Club's mascot, Blackie the cat, was reported lost, its disappearance was blamed for Stoke City's defeat by Wolves!

APPALLING CUP-TIE DISASTER

28 Killed in Crowd Turmoil at Bolton-Stoke Match

| ANY MORE TAKEN TO | *Crowd Invades the Pitch:* 26 Minutes Hold-up | AMATEUR SWIMMING | Arson Expert Inspects the Queen Elizabeth | News In Brief |

Much of Stoke's hand-me-down housing condemned people to living in squalor reminiscent of Dickensian times. Some, marginally more fortunate, were rehoused in utility prefabricated concrete houses (prefabs), remaining part of the local landscape for decades. New housing would be theirs one day, but when? It was 'jam tomorrow', all over again!

Hanley in the late 1930s

Almost everything was in short supply, rationed by a Labour government gamely grappling with huge social and economic problems.

Keele Hall in the 1930s

So it was perhaps surprising that the future of higher education should appear on the political agenda. One, amongst many, was a proposal to create a university for Stoke-on-Trent. Rev Thomas Horwood, vicar of Etruria, leader of the Labour group on Stoke City Council, worked tirelessly for that cause. With Lord Lindsay of Birker (Master of Balliol College) this far-reaching plan slowly received acceptance and credibility. Negotiations to secure a site began. Finally a deputation approached Col. Sneyd at Keele, near Newcastle under Lyme with a view to acquiring the Keele Estate, the Hall and 640 acres of rolling parkland.

Founding a new university in 'Austerity Britain' should not be underestimated and would have defeated anyone less determined than its two main promoters. In October 1950, the University College of North Staffordshire opened. Lord Lindsay and the battling clergyman from Etruria had worked miracles but were about to face enormous challenges.

New challenges, of a different kind, faced local clergymen. In Spring the vicar of Edensor, Rev. Francis Noble, moved to St Mark's, Basford; in the autumn, Rev. Robert Bell, Vicar of Holy Trinity, Meir, appointed by the King to the vicariate of St Mark's, Ocker Hill, Tipton, departed with unique memories of wartime Meir, its parishioners, service personnel and the turmoil of the late 30s and 40s. Rev H.V. Woodward, a curate at Holy Trinity, slipped effortlessly into the shoes vacated by his predecessor. Whatever the future had in store, it was difficult to imagine a period in history as demanding as the previous decade. A pattern of regular Sunday worship was still part of peoples' lives, although in November, 1946 the sale of a Hanley Church was blamed on 'falling attendances.'

August was damp and depressing, the wettest since 1917, when only those who had recently dismantled the Andersen shelter in the garden and re seeded the lawn, would be cheering as close to 5" of rain tumbled from the skies.

With no television, many went out in the evening after work. The pub and the 'pictures' were popular, but recitals, the theatre and concerts (Richard Tauber, Gigli, Paul Robeson and Rachmaninoff all appeared locally) broadened the choice. For those seeking cerebral stimulation, a talk or seminar given by an expert in his field was popular. One of the first lectures at the Reginald Mitchell Memorial Theatre, Hanley was given in October by the distinguished aeronautical engineer, Air Commodore Sir Frank Whittle C.B.E., designer of the world's first jet engine. 'Standing room' only.

The Canberra, the jet aircraft developed from Frank Whittle's invention.

Whittle Road, Meir, ensures a link with Meir's aeronautical past.

On this occasion his talk revolved around the Spitfire. Given the aircraft's pedigree, and association with Reginald Mitchell and Stoke-on-Trent, it proved popular. A guard of honour from the Air Training Corps came to attention, greeting Sir Frank as he entered the theatre. In Meir his name is honoured in the naming of Whittle Road.

In a short space of time, the jet engine created by Frank Whittle increased the capabilities of aircraft massively. Two years on, in 1949, the Canberra, a twin-engine fighter bomber, made by the English Electric Company at Stafford, flew at the Farnborough Air Display. In the early 1950s the Hawker Hunter captured the world air speed record and the world's first jet passenger aircraft, the Comet, appeared.

The future of Meir aerodrome still plagued City Council meetings but a decision taken during the few days falling between Christmas 1946 and New Year offered new prospects:

'Following a recent visit to the city by officials of the Ministry of Civil Aviation, it is announced that the Stoke-on-Trent aerodrome at Meir is shortly to be de-requisitioned. The aerodrome was in the course of being developed as an airport when war broke out in 1939 and it was immediately requisitioned by the government, who erected new hangars and made extensive alterations. After the Ministry of Aircraft Production, it was transferred to the Ministry of Civil Aviation but for many months the place has been lying idle, although some of the new buildings are being used by industrial concerns. The Aerodrome Committee has plans in being for developing the aerodrome as a municipal enterprise.'

Although the Meir 'shadow factory' was small nationally, the release of other 'shadow factories' to commercial use gave employment to 200,000 workers, as the country staggered back to its feet. In late 1945 the bizarrely titled Projectile and Engineering Company Limited of Battersea moved into the empty factories on Meir aerodrome, manufacturing colliery mechanical and loading equipment and also refrigerators. But what did 'a municipal enterprise' mean'? As usual the Ministry men left everyone guessing.

Winter 1947 was one of the severest in modern times and came at a time of serious fuel shortages. Although victorious in war, many now shivered in the intense cold. From January 24 to March 14, a continuous blanket of snow covered the ground at Harper Adams College, Newport, Shropshire. Blizzards cut off the moorland villages at Alstonefield, Ilam, Butterton and Grindon and relief supplies were flown in. Tragically a Handley Page Halifax sent on this mission came down in poor weather on bleak Grindon Moor, killing the eight crew. A plaque in Grindon Church to the courageous airmen records this selfless but tragic act in that bitter winter.

Chilled to the marrow, few gained satisfaction in the possibility that this could be the last time they would have to suffer, as the creation of a new National Coal Board promised a state monopoly that would be better than a fragmented privately owned industry.

Meaford power station, near Barlaston, neared completion. At a cost of £5m its opening, 6 months later, prevented a recurrence of the power shortages. Labour stalwart 'Manny' Shinwell opened the new complex in October 1947.

The wartime standby, Double Summer Time returned from April 13 to August 10 to eke out meagre stocks of coal. Eighteen months after the victory, the effects of the war still exerted a debilitating effect on everyday life. Some sought new horizons. Local newspapers told the tale of one Meir resident under the banner headline, 'From Meir to Melbourne'. It was difficult to think of anything more dramatic. Was it to avoid winter's icy blast or a depressing future? Was the grass really greener in the Colonies?

The marriage of Princess Elizabeth and the Duke of Edinburgh in November 1947 pierced the winter's gloom with its pageantry. Few saw the ceremony but listened huddled around the radio, celebrating the occasion with jam tarts, slab cake and tea. There might even have been ham sandwiches - if you could clap your hands on any ham, which was still rationed.

In early 1948, England and Wales recorded the lowest infant mortality ever - 52 per 1,000 live births. It was one of many benchmarks used to judge the progress of social improvement in the country. Remarkably during the 60 years from the gas-lit end of Victoria's reign, infant mortality was now one third of that in 1889 and great credit to those who had introduced public health regimes. Real progress had been made.

Meir Golf Club spluttered on fitfully. A depleted membership, reluctant to raise the money to rejig the course and club house searched for a 'white knight' for their cause. Help was at hand in the presence of Dr C.W. Healey, a local GP and Consultant.

Former Sergeant Ernest Albert Egerton VC, a veteran of the Great War, attended the opening of Blythe Bridge and Forsbrook War Memorial in April. It was most fitting that he should be chosen.

Although food production increased, *'because of shortages on the land, former German prisoners of war were to be used to increase food production'*, even though they were still classified as aliens.

Another local hero from a long forgotten 'heroic' age appeared fleetingly across the obituary columns of local and national papers. Able seaman Joseph Leese, assured of a place in polar history through his deeds with Captain Scott (1910-1913), died at his home in Meir in the days before Christmas, 1948. His claim to fame, a classic case of being in the 'right place at the right time' had ensured his immortality.

BBC television service, the first in the world, shut down in 1939, resumed broadcasting TV programmes in April 1949 to 400 viewers. TV sets, in short supply, cost 48 guineas, and due to their scarcity a new phenomenon appeared, 'TV viewing parties.'

In February the County produced a record bill for education, reiterating the Labour Government's commitment for improvement. Stoke-on-Trent, the 11th largest city in England saw tangible evidence of that as their 'local' university prepared for opening.

A memorial stained glass window in the crush hall at Longton High School, now Sandon High in Sandon Road, Meir was unveiled in April 1949. Measuring twelve feet square and inserted above the main entrance door to the school, this War Memorial Window detailed the 27 Old Boys of the school killed on active service with the forces of the Crown during the Second World War. It was dedicated on May 7th, 1949.

The window depicted John Bourne, Professor W.T. Astbury FRS, distinguished old student; Arnold Bennett, author; James Brindley, Civil Engineer; Sir Oliver Lodge FRS, physicist and inventor; Reginald Mitchell, aeronautical engineer and Josiah Wedgwood, master potter. It was moved to Longton High School, Box Lane in the early 1960s

Originally situated in Trentham Road, Longton and founded by John Bourne in 1760,

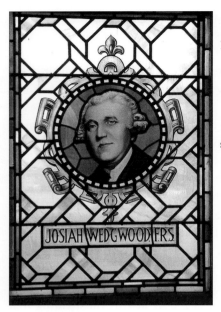

Panels from the Memorial Window at Longton High School, Box Lane, Meir. The window was originally in the Sandon Road school.

Right: The original school crest and motto 'Renascor'.

Longton High School was relocated to Sandon Road, Meir before the Second World War. It was never occupied by students before its requisition by the Army, the Royal Military College of Science.

Grammar school students - pupils who had passed their eleven plus - were admitted post war. Evidence of former military occupation abounded with 'Bull's eye targets' on many walls. Despite numerous post-war shortcomings, many pupils left for demanding careers and responsible positions in society.

The original Longton High School founded by John Bourne in Trentham Road, Longton.

CHAPTER 7

"The events of life are mainly small events - they only seem large when we are close to them."   Mark Twain 1835-1910

By 1950 the Keele Estate, its hall and parkland had been acquired by the City of Stoke-on - Trent and Staffs County Council. Six months earlier in January 1950 Major Ralph Mowbray Howard succeeded to the Keele estate. Bidwell and Sons, with Heywoods of Newcastle, acted as agents for the disposal of the Sneyd Estate of 4,500 acres, with three pubs and land held by the family since the time of Edward III. Frenetic preparations continued to enable the University College of North Staffs to open its doors on 16th October in 1950 to its first student, K B Ellis of Wolstanton. Were there any from Meir?

The Korean War ground interminably on. Because of United Nations regulations, combatants fighting under their flag had to be 19 years of age. It was not uncommon for 18 year olds to receive their call-up papers and be shipped off to Japan to be kept there under training conditions until they crossed the 19 year-old threshold. Many Second World War veterans, hardened by fighting in Europe and the Far East became embroiled. The capture of UN forces at the Imjim River by the Chinese was a low point in a bitter struggle when prisoners of war were sometimes forced to walk through ice cold rivers over rough stones to punish them.

Mr H. Marriot a member of the Royal Electrical and Mechanical Engineers, saw action in Korea with the UN; on his return he worked for Longton Transport.

The Festival of Britain in 1951 in London was designed to lift the spirits after the misery of the 1940s. Many recall the Festival's famous Skylon, a pencil-shaped structure reaching upwards almost floating on air, which cynics likened to the British economy - with no visible means of support. Its breezy literature and pavilions promoted a bright tomorrow, the shape of things to come, overshadowing the past. The truth was somewhat different with labour shortages, a downturn in the British economy in 1951 and firemen pressing for a 60-hour working week.

By visiting the University College of North Staffordshire at Keele in April 1951, Queen Elizabeth, the Queen Mother, forged a royal connection, which through Princess Margaret, as Chancellor, lasted well into the 1980s.

Many took more holidays in summer 1952, as life slowly returned to normal. Few owned cars still, and a mass exodus during the 'Potters' Wakes' from stations at Meir and Stoke was routine.

Women came more to the fore in all walks of life. The Second World War had proved they could perform just as well as men. In early January 1953, the WRAC/TA at their TA display formed part of a national campaign to boost numbers in the Women's Royal Army Corps/TA. Recruiting offices were set up at TA depots at the Meir, Cobridge and Stoke.

In 1953 Sherpa Tensing and Edmund Hilary reached the summit of Mount Everest under the guidance of Col. John Hunt while Stan Matthews' dazzling performance at the Cup Final elevated him to the ranks of the immortal. Many in Stoke still cheered even though he had long since left the 'Potters'.

The Longton High School Dramatic Society players appear after a performance of *The Ivory Door* by A.A. Milne on May 1-3 1951, their contribution to the Festival of Britain.

Queen Mother seen at the opening ceremony for Keele University with the Chancellor Lord Lindsay.

A new Elizabethan age began with the Coronation in Westminster Abbey in June, the entire ceremony costing about £365,000. It contrasted conspicuously with continuing scarcities, particularly of basic commodities like meat. A deal between the United Kingdom and Argentina to ship 1,800,000 tons to Britain plus an agreement to buy $1 million of Canadian bacon eased the situation. And much to the delight of small boys and girls, sweet rationing was relaxed - only to be re-rationed later.

Although 4,705 died in road accidents in 1952, the lowest since 1930 and 545 less than 1951, it was of scant consolation to bereaved relatives. Officially 'Fog' was thought responsible for the decline, slowing, as it would, errant drivers. The Clean Air Act in towns and cities augmented a massive programme of conversion to gas, eliminating these insidious fogs which in London killed more people than the great cholera outbreak of 1866. Fifty years later, the annual road death total in 2002 was down to 3,650.

The abolition of the Motor Trade Covenant Scheme, prohibiting the re sale of cars for 12 months after purchase, ended in 1953 giving a much-needed fillip to the motor trade. New models quickly appeared in dealers' windows and the Earls Court Motor Show, bringing a plea from the authorities "Do NOT speed!"

Local miners broke all records at three pits: Norton, Park Hall and Wolstanton: 433,000 tons was dug up in 1952, 13,000 tons more than the previous record. With severe winter weather in February, and an especially heavy fall on the 13th, snow cut off several Moorland villages. Doubtless the doughty miners received many a cheer throughout the area for their backbreaking efforts.

The intention to build a new housing estate in the city at Bentilee, 10,000 houses, was announced. Given 2,250 homes were built in 1953, this was achievable, reinforcing the City Council's resolve to rehouse many city families. Bentilee became the largest council estate in Europe, where formerly Bertram de Verdon, Lord of Ubberley, founder of Croxden Abbey in the reign of Henry II, once dwelt!

Although Meir was now more urban than rural, occasional glimpses from its agricultural heritage still emerged. Meir's own Meir Smithfield Market was still alive and kicking on December 16th 1955, with young cows fetching £6.4s and ewes £4.10s live weight. Originally situated behind the old King's Arms Hotel in Uttoxeter Road, it was moved, when Messrs John Joules rebuilt the hotel in 1935, to Catchem's corner, off Caverswall Lane alongside the main Crewe Derby railway line. Beckenham Close stands on the site today, a housing development built by Coupe's in the late 1950s. Was this how Cathchem's Corner got its name? Up until 1932, when the old Saracen's Head was demolished and rebuilt higher up in Sandon Road, sheep and other stock were still sold from behind the old pub, opposite to the King's Arms.

While Meir town centre grew up around a crossroads, figuratively speaking, in the mid 1950s it found its future development at a similar juncture, at a crossroads. But which way would it go? Highlighted in a wide-ranging survey, its dilemma became apparent:

'Little more than 30 years ago Meir was a scattered village on the outskirts of Stoke-on-Trent. Today it has grown into a town within the city, the home it is estimated of something like 20,000 people with their own social, shopping and educational facilities. Council

An auction sale in the First World War for the Red Cross.
Centre L to R: Mrs James Barlow, Mrs Rittner of Weston
Coyney Hall, Claude Hill and Mr C. Averill.

The pub sign which refers
to the former cattle market
200 yards further down
Caverswall Lane.
The pub is at the eastern
end of the new A50, at the
corner of Caverswall lane.

building has been responsible although there has been a great deal of private development. Twin estates which stretch north and south from the main Uttoxeter Road, contain over 2,200 council houses and 700 more have yet to be built. Although primarily residential, Meir finds employment for 500 workers in a smokeless industry - a successful pottery enterprise launched only five years ago. It also possesses, as is well-known, the city airport which is to assume new importance with the introduction of a summer holiday air service.

Not surprisingly, in view of its rapid expansion, Meir is suffering from what might be called 'growing pains'. Although developed by the city within its boundaries, it is yet sufficiently separated physically to be a place apart. Its very plan based on a central focal point with self-contained facilities tends to give it an entity of its own. Meir residents are aware of this. Gradually they are severing their old connections with Longton and other places where they originated and where ,of course, they mostly still work.

Local shops are being better patronised and the trading centre is growing to meet the increased demand. There is a tendency to seek entertainment locally and young couples are marrying in their churches instead of going outside the district to their old parishes - as mostly was the case before the last war.

But in spite of these trends, social workers feel that Meir lacks community spirit. They want to see Meir not just as a dormitory suburb but a live individual unit, supporting its own communal organisations. At present, apart from extremely active church life, achievement of this seems a long way ahead. One of the obstacles seems to be an invisible barrier between the people's of the twin estates - Meir and Sandon Road. "The two refuse to mix. The Uttoxeter Road might as well be a 10 feet high wall." This apparent allergy to each other is partly held responsible for the fact that the Meir Community Centre is not better patronised.

The young folk however are showing the way. The extremely active Meir Youth Club which meets in Meir County Secondary School five night a week draws its membership of 220 from all parts of the area, and a friendly spirit is a feature of its activities. Possibly a Ratepayers' Association or similar organisation would help bring Meir people together if only to ventilate and find support for their complaints. Complaints there are. The biggest grumble concerns the lack of a park and suitable playing fields for the district's child population. Residents are bitter that the 42 acre golf course so conveniently situated was not converted for this purpose and that it is now to be used temporarily as playing fields for the North Staffs Technical College. A Weston Road trader: "There is nowhere for old people to go except a seat by the main road roundabout where they get all the petrol and diesel fumes and dust".'

Other residents pointed out that large amounts had been spent on improvements to existing city parks, while Meir remained a 'Cinderella', entirely without. Mrs V.E. Jackson, one of the district's City Council representatives who had pleaded the case for a park since her election in 1945, was still hoping to see the golf course used for the purpose. *'Any move to build on it, we shall bitterly oppose!'* The planners' answer to these complaints was not only has provision been made for individual football and hockey pitches and tennis courts on the estates, but that Weston Sprink, 35 acres of common, almost as big as Hanley Park, is available for Meir residents' use. To enable the public to use the Sprink, an official of the Reconstruction Department said, *'One marlhole has been drained and others filled in.'*

Meir's comment on this was brief - *'it is too far away'*.

Among other complaints residents ventilated were conditions in the original village school which was still lit by gas, poor street lighting, the undoubted shocking condition of roads on the new estates and lack of facilities at the local police station which consisted of the front room of a constable's house:

'In spite of the grumbles the planners are doing a fine job at Meir. Non residents are apt to describe it as 'a sprawling suburb of council houses' but that is inaccurate as well as unkind. Meir has grown, not haphazardly, as have so many towns of comparable size, but according to preconceived plans. This development has largely been dictated by council building. Between the two world wars, the city built nearly 2,000 houses in the district and another 454 have been completed. At present, plans are for 650 more on the 50-acre Wood Farm estate with auxiliary shops and a games centre, and this, it is expected, will be completed in about three years time. In the centre of Meir there is provision for the shopping centre to expand and here too will be provided the new police station and a new library.'

Criticism levelled at some of Meir's institutions brought home the disparity between the old Meir and the newer emerging face of the town, two schools providing stark comparison of what was and wasn't acceptable.

Opened in 1953, and demolished in 2003, Lyme Road County Primary and Infants school, under its headmaster Mr C.H. Deakin, was a modern light and airy building looking out on 9 acres of fields, lawns and gardens. Already with 306 children, following the expansion of the Wood Farm estate, it was planned to add a wing of eight more classrooms.

Its Victorian equivalent, the old Meir village school in Uttoxeter Road, opened in 1873 and had dark pokey classrooms. Inefficient gas lighting, old-fashioned furniture and high windows, through which nothing could be seen except the sky, added to the malaise. Its headteacher Miss M.C. Hamer, in post since 1946, intimated that much needed doing quickly. Old air raid shelters in the playground restricted playing space, and the provision of hot water and the replacement of chipped wash basins were items needing swift attention. But although it was now nearly 75 years old, Meir School provided a link with Meir's past life, barely a village in the 1880s:

'The number of children attending this day school, a good yardstick of Meir's size in 1887, was 232; in 1888, dropping to 212 while returning to 236 in 1889. Average attendances were 172, 167 and 173 over the same years. The efforts of a dedicated teaching staff were reflected in the passes they achieved - 88, 82 and 88%. Financially as well as academically, the school was flourishing as the income showed a rise from £267 17s 9d for 1887, £251. 1s 8d the year after and £371.14s.6d for 1889. Total receipts on the average attendance for the same period were £1 11s 4 1/4d per head viz. from grants 16s 41/2d; from fees, 14s 13/4d: from sales and rents,1s 5d. The total costs on the average attendance were £1 16s 51/2d; the deficiency, made up from the rates, was 4s 61/4d per head.'

The self-same buildings, which during the week reverberated to the 'times tables' and swish of the cane, on Sundays resonated with hymns sung by the faithful during Christian worship: *'The Harvest Festival was held on Sunday* (12th October 1890). *At morning service, the Rev T.H. Masters preached the sermon and in the afternoon, the Rev.J. Beckett, vicar of Dilhorn(e) occupied the pulpit and in the evening the vicar of the parish (the Reverend J.G. Addenbrooke) preached to a crowded congregation. The room was tastefully decorated and a large quantity of bread and vegetables were given to the poor. The anthem "and God said, Let the earth" by Caleb Simper was well rendered by the mission choir. The offertories amounted to £ 8 7s.'*

Eight years later it witnessed a ceremony to recognise a gallant attempt to rescue a young boy. During November 1898, a drowning accident involving young Thomas Barker in a pool at the Meir in trying to rescue his 3 year old brother, made the newspapers. Young Tom's death touched the hardest of hearts, prompting a nomination from his many friends for his bravery:

'On Monday evening at a concert held at the Meir Board Schools, in aid of the Sunday School Building Fund - Mr T B Cull presiding - certificates of the Royal Humane Society were presented to Charles Henry Barker and John Harvey respectively. Barker's certificate was "In Memoriam" of his son, Thomas aged 8 years who lost his life nobly endeavouring to save that of his younger brother, Willie, who had fallen into a pond at The Meir. The other was in recognition of distinguished bravery in gallantly rescuing William Barker. The presentation was made by Mrs Alfred Mear.

The Rev. Charles Addenbrooke spoke on the work of the Royal Humane Society and took occasion to mention the efforts being made to free Meir church from debt. They had, he said, a generous offer from Mr Cartwright, one of the trustees, of £67.10s - being half the debt - if they would make up their share, of which some £15 or £16 had yet to be subscribed. Mr Cartwright had further promised to make his donation up to £100 in 2 years. This he added should encourage others to assist in the project.'

Holy Trinity Church - then with no hall of its own - used the school premises on various less sombre occasions:

'The annual distribution of prizes to the children attending the Holy Trinity Church School, the Meir, took place on Monday evening at Meir Board Schools. The vicar of Caverswall, the Rev J.G. Addenbrooke presided, being supported by the Rev T.H. Masters and there was about 250 scholars present, besides a large number of their parents and friends. The prizes were distributed by Mrs Stephen Mear. At the end of the evening each child received a parcel of warm clothing, the results of much hard work willingly given by the many friends interested in the new church at the Meir. It is intended that clothing shall be distributed annually as Christmas gifts.'

Even in 1955, Meir airport was in almost daily commercial use by Staffordshire Potteries Ltd., which even then also provided day nursery facilities for children of working mothers among its 500 workforce. Its main factory, in one of the hangars formerly used by the Royal Air Force and leased from the City in July 1950, covered 45,000 square feet. Chinaware Limited, also producing competitively priced ware, occupied the second.

The basic idea conceived by Mr G.C. Bower, Managing director of Staffordshire Potteries Ltd, and of the group of companies of which the firm was the chief subsidiary, was simple yet effective. The factory, adjacent to the runway and with its own aircraft, a Dragon Rapide, could deliver finished ware in around an hour via Elstree airport, to the heart of

London. As a measure of its success, the Rapide was quickly superseded by a twin engine de Havilland Dove with on-board facilities for business meetings at tables while en route.

The pilot of the aircraft, Neale W Fagg, a New Zealander, had 5,000 hours flying time to his credit. After joining the Royal New Zealand Air Force in 1941, he later saw action with Fighter Command, flying Spitfires. Flight Lieutenant Fagg also flew Liberators for RAF Transport Command taking troops to Karachi.

News of various dignitaries landing and taking off were common place. In April 1955, the Lord Mayor was shown arriving, after opening the new headquarters of No 45 squadron Air Training Corps the previous Sunday. At Longton High School in Sandon Road, Air Vice Marshal Cox DFC OBE reinforced Meir's links with past when he landed in a helicopter on the playing fields behind the school.

Air Vice Marshall Cox DFC OBE landing at Longton High School, then in Sandon road.

Vickers Supermarine later informed the Lord Mayor, Harold Naylor, they had a model of a Spitfire which they were happy to turn over to Stoke-on-Trent City Council to commemorate the birthplace of Reginald Mitchell, its designer. Nearly 20 years after his death, and with precious little otherwise to show the link between one of the most beautiful aircraft of all time, the offer was accepted graciously.

In 1957 if anyone doubted Meir airport was still in business then photographs of a group of the 1st North Staffs Women's Junior Air Corps on their annual training flight from Meir Airport dispelled their doubts. Despite the dangers, their enthusiasm was unbounded.

But danger lurked below as well as above ground. News of a fatal accident re-emphasised the dangers miners faced throughout their working days. Whilst trying to clear the track Reginald Denny Cotton of Mollison Road, Meir lost his life after being struck by tubs on the underground railway at Parkhall Colliery.

Now open almost ten years after wartime occupation, the curriculum at Longton High School in Sandon Road had 'found its line and length', the shortages of the early post war years all but gone. Numerous societies and clubs at the school sought to widen the horizons of pupils beyond the limits of the four walls of a classroom. Foremost in this was the annual

Longton High School RAF section at summer camp RAF South Cerney, Glos. July 1958, in front of an Avro Anson Mk 19 of RAF Transport Command. L to R: Cadet G. Mottram, Sgt R. Williams, Warrant Officer C.O. Massey, Cadet K. Jones, Cadet N. Harrison, Cpl P. Geary, Cadet R.G. Smith, Cadet N.J. Cartlidge, Cpl J. Cooke, F/Sgt M.A. Fowell, Cadet I.G. Ray, Cpl Marshall, Cadet G. Edge, Flt Lt D.A. Potter RAFVR(T), Flt Lt T. Purcell RAFVR(T), Flg Off D. Hiscox RAFVR(T), Cadets N. Whitmore, P. Bailey. A. Le Rolland, G. Price, C. Lees, M. Edwards, D. Sims, A. Cartwright, P.L. Hull, D. Leak, K. Insley, and Sgt Hancock.

school play. Produced by Mr Ken Lowe, most were a triumph, considering the inexperience of those called on to perform. Two years before they had produced George Bernard Shaw's *Arms and the Man*. A year later the school players tackled a Gilbert and Sullivan favourite, *The Pirates of Penzance t*o great acclaim. On March 25, 26 and 27, 1958 *The Taming of the Shrew* was applauded. Robert Jamieson played Baptista, Jeffrey Wainwright, Katherina while David Wade excelled as Vincentio. As always Paul Howes as Biondello was magnificent, his later tragic early death deprived the stage of a prodigious talent.

It was still prudent sometimes in Meir to look where you put your feet. The pleasant smell of cattle still tainted the air at the Meir Smithfield Market. Cattle Dealers Messrs W. Bagshaw reported 'Fat cows' fetching 97s per live cwt and calves up to £7. The market closed at the end of the 1950s - as did that at The Smithfield at Blythe Bridge.

More than ten years after the war, reminders of its horrors still scarred the local landscape. Whilst rumours of military equipment and old aircraft being buried at Meir aerodrome were common, its presence was hard to detect. In Longton it was quite the reverse. Air raid shelters at Longton Bus Station that had protected residents in their hour of need were demolished, finally and irrevocably. When the Bennett precinct occupied the site, a new bus station in Commerce Street, Kingcross House opened. Never successful, bus passengers were liberally soused with exhaust fumes, and it closed during the 1990s, a crumbling ruin.

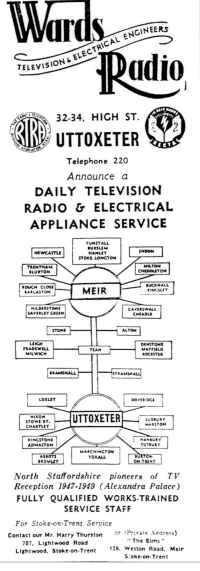
Car ownership increased rapidly through the 1950s. British car manufacturers, then second only in world production to the United States, produced a wealth of models. Traditional as the British Sunday roast, the Morris Oxford at Pepper's in Hanley cost £575 plus £288.17s.0d tax. Then new technology and design produced the world beating 'Mini' at around £500. Car adverts reflected a new felt optimism, a sense of having 'turned the corner'. It was optimism shared by the Tories who achieved a 'Tory hat trick', winning the General Election with a majority of around 100.

A forecast by Sir Howard Roberts of the Royal Society for the Prevention of Accidents (ROSPA) that *'6000 would be killed on the roads'* seemed overly pessimistic, but RTAs were increasing and he had every right to be concerned.

Longton High School production of *The Taming of the Shrew*, March 1958.
David Wade is extreme right, back row. Paul Howes is seated front.

Longton High School production of *Patience*.

A bus and coach standing in Saracen Way, Meir, in the early 1960s. The terraced housing, typical of Meir, ran from the town centre to Catchem's Corner. All were demolished for the new A50.

The opening of Meir station in 1893. It was built in a deep cutting. A few years later the station staff would regularly see Reginald Mitchell boarding the train for Southampton and the Supermarine works.
The Meir station closed in the mid-1960s although the passenger line from Crewe to Derby
still has a station at Blythe Bridge.

CHAPTER 8

"If you can remember the sixties, you weren't really there." Anonymous

The new decade breezed in. The Beatles, the Rolling Stones and Mary Quant typified 1960s' Britain. To be young was invigorating, everyone's living standards improved dramatically. In Prime Minister Harold MacMillan's words, *"You've never had it so good!"*

In 1960, the departure of Holy Trinity's Rev H.V. Woodward, after 4 years, heralded the arrival of Rev H.A. Richards. According to Rev T.J. Harvey (1977-1986) the church had a wooden floor which was taken up by Rev Richards to provide an under-floor heating system.

Meir residents also expected to see visible signs of progress. The town having grown rapidly found itself without the trappings of suburbia which others took for granted. Was geographical lay-out the reason for its dilemma or was *'a split community, the Meir estates' biggest problem'*, as the newspapers suggested?

'Meir's first housing estate appeared on the north side of the railway where now stands Colclough Road, North Walk, South Walk and the Square quickly followed by a second estate - Leason Road - and adjoining streets up to Weston Road. With plans to develop Lewis's Lane, now Sandon Road, it meant many adjoining fields - and Meir's Green Belt - would disappear permanently.

Between 1920 and the outbreak of the Second World War, 1,758 houses went up on 6 sites in Meir, some, to re-house families from Longton, which - due to slum clearance - lost 846 houses in 32 slum clearance orders. Since the last war, 1,138 houses were added to this tally on two main sites at Lyme Road and Wood Farm as well as at Bartholemew Road,

A view of Meir roundabout in the 1950s, looking towards the King's Arms.
Note the Victorian housing, centre field, which appears also on the opposite page.

Brick Kiln Lane, Pickford Place, Waterhead Road and Parkhead Drive. In the same time frame 12 more clearance orders demolished 726 houses in Longton which boosted the population of Meir in 1922 between 2 and 3 thousand and in 1939 to 14,000 to an estimated 20,000 in 1960. It had increased about 1000% in half a human lifetime.

One aspect which irked Meir residents was the lack of a park for children to play in. There was also no public library in Meir, although it was under construction as people moaned. At one time housed in the TA building it had since moved to the Holy Trinity Church Institute in Box Lane.'

A popular statement of the day *was 'the population of Longton has moved to Meir, but some facilities are still in Longton!'* Mrs V.E. Jackson councillor for Meir said a scheme for a kiddies play ground off Stansmore Road had been approved. It was certainly not true of Longton High School then in Sandon Road which had been part of Meir life for two decades. Plans for a new Longton High School were considered by the local authority to augment the 1939 school. Undaunted the old school carried on and by the end of term had produced another of Gilbert and Sullivan's Savoy operas, *Patience* with Paul Howes as Reginald Bunthorne and Keith Ollier as Patience. Frank Gilson played Archibald Grosvenor. After leaving school, his fine voice and talent for music led him to study in Birmingham, afterwards becoming a vicar choral at Lichfield Cathedral. He died in 1985.

Now the lack of a purpose-built post office was another annoying gripe, particularly if you were one of its 20,000 customers. The post office was in part of a grocer's shop at that time. A 42 page petition calling for a new post office was signed and given to Mrs V.E. Jackson to be delivered into the hands of the Town Clerk.

The focus of Meir's Social Activities, the Community Centre and Youth Club headquarters, was housed in a former public house in Uttoxeter Road, adjacent to the A50, later to be used for the Meir Play Group for toddlers.

The newspaper article gave no suggestion as to why Meir had grown into two separate parts, but there was widespread belief that the Uttoxeter Road had been responsible. There was no reason for people from one side of the road to *'expose themselves to dangerous fast flowing traffic, to reach the other part of Meir. It was definitely NOT snobbery.'*

Situated less than a half mile from Meir lay Meir Heath, a small enclave with a more upmarket atmosphere than its scion of Meir - the suffix Heath some thought, imparting an aura of exclusivity. At almost 1,000 feet above sea level and always a few degrees colder than 'down in Meir', it was not a place to linger particularly during the winter of 1947, when cleared snow lay piled to the tops of telegraph poles. Uniquely Meir Heath had its own windmill - or what was left of it, a landmark and beacon to drinkers from time immemorial heading for the eponymous public house lying at the junction of the roads to Blythe Bridge, Hilderstone, Rough Close and Meir.

But with news of proposed boundary changes, and a threat of more urbanisation and encroachment, the inhabitants of Meir Heath and Rough Close were concerned it might signal the destruction of *'their corner of Eden.'* It was a familiar theme. The development of the Grindley Lane site, with the Simplex Works as a nucleus, meant more housing. But in the years that lay ahead, Stafford Borough Council built a few houses off Grindley Lane and a private developer added considerably to the tally of homes, but generally the area retained its air of quiet contentment.

The Potters Union tried to get a 42 hour week for its members in 1960 as post-war stagnation slowly, painfully slowly, receded. Consumerism was beginning to rear its head seen most obviously in the increasing number of car owning families, leading to plans for more roads. In the early 1960s a new breed of highway began to be built, the motorway. Carrying a price tag of £24.6m, the M6 and built by John Laing, running through Staffordshire and Cheshire, was announced. With 19 road deaths every day in Britain, a new safer approach to high-speed private transport was overdue. The M6, completed in 1962, with three lanes each way, was designed for traffic flows of 72 000 vehicles a day.

For sheer audacity, the theft in March 1960 of a load of timber, along with the lorry, in the Strand in Longton, took some beating. The driver, experienced Mr F.K. Mooney of Hartwell Road, Meir, shocked and stunned by its disappearance, said it had never happened to him in years of driving. It had gone, *"Just like that!"*

The loss was nothing like that of a valuable facility in Meir - the Sports Ground. Occasional references to it arise but only a few indicate its precise location. Some point to its being the moribund Meir Golf Course off Whitcombe Road. In the early spring of 1960 it was the venue for the 'Meir inter-college sports event' which began at 3 pm with North Staffs Technical College the hosts. What would the old diehards of the Meir Golf Club have said as javelins and shot putt peppered their hallowed greens.

The 'feel good factor' of the 'swinging 60s' now found its way into Meir domestic life. People expected more and to match those hopes, the town had tried its best to comply. Back in the Holy Trinity Church Institute days a fledgling Community Centre had evolved from those humble beginnings to the point where it was able to offer an immense range of activities. Once the old Waggon and Horses public house in Uttoxeter Road, it was no longer just a place under whose roof old codgers met to play dominoes with their chums - the town centre public house, the King's Arms, could satisfy that need. By 1962, Meir Community Association and Youth Club with its warden, Mr R. Lockett, boasted a whole raft of pastimes and hobbies.

Netball, cricket, basketball and swimming were also on offer for the residents of Meir. Swimming at Sandon Road Junior High School, formerly Longton High School, was also available for 2/6d a session, and you got an experienced instructor to keep an eye on things.

For the less physically energetic, Miss J Rogers ran dressmaking sessions and with membership at more than 120 it necessitated 8 classes weekly! Cookery and beauty demonstrations, also a feature of the Centre, added to the expanding range.

Expansion topped the agenda at a meeting concerning Grange County Primary School where plans to enlarge the site meant a recommendation to *'appropriate 1.29 acres from the Airport Committee'*.. Would the Meir Aerodrome end its days in death by a thousand cuts?

In secondary education, Longton High School's stalwart headmaster, Mr M.V. Gregory, lay ill in hospital. Often seen at the wheel of his Riley Pathfinder saloon on the poplar-lined drive to the school, he was responsible for the formation of the war time ATC units, and in peacetime, the Combined Cadet Force. He was due for retirement in July

1962. Along with Mr Tom Meredith, his deputy and enforcer, he formed an unholy alliance which many former pupils will agree produced an enduring influence on their development and behaviour during their adolescent years.

In higher education too, 1962 was a milestone. From amongst a cluster of old army huts and totally inadequate facilities, the University College of North Staffordshire (UCNS) at Keele had opened its doors 12 years earlier. Lord Lindsay of Birker was its first vice chancellor and his name lives on in perpetuity in the Students' Hall of Residence, Lindsay Hall and also in the famous Lindsay String Quartet. These musicians under the leadership of Peter Cropper achieved worldwide fame and recognition for their concert and studio performances of classical string quartet music. They were formed from Keele undergraduates.

The University College was formed from a noble idea to educate the citizens of Stoke-on-Trent, Stafford and Burton on Trent, by virtue of the University of Keele Bill. Passed by the Lords examiners, it enabled the transfer of all the debts and assets to the new establishment, the University of Keele.

Keele Hall in its early University days.

Although by this time Meir aerodrome/airport was not in commercial use, less than 30 miles to the south in what was a similar situation, an event occurred at RAF Seighford which seemed to augur well for its future as a commercial enterprise where Meir had faltered. A Vickers Viscount with 37 test pilots from Farnborough flew into Seighford aerodrome to demonstrate the possibilities for its use as a civilian airport for the West Midlands. At the time it was leased from the Air Ministry by Boulton Paul Aircraft of Wolverhampton. A meeting with Stoke-on-Trent City Council, Staffs County Council, Wolverhampton and Stafford Councils to discuss this was proposed. Seighford had a 2,000 yard runway - OK for the Vickers Viscount.

Could Meir airport have developed in a similar fashion if those on the city council had shown vision? Well Meir was not 'down and out' just yet. In April 1964, a plan showing

One of the Mercury planes of Railway Air
Services that used Meir Airport in the 1930s.

Right: Mr Claude Graham-White landing in
Staffordshire during his London to
Manchester flight in May 1910.

Amy Johnson, here seen landing in South
Africa, flew into Meir.

the gradients of Meir Airfield was sent to the Ministry of Aviation by Stoke-on-Trent Corporation. They hoped for a licence to reopen the field for club flying. It had been originally granted a licence for charter flights by holiday planes, but this was withdrawn because of the condition of the runaway. Local enthusiasts pressed for a flying club at Meir, even offering financial help towards the cost of resurfacing the runway. The Corporation agreed to the letting to the Staffs Gliding Club of a hangar formerly used by the Air Training Corps. For Meir aerodrome, the wait and see approach was the worst of all worlds.

Meir was also awaiting for news of a new local relief road, as traffic volumes steadily rose. To the chagrin of many, plans for the long-awaited Blythe Bridge by-pass - a mile from Meir - did not feature in any proposals for the four years till 1968. Various wags said if the decision was delayed any longer, the Great Train Robbers, collectively jailed for 307 years, would be free again before it was constructed.

A mile from Meir, in Longton, a new shopping arcade named after Alderman A.E. Bennett, NOT the novelist Arnold Bennett, opened at a cost of £750,000 a year later. Meir, without a recognised shopping arcade, relied on small local tradesmen and women.

Also opening in 1964 was a spacious and pristine health centre, situated behind a parade of shops in Sandon Road, which offered patients a wide range of treatments right on their doorstep: *'The £41,000 Meir Health centre in Saracen Way, designed to serve 2 vital purposes on a grand scale, was opened by Mrs V.E. Jackson, the chairman of the committee. It would provide a population of 16,000 with schools health services and a baby*

Meir Health Centre, Saracen Way, Meir. It was opened by Mrs V.E. Jackson in 1960s and was built at a cost of £41,000. It has recently received an extensive refurbishment.

clinic.' In the days before 'the politically correct' had infused the council chamber, to see Mrs Jackson referred to as a 'chairman', plain and simple, is refreshing. On the ground floor - complete with pram bay - was the maternity and baby clinic, whilst upstairs and designated for use by Schools Health, was a physiotherapy room, an ophthalmic room and areas for dentistry and the treatment of minor ailments

Mrs V.E. Jackson, chairman of the Schools and Welfare Sub Committee, said: *'The new centre fulfilled a long felt need for modern facilities for the care of babies and schoolchildren. Mothers from Meir who had to travel to Longton with their babies now had the amenities at hand and could take advantage of the chance to prevent disease rather than have the worry of having to cure it.'*

Meanwhile I watched the fortunes of former Longton High School pupil and now international tennis star, Keith Wooldridge. As a schoolboy I had the honour to partner Keith in a house tennis match at school, mine being something of a walk-on part. By the age of 20, Keith was in the ranks of Britain's Davis Cup squad and amongst the best half dozen men in British tennis. In June 1966, he had his best run at Wimbledon beating Americans James Mcmanus and W.H. Hoogs to reach the third round. He was defeated by Stan Smith in the next round on the Centre Court. When he bowed out of major competition he carried on in tennis, becoming manager of the British Women's team.

For those for whom vigorous exercise was an anathema, supporting Stoke City Football Club was a way of letting off steam. Playing at the Victoria ground in 1964 the Potters took on Manchester United, a match Stoke won 3-1 before a crowd of 45,697. The following year saw the testimonial match of soccer's greatest ambassador, Stanley Matthews. Unable to see the match I wrote to the great man who, politely replying in his own hand, wished me good luck. His letter, a testament to the humble nature of this remarkable and unassuming son of the Potteries, is a treasured keepsake.

1964 was election year when the temperature on Easter Monday was colder than Christmas Day. Undeterred, in April, Miss Edna Newnes of Meir, representing Wild's St Mary's Works, Longton, and wearing thermal underwear, was triumphant in carrying off the title as "Pottery Queen" at Trentham Gardens Ballroom. Hooray!

The four-year tenure of Rev W.A. Richards as parish priest at Holy Trinity church ended in 1964. The following year Meir church welcomed Rev F.W. Osborn who imbued the parish with a sense of stability and support for many varied charitable causes, perhaps it might be argued, at the expense of the buildings

In World Cup final year, 1966, nationally trade was good; the deficit was down to £5m and exports 'hit the jackpot'. But some local council services were still being reined in. Stan Bourne, vice-chairman of the City Baths Committee voiced proposals to close Longton's Turkish Baths - *'It costs £7,000 per annum to maintain!'*

The aspirations of those seeking to make a commercial success of any Staffordshire airfield were dashed when a fateful decision was leaked to the press. In March 1966 the newspapers revealed *"Staffordshire County Council agrees NOT to proceed with plans for development of the wartime bomber station at Seighford as a municipal airport."* Was this the end of the road? Thirty years later and with hindsight, the advent of cheap flights from

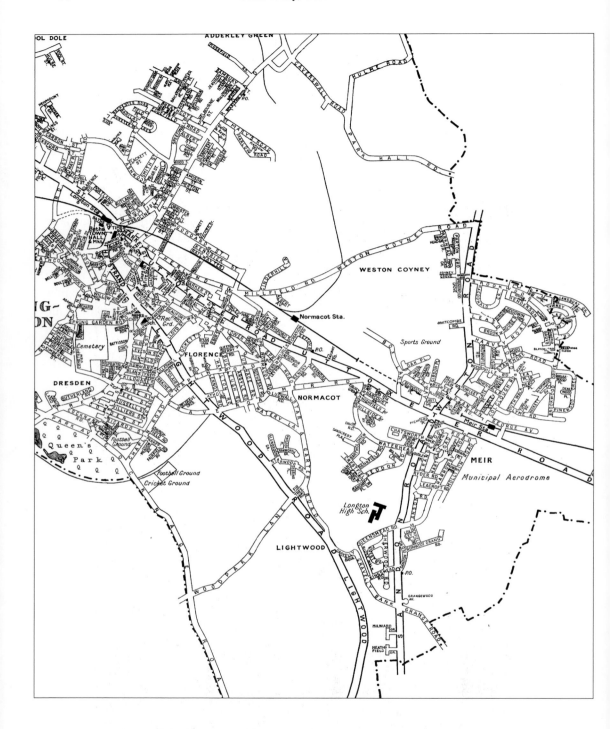

Meir and its neighbours in the 1950s. The Municipal Aerodrome was still prominent.

the likes of Easyjet might have made Meir Airport had it been operating.

For Meir Airport the outlook was bleak and its 400 acres would now be the site of various housing developments. Meir, like Stoke-on-Trent, was seen to be growing. The pottery industry still employed over 50,000, although old industries were already in decline. Regional and local projections were made. Estimates by the City Reconstruction Department, with the County Council Authority, foresaw a target population in Stoke on Trent of 280,000 by 1981. This was wide of the mark - in 1991 it would be only 240,000. People have voted with their feet, leaving the city to seek their fortunes elsewhere.

The old wartime 'shadow factories' at Meir in this 1970s shot became the home of Creda .

If it heats, washes, spins, cooks or tumbles, it's a Creda.

If it warms, glows or blows, it's a Sunhouse.

TI Creda Ltd., Blythe Bridge, Stoke-on-Trent, ST11 9LJ.

CHAPTER 9

"The rule is, jam tomorrow and jam yesterday - but never jam today."
                                        Lewis Carroll 1832-1898

A thumbnail sketch of Meir published in the souvenir programme for the Broadway Cinema opening in 1936, thirty years later basically still held true. There were more houses and people, and the town had expanded and a few companies, by relocating to Meir, now gave employment to several hundred just as the wartime 'shadow factory' had done.

In the 1960s Johnson Matthey and Staffordshire Potteries, on the edge of Meir Airport, parallel to the main A50 on the eastern side of town, were two prominent enterprises. New buildings appeared quickly, but did Staffordshire Potteries still use the old hangars from Meir airport into the 1960s? Photographs seem to hint at it.

Staffordshire Potteries Ltd prospered. Chairman Mr R.A. Harding in 1968 delivered a "cheerful report" to the company's shareholders.

'Despite increasing costs due to devaluation, Staffordshire Potteries with its broader based range of products will retain an expanding share of world markets. Although half yearly sales in December were basically the same as last years figures, exports had increased substantially.'

Bad weather, with snow ploughs on the M1, blizzards isolating villages from the outside world and local roads engulfed by a 12" fall in early February, didn't dampen the success enjoyed by a quartet of local lads:

Four Longton High School pupils-in Box Lane, Meir-were awarded scholarships to Cambridge and Oxford Universities: Michael R Povey of Weston Road, Paul Wilcox of Dresden, Terence Meredith of the Westlands and Robert Harman of Fenton.

Their adult lives were just beginning. That of William Henry Amison of 291 Weston Road, ended in June 1968. He had received the Distinguished Conduct Medal in the Great War, and in the Second World War he became the Divisional Warden for Longton, Meir and surroundings in the Air Raid Precautions (ARP) service. A former member of the Pottery Manufacturers Association, he was a pillar of society and a gallant English gentleman.

A battle raging in the countryside had claimed a huge number of cattle and sheep but the epidemic of foot and mouth disease had in 1968 turned the corner. 30 years before with its Smithfield livestock market at the old King's Arms Hotel in Uttoxeter Road, the town was still a farming community, but in the 1960s, fewer in Meir now depended on the land.

Meir Airport, finally lost in 1968, became housing, with estate agents' boards announcing *'mod. det. res; lounge/diner; 3 bedrms, GCH; and Dble garage',* across its rolling acres. Newspaper headlines said:

'Meir aerodrome had been re-zoned for housing which highlighted the importance of the old RAF base at Seighford once more. Now a survey carried out by a firm of consultants at a cost of £4,550 has confirmed Stoke-on-Trent City Council's enthusiasm for the scheme. Staffordshire County Council were 'lukewarm.'

In April 1970 Staffordshire Rural Council turned down Stoke-on-Trent's application for Seighford saying *'it would injure the rural appearance of the area, produce an unacceptable amount of noise and the roads serving it would be inadequate';* a familiar story in fact. Town Clerk, Mr L.K. Robinson, described the Rural Council as being 'misguided and prejudiced.' An appeal to the Ministry of Housing and Local Government proved unsuccessful. 'Nothing ventured, nothing gained' says the old axiom. Did the result of this indifference condemn Stoke-on-Trent to a place in the 'also rans' table of civic amenities, from which it would find it difficult to recover? The hopes and aspirations awakened by those pioneering aviators, Amy Johnson and Jim Mollison, the visits of distinguished guests, royalty and civic dignitaries would now be just history, endlessly embellished over a pint of Joules' Stone Ale at the King's Arms. Undaunted by the depressing cycle, a few 'magnificent men in their flying machines' carried on using Meir airfield, albeit at the margins, well into the 1970s, but an argument in allowing limited private use was dealt a hammer blow after a tragic accident.

'A glider and a Tiger Moth aircraft collided over Meir as a result of which Board of Trade representatives were sent to investigate the crash. The Tiger Moth pilot, Mr Ken Sherriff, 40 of Hardy Farm, Bramhall, Cheshire was killed. The wreckage was scattered over a large part of Meir and Weston Coyney. It is expected the inquiry will last one day or maybe two days. The glider pilot, Dr Peter Bradwell of Uttoxeter Road, Blythe Bridge parachuted down into a tree yards from where the Tiger Moth plummeted to the ground with the glider still in tow. He broke his arm and was today at the NSRI recuperating.

The aircraft crashed in the playing fields belonging to the North Staffs Polytechnic, missing a housing estate by 150 yards. The dead pilot was an instructor of the Staffordshire Gliding Club based at Meir. Dr Bradwell also of the Gliding Club, was their chief flying instructor. Mr Charles Webb, the deputy chief gliding instructor, said it was "the first accident since the club was formed seven years ago!'

At the inquest on Kenneth Worsley Sherriff, the pathologist, Group Captain Mason, stated the body had been identified by the fingerprints. Death was due to 'multiple injuries.'

Fred Holdcroft, whose motorcycle shop on the junction of Broadway and Uttoxeter Road was a mecca for two-wheeled aficionados, owned a private-pilots' licence. A frequent user of the airstrip, the Evening Sentinel said Fred was the last person to fly from Meir airport. In a strange way they were correct, but in its printing someone inadvertently got hold of the wrong Fred. Emigré aviator, Eric Clutton, now living in Tennessee, USA, claims the honour as the *'last pilot to take off from Meir Airport'.* Piloting his own aircraft named "FRED", Eric Clutton is in the record books as *'The last man to...'* before the builders' profile boards went in.

The airport site had other uses. Stoke Rugby Club, for a while, used it for club matches. Until its relocation to Box Lane, Longton High School in Sandon Road had several rugby pitches there. High School cross-country runners also had cause to recall its enormous scale with some regret. After a gruelling seven mile race that had taken them up Sandon Road, along Hilderstone Road and Stallington Lane, the final mile following a diagonal from Grindley Lane to Old Sandon Road seemed eternal in the face of a stiff breeze.

The Air Training Corps until the mid 1960s also had a crumbling presence there.

The last plane to fly out of Meir aerodrome before it closed, FRED - seen here in Tennessee USA - was piloted by its owner, Eric Clutton.

One of the largest planes to ever land at Meir Aerodrome during WW2, the B-24 Liberator, is also seen here in model form.

Below: A blown-up aerial photograph showing actual B-24 Liberators parked at Meir Aerodrome, August 9, 1945.

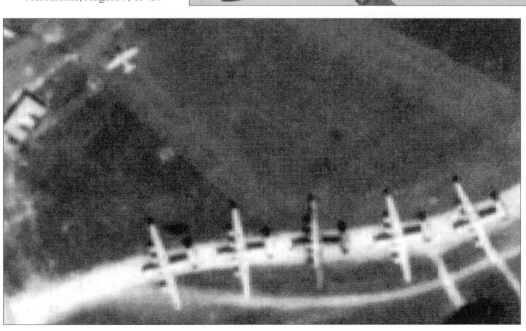

1037 Squadron ATC at Meir Aerodrome 1965
Front L to R: Mr S. Wright, W/O L. Nixon,
Flt. Off. J. Carter, Flt. Lt. J.D. Davies,
Flt. Off. J. Cooke, Mr K. Wetton, Miss Mansell.

Flying Officer John Carter RAFVR(T) and
Flying Officer John Cooke RAFVR(T),
1037 Squadron ATC.

The new and as yet incomplete ATC headquarters behind the
Territorial Drill Hall in the heart of Meir which replaced old
WW2 premises on the Aerodrome.

The ATC, created as a 'junior RAF', was extremely popular with boys aged 12 to 18. The ATC gave youngsters a taste for service life in the Royal Air Force, plain and simple.

The Meir detachment, 1037 squadron, occupied the decaying remains of two war time wooden huts at the airfield perimeter, the archetype for producers of Second World War movies. Commanded by the highly personable Flt Lt Dennis Davies, his adjutant, Pilot Officer John Carter and Pilot Officer John Cooke, they achieved a courteous bonhomie rare today. Pilot Officer John Cooke was later Officer Commanding 239 Squadron when it was renumbered. With two civilian instructors and a catering manager, Ken Wetton, who had the happy knack of appearing with a cheering cup of tea or coffee, cadets assembled for twice weekly parades, emulating airmen in war time. How many times did they wonder what it was really like during those grim days?

Several Meir ATC cadets enjoyed exchange visits to Germany, while many attended summer camps at RAF Bassingbourn, Cambridgeshire and RAF Kinloss in Scotland. In a time of nuclear capability V-bombers, Kinloss's Avro Shackletons, powered by 4 Rolls Royce piston engines, flew maritime reconnaissance missions over the North Sea shadowing aircraft of the Soviet Air Force.

With new premises behind the Territorial Drill Hall in the town centre, the new ATC HQ promised Meir cadets a brighter, drier and less draughty future.

As the wartime huts disappeared, many asked when would it all end? The whole town seemed in turmoil. Now, Park Hall, renamed the Safari Lake Club, and originally erected in 1760, was demolished. An exclusive educational establishment in Georgian times, in the 1800s the home of the Sheriff of Staffordshire, it had served many masters. The insatiable demand for land for the housing boom, meant the old Hall now received the attention of the demolition wreckers' ball. Two centuries of history was excised: Weston Coyney Hall, the former home of Captain and Mrs Rittner and a Home Guard post during the Second World War; Longton Hall, the seat of the Edensor Heathcote family where porcelain was produced in middle of the 18th century; and Meir House, once opposite Holy Trinity Church, the residence of Charles Harvey, now destined to appear only between the pages of a history book.

The 'new broom approach' was everywhere. The past, gone in an afternoon, was supplanted by 'a vision of the future'. The new Blythe Bridge by-pass, with a start date of August 1970, costing £1.25 million, was a prime example. James Musgrave hoped it could be finished by early 1971: '.....*a complete link between the M6 and the M1 within 5 years.*'

The pressure for new roads to cope with the flood of new cars and vehicles, grew. The Derby Way, designed as a 6 lane urban motorway, followed the track of Uttoxeter Road in Meir. Plans though in the local press gave little away as to how the civil engineers were to shoehorn this environmental dinosaur into Meir's landscape.

The genial Carlo Witasek, originally from Yugoslavia, the driving force behind a local action group, foresaw many of the problems should the road be constructed. With Duncan Ross and several others, alternative plans were suggested. The group he led, the Keyhole Committee, derived its name from a comment made by a Department of Transport official that '*the section outside the TA and Holy Trinity church in Meir was the keyhole to the entire*

Stylish Weston Coyney Hall, the former home of Captain and Mrs Rittner,
part of which was later used as a Home Guard facility during WW2.

Park Hall, once the seat of the Sheriff of Staffordshire and a school for 'young ladies' was converted to the
Safari Lake Club before demolition. A housing estate stands on the site today.

scheme.' This proved to be true. A road similar to the Derby Way had been built in Reading, Berkshire in the mid 1960s. In 1972 a party drawn from the serried ranks of the Keyhole Committee, Meir businessmen, householders and academics went to Reading to see for themselves what it was like.

The shock on seeing the bridges and carriageways in Reading is difficult to describe. It was immediately obvious that the plans for Meir in local newspapers were a very long way from reality. The Derby Way called for destruction of property and amenities on a massive scale. Many returned, depressed. Should the Derby Way be built, old Meir would disppear.

Detailed plans outlining the Derby Way road scheme appeared, suggesting by its sheer size Meir would be relegated to the modern equivalent of a 'turning point' in the 1930 air races. The town would be reduced to no more than a 'passing place' on the national road network. Innumerable improvements, dozens of brochures, maps and diagrams followed along with meetings and discussions in Longton Town Hall implied according to American, Professor Les Fishman of Keele University, *"They're gonna build that road!"*

There was universal uproar in Meir. A petition started by Cliff Hathaway soon reached enormous proportions after appearing in local shops and businesses. At the final tally, thousands wrote of their opposition. But was anyone listening and more importantly would it have any effect? The petition was handed over to a representative of Staffordshire County Council by George Stevenson MP. It then disappeared, sparking fears it had been put to one side to be quietly forgotten. It failed for a memorable cartoon drawn by the late Dave Follows, of the Evening Sentinel caught the mood perfectly.

Proposals of mass housing on the airport site appeared in 1972 but was a statement implying a *"Garden City image for new Meir Estate"* more tongue in cheek than reality:

'A multi-thousand pound housing development project aimed at attracting business executives to Stoke-on-Trent was given the go ahead yesterday. The scheme involves building 57 on the former Meir Airport site. All have price tags in the £10,000 region but a double garage and oil fired central heating will be among standard fittings..... Building is expected to be under way by August. Chairman Harry Smallwood said. "With large areas of space, it will have a 'garden city' image with access to the new Derby Link road and the Blythe Bridge By Pass." Two thousand homes will be built on the site. The former Meir airport covers 420 acres and in the region of 220 acres are set aside for housing, but almost half the 'housing area' will be left as public open space and will be landscaped. A further 15 acres have been set aside for schools, shops and other amenities. The initial work is by Percy Bilton Limited. Development will take from 5 to 10 years and talks are to be held shortly with Staffs Council delegates on building on the other sections of the site.'

In 1972 industry and commerce were disrupted on an unprecedented scale when the miners' strike affected everyday life. Coal shortages in February 1972 and a coal famine closed more than 30 City schools.

It had become so severe that Prime Minister Edward Heath appeared in a television broadcast. 200 North Staffs pitmen lent their considerable bulk to a protest march through London streets on the afternoon of February 15, 1972. Local evening classes were soon affected by the coal crisis. Before long 50,000 workers were on short time.

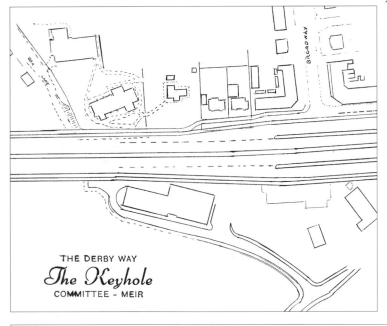

THE DERBY WAY
The Keyhole
COMMITTEE - MEIR

The Keyhole Committee of Meir seen here in Reading 1972. L to R: Mrs D. Moss, Carlo Witasek, Jean Witasek, Russell Finney, Mrs L. Beale, Peter Hyland, Mike Lowndes, Jack Lavick, Prof Les. Fishman, Arthur Talbot (civil engineer), Alan Key, ----, ---- (engineers), Nicholas Cartlidge, Duncan Ross, Eddie Dale.
Photo by Gerald Mee.

Part of the Keyhole Committee's amended plans for the Dept of Transport's ill-fated Derby Way, showing the area around Holy Trinity church.

The 'Save the Meir' petition which illustrated the enormous opposition in the town to the Derby Way.

SAVE THE MEIR

WE THE UNDERSIGNED REJECT THE PROPOSAL TO RECONSIDER THE DERBY WAY PROJECT AND RESPECTFULLY URGE THE MINISTER TO GO AHEAD WITH THE PLANNED STOKE-ON-TRENT SOUTHERN BY-PASS THUS AVOIDING THE HEART OF OUR COMMUNITY.

Reading, Berkshire photographed by Gerald Mee.

In 1972 the Keyhole Committee, from Meir, visited Reading to see a road similar to the 'Derby Way' proposed by the Dept of Transport for Meir.

Below: An aerial view showing the Reading underpass and roundabout which was proposed for Meir ((later reappearing in the guise of the 'Chalker Cut') but turned down by public opinion.

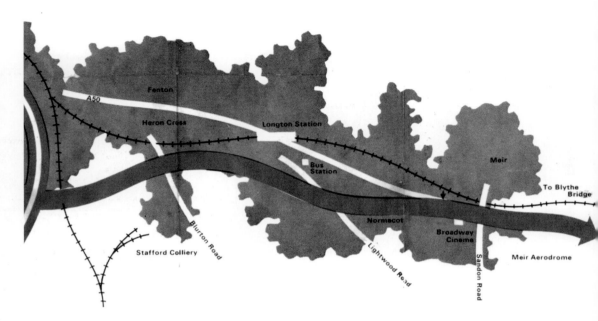

Part of the Department of Transport literature illustrating the Derby Way in the early 70s. The proposed route, shown by the bold line on the lower half of the map, was uncannily similar to the new A50.

A bleak view of the Reading scheme which was a blueprint for the DoT's Derby Way scheme for Meir.

Meir struggled on. Nothing though could dampen the enthusiasm of the victorious Stoke City team and its supporters following the victory over Chelsea at Wembley on March 4, 1972 in the Football League Cup Final. Who will ever forget the scenes around the Broadway Cinema when the entire centre of the town, a sea of faces, proudly proclaimed the Potters champions?

With lighter nights and Spring on its way, old mens' fancies turned to other things - like bowling. Professional bowling - better known as the 'panel' game - was staged for the first time at the King's Arms Hotel on a Sunday towards the end of May. The John Joules public house was very fortunate to have a bowling green when newer public houses were going up with enormous car parks ignoring this traditional and fascinating game of skill.

Stoke-on-Trent, the birthplace of one of the country's foremost engineers, Reginald Mitchell, had no example of his immortal creation, the Spitfire on display. Now in 1972 that was about to be rectified: *'A Supermarine Spitfire Mk XVI was manoeuvred into position in Bethesda Street, Hanley before being housed in a custom-made perspex hangar. It was given to the City of Stoke-on-Trent by the Ministry of Defence in recognition of Reginald Mitchell's outstanding contribution to its design.'*

William Havergal Brian, former organist at Holy Trinity church, was a nationally recognised composer by now and was at a point in his life when he didn't have a great deal of time to kick his heels. On the contrary municipal approval was never to be hurried: *'Stoke-on-Trent City council were told at the regular monthly meeting that the General Purpose Committee has DEFERRED consideration of formal recognition of Havergal Brian, the Dresden composer, who is now 96. Brian who has written 32 symphonies 5 operas and numerous choral works, now lives at Shoreham by Sea. Composing since he was 15 some of his early choral work and orchestral pieces received their first performance by local choirs and orchestras.'*

1974 in Meir nearly began with disaster: *'Three children were ushered to safety by their parents as fire ripped through their parents' grocer's shop. The fire damage was estimated at £3,000 to Mr and Mrs Nick Ainsworth's shop at 42 Broadway.'* Mr and Mrs Ainsworth were awakened by their 8 month old baby, Melissa crying. Mr Ainsworth, aged 28, dashed into the children's bedroom over the shop, where 5 year old Shona and Fiona, 3 were sleeping. *'The smoke was really thick I put damp towels over the children's heads and led them to safety.'* Pat Ainsworth said ruefully, *'Business was building up well but I don't know when we'll be open again.'* Mr and Mrs Ainsworth moved from Bury to Meir last December and had just decorated, installed new central heating and fittings in the shop.'

Better news for two 'golden oldies'. The best glasses from the sideboard were filled to toast the health of Mr and Mrs Tom Deakes on January 16th 1974, celebrating their golden wedding anniversary. For almost 40 years they had lived in Waterhead Road, Meir. If Tom had been a Stoke supporter he might have just sunk a second glass of cream sherry at the news that Stoke City had signed Chelsea and under-23 England star Alan Hudson for £240,000, a British record. Stoke borrowed £200,000 to help finance the deal, but with crowds close on 33,000 for a home match against Liverpool in the same month, the money was coming in.

A class at St Augustines School, Meir with Miss Anne Marie Coghlan on the left, in the early 1980s when school closure plans were announced.

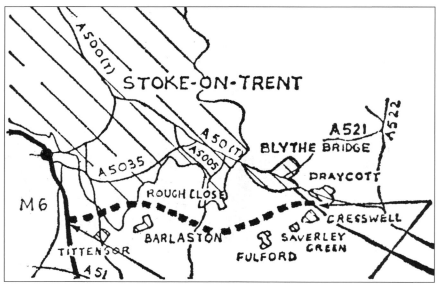

The Stoke Southern By-pass proposal 1979

CHAPTER 10

"Politics is perhaps the only profession for which no preparation is thought necessary."
                                                                Robert Louis Stevenson

How did the rhyme go? *Plant a tree in '73, plant some more in '74, still alive in '75 and dry as sticks in '76.* After an immense effort to make the country a more green and pleasant land, the weather had the last word. The ferocity of the summer caused havoc. Water shortages followed and as if that wasn't enough, a series of earth tremors rocked certain parts of Stoke-on-Trent, caused, it was said, by the Department of Geology at Keele, by the collapse of old mine workings abandoned long ago.

In the heat, contractors toiled on the D road, the A500 in Stoke, in temperatures only slightly less than those endured by prisoners of war in building the Burma Railway. Hopes were raised that the A500 would be concluded by 1977. Three miles long from Hanford to Etruria, two vital roundabouts were omitted, to be added in 2004-5 - at three times the cost.

The heat affected people's behaviour and the way they worked. Those embroiled on production lines in hot and stuffy factories suffered more than others. By reorganising the working rota for the firm's 1,200 employees to begin work three hours early at 6am, Dave Carryer, the Production Director of Staffordshire Potteries in Uttoxeter Road, became universally popular. It meant ending the working day at 2 pm, leaving them time for sunbathing. Good bloke that Dave! Dave Cartlidge, Personnel Officer said, *'It's going extremely well and we're just as pleased with the way it's working out as the people involved. It's terribly hot working in the factory and anyway this lovely sunshine is enough to tempt anyone away!'*

A furore erupted in the House of Commons at an order for £20,000 placed with Rosenthal, a German company, for china for the House of Commons. To call it 'unpopular' was an understatement. Extrapolated nationally, it wasn't difficult to see how the worst jobless total since the Second World War with 1,250,334 was being attained

Some of Meir's facilities, accumulated over many years, slowly vanished as suburbia's need for housing gathered momentum. Green acres, pillaged extensively during the 1920s and 1930s to relocate Longton's poorly-housed residents, were now decimated. Would it ever end? In 1975, a small parcel of land, in private ownership since the 1940s and part of the former Meir

Watchfield Close off Box Lane, Meir, built on former Holy Trinity church land, sold in 1976. The first two houses are the site of the 1903 Church Institute demolished in 1977. Other parts of the plot contained the tennis courts.

Golf Course was sold off. Next door, at Holy Trinity church, what remained of the once well-used tennis courts was deemed by the Commissioners *'surplus to requirements'* and auctioned off. Courts which in former days on fine summer evenings rang to the shouts of 'fifteen love', and saw Florence Dayson, the future wife of Reginald Mitchell and other loose-limbed girls, practising the overhead smash, would be supplanted by tidy 3 bedroom houses.

The sale of this land would be one of the last acts involving Rev FW Osborn (1965-1976) before he departed Holy Trinity Parish. Originally coming from Longsight, Manchester to Meir he returned to his roots becoming Bishop's Officer for the Homeless at St Benedict's. Many were surprised and pleased when the announcement that Meir's new priest was to be *'an old boy of the parish'*, the Rev Trevor J Harvey.

Adjacent to the church, the Holy Trinity Church Institute opened in 1903. Now in an age of spiralling coal and oil prices, its high vaulted rooms, large and difficult to heat were a handicap. The external fabric too had seen better days. Times had changed. Once the home of Meir library during the late 1940s, the Institute had seen many celebrations, been the venue for social functions and moments of great import through two world wars. A small area was the home in the 1930s of Joseph Leese RN. The Institute was demolished in 1977 and supplanted by a newer smaller church hall, attached to the church by a passage, along with a new Sacristy and Vestry. As Rev Harvey wrote: *'The present church hall is a*

The Lord Mayor of Stoke-on-Trent, Mrs Mary Stringer, and the Lady Mayoress, Mrs Suzanne Morley, with Father Trevor Harvey, parish priest of Holy Trinity church, far right and former incumbents, Father F.W. Osborn (2nd right) and Father H.V. Woodward, at the dedication of the new church hall in 1979. *The Evening Sentinel*

far cry from the original version of the vicar and men of the early 1900s who had a vision of surrounding the church with all the gentlemen of that time might need by way of leisure activity - tennis, bowling, billiards etc.'

Holy Trinity's new vestry and church hall was officially opened on June 11, 1979; Rev. Trevor Harvey accompanying the Lord Mayor and Rev. Prebendary H.V. Woodward, parish priest during the 1950s, at the ceremony.

Although the church hall had been slimmed down, the extensive grounds surrounding the church had not. To keep this semi-parkland setting tidy, an oasis amidst a sea of seething traffic, required a weekly trim in summer to sharpen up its text book appearance. Aided by a band of parishioners, Rev. Harvey maintained the grounds to such a high degree, the church won many awards in the Lichfield Diocese over several years. Judged the *'best churchyard where there are no burials',* praise for the church which had a *'beautiful garden'* were profuse and richly deserved.

Rumours began circulating concerning the closure of some Roman Catholic schools in the city. The staff and governors at St Augustine's in Meir, fearful the school might be included, took evasive action. A committee under Father W.A. Oddie, the parish priest, was formed as the rumour acquired authority. It needed a strategy for the school to survive.

The Silver Jubilee of the Queen's accession to the throne on the death of her father George VI on February 6, 1952 was celebrated in 1977. In the interim most families' living standards had improved greatly, many owned a car, a washing machine, a refrigerator and a television set. It was far removed from the grey days of Coronation Year in 1953 when owning a TV set made you very popular, your front room always knee deep with your immediate neighbours, who just happened to be 'passing by.' The pottery industry was as usual quick off the mark to produce a whole raft of commemorative plates and cups, of markedly better design and taste than those of 1953. Most of all, Jubilee Year provided a slight diversion from strikes and industrial unrest, never far from the surface since the early 1970s. James Callaghan, Prime Minister after Harold Wilson's resignation in March 1976, would soon feel the full force of the industrial turmoil again.

Through the 1970s, starting dates for the Derby Way slipped silently into oblivion. Months passed into autumn, Winter and Spring. When would a decision be made? The answer came in a banner headline of September 17, 1979: *'DERBY LINK NOT TO CROSS CITY'*, a landmark decision by Central Government. News that tens of thousands in Meir and Normacot would not have to endure years of siege, acres of concrete and piling machinery was greeted with great relief.

But in Barlaston, a tiny village, 3 miles away, it produced 'fury' on learning the Stoke Southern by pass, the preferred route, would pass a half mile away from their rural retreat. For the moment, Meir and Normacot could breathe again - cooking sherry flowed like water. In a gallant attempt to redress a terrible wrong, Councillor John Wallis asked for compensation from Central Government for some home owners whose houses had been threatened by blight for 20 years. Thousands were involved. He realised the city could not reimburse those affected.

His views were reinforced by a *'clear the air statement'* of the future of houses on the route of the Stoke-on-Trent to Derby link road by City Highways Committee chairman, Mr George Stevenson, who told council that, *'As far as we are concerned a Government announcement rejecting a possible route through Normacot and Meir to Blythe Bridge has removed the blight from the properties. When the statement was first issued earlier this month officials made it clear that 400 houses on the route of the link road had now been reprieved.'* But later, Council leader Mr Arthur Cholerton threw the entire meeting into confusion by saying, *'that until there was actual legislation taking the road on a route outside the city, the blight could not be said to have been lifted!'*

Asked by ward councillor John Wallis to explain the position, George Stevenson said, *'The Minister's letter made it clear that a city route for the Stoke to Derby Link had been rejected. You can't get it any clearer in a letter! It would seem that the planning blight no longer exists and I think that a lot of people will be pleased to hear that.'*

But the forces of opposition, small in number, were massing. *'Fulford Parish council will support a plan for informal talks with Barlaston and Swynnerton Parish Councils about the Stoke to Derby Link Road.'* Eddie Hill of Fulford Parish Council said. *'The economic viability of the road should be investigated before a definite decision was made. Even this route - not through the city - was not without risks.'*

Another group from Tean now handed a 2,500 name petition, to chivvy the planners, to David Knox MP for a start to the Blythe Bridge to Uttoxeter section of the A50. Two days later, as if to endorse the validity of their case, a juggernaut travelling along the old A50 crashed through a wall of Mrs Mabel Turland's Tean cottage, while she and neighbour, Mrs Dorothy Lomas, looked after Mrs Turland's 2 year old great-nephew, Giles. Falling masonry buried the tot, who was dusted down, fortunately none the worse for his experience.

And what about rail? *'A major call for the reopening of the once busy Meir Railway Station was voiced today. British Rail are being urged to consider this action which would be of 'great*

"BY THE WAY, ANY IDEA WHAT BECAME OF THE MEIR A50 PETITION THAT WAS HANDED IN SOMETIME AGO?"

benefit' to the thousands who live in the south of Stoke-on-Trent. The plan has come from Longton and District Chamber of Trade who feel that the service from Blythe Bridge to the city should include Meir.'

It was all a far cry from the unbounded optimism almost 85 years earlier: *'In view of the rapid growth of the Meir District, representations were recently made to the North Staffs Railway Company with the object of inducing them to provide a station for the accommodation of the inhabitants of that district and it is satisfactory to note that the company have definitely decided to accede to their request. The station is to be situated near to the bridge beyond the Normacot tunnel and near to the water works. Most of the land in the neighbourhood is being laid out in building plots and a still further development of the district is to be hoped for. The company will endeavour to have the new station completed and opened by Wakes Week.'*

Now Chamber of Trade President, Terry Steel argued, *'I'm sure it would cost comparatively little to reopen this station when one considers how well it could be used. Trains already use the link and all they have to do is make an extra stop.'* Trader Mrs Anita Liberson said, *'Blythe Bridge station was well used by shoppers travelling to Longton and the same could apply to those at Meir.'* Builder Mr David Fitzgerald commented, *'The roads get worse and worse and this, I feel, would ease traffic congestion.'* The Chamber retired for the night after deciding to write to British Rail.

The onset of autumn stirred the malcontents in the Trade Union movement for an assault on the Labour government. Britain was strikebound. Inflation spiralled as wage demands ballooned, rubbish filled the streets, the dead went unburied. Labour Prime Minister Jim Callaghan arrived home from aboard with a spectacular statement, *'Crisis, What Crisis?'* Dubbed *'The Winter of Discontent',* it provided the springboard for Margaret Thatcher to become the first woman Prime Minister.

Although memories of Meir airport had all but faded, a reminder of Meir's past association with the Royal Air Force and the Air Training Corps was rekindled by a milestone during September 1981. Wing Commander S.D. Little, the officer commanding the Staffordshire Wing of the Air Training Corps, presented Flt Lieutenant John Cooke, Commanding Officer of 239 Squadron Meir ATC, with a clasp to the Cadet Forces Medal awarded for 20 years commissioned service. Flt Lt Cooke had given over 1,000 hours of his voluntary time to air cadets in the Meir, a remarkable record.

Blythe Bridge station as it was in the late 1930s.

Ewie Hollinson's shop at the junction of Meir Road (A5035), left, and Uttoxeter Road (A50),
boasted one of the Potteries' first ice cream parlours. Later the entire building fell victim
to the new A50, and the junction, with car access to Meir Road, has gone.

An earlier view of the Uttoxeter Road/Meir Road junction c 1920. *Priestley Collection.*

CHAPTER 11

"Political language is designed to make lies sound truthful and murder respectable and to give an appearance of solidity to pure wind."

George Orwell

For almost two years Prime Minister Margaret Thatcher grappled with the economy, unemployment and inflation. More people were unemployed in 1982 than in the 1930s, and these domestic problems were exacerbated by a war against Argentina in the Falklands. All these events were to upset the carefully laid wedding plans in the Meir.

Henk DeJager, now 30, was a lieutenant in the Royal Marine 42 Commando and had been married for only 48 hours to his childhood sweetheart, American girl Samantha when he received his orders to report for duty in the Falklands conflict. DeJager a former pupil at Longton High School in Box Lane decided to read medicine and become a doctor, but 2 years later changed career, applying for a commission in the marines. Now at Plymouth Training College he had confirmed he had made the right choice by being awarded the 'sword of honour' for best officer in that year. His mother, Mary DeJager taught at Meir Middle School for 20 years.

For Susan Anne Barnes of Beckett Avenue it was a good year when she acquired the Queen's Scout Award. But Deputy Head Frank Huson at Sandon High School would remember it for all the wrong reasons. Referred to as the "the stud in the ear Saga" a contra-temps arose when a pupil arrived at school wearing a stud in his left ear, and was sent home. The national newspapers took the case up in full cry!

The proposals affecting St Augustine's Roman Catholic School in Meir gathered pace. The Local Authority proposed to cease to maintain the school from August 31, 1984. Pupils would transfer to St Gregory's in Longton or to Grange County Primary School in Harrowby Road then operating as Grange County Middle School.

The case offered by the Chief Education Officer seemed on the face of it a strong one. It was estimated there would be 1,000 surplus school places in Roman Catholic schools in Stoke-on-Trent in January 1984; two out of five places had to go. Father Oddie and his group pointed out that young children would be travelling by bus to Longton during dark winter months, and made reference to the school's past achievements, academic records, and the loss of a Christian education and social centre .

The church of St Augustine, Meir, was founded by Fr William Walsh on a large property in Sandon Road (formerly Lewis's Lane) called Highfields. It followed preliminary work by Fr Joseph Emery of St Gregory's, Longton, for a new church in Meir. For those who knew their history, by sending clergy from St Gregory's to Meir to establish St Augustine's, it paralleled the instructions from Pope Gregory to St Augustine to go to England to form a church nearly 2000 years earlier.

In 1934, the new parish was established formally by the Archbishop of Birmingham. Named after St. Augustine of Canterbury, its first parish priest was Fr Timothy O'Connor. Despite lack of creature comforts, no electricity, water drawn from a pump in one of the

St Augustine's RC School pupils in 1986 after the school closure threat was defeated. Miss Mary Tunney (head), left. Mrs Jean Hailstones (class teacher), right.

Mrs Florrie Scott.

outhouses and no furniture, one of the outbuildings, a stable, was adapted to serve as a church. And so it came about that the Parish of St Augustine began at midnight on Christmas Eve 1934 in a stable. According to Mrs Florrie Scott, *'The original church, the stable, had an extension added shortly after its opening. Several pieces from old Nissen huts were attached to the stable which made the building L-shaped. Mr Farmer was our first organist, and his son succeeded him.'*

For three years church services continued in the converted stable until St Augustine's school was ready. Built in 1937 with 'shilling bricks' paid for by the parishioners it had four classrooms, staff room, offices, toilets and wash rooms with hot and cold water, and a hall which became St Augustine's church for almost twenty years.

Father Tim O'Connor departed in 1935 leaving Fr Thomas O'Doherty to nurture the fledgling church until 1940. During the war years three priests served: Fr James Crichton, Fr O'Doherty and Fr J. Denis McEvilly. Fr Patrick Wall followed and then Canon Bernard McKenna completed two decades at St Augustine's to 1966 and during his ministry the much-needed new church was begun. The commemoration stone of May 25th, 1957 was laid by the Most Revd Francis Grimshaw, Archbishop of Birmingham and the church finally opened later in 1957.

In 1966 Fr W.A. Oddie arrived. His robust refusal to allow St Augustine's school to be downgraded or closed preserved the future of Catholic education in Meir. Fr Bernard Anwyl followed from 1994 till 1998, giving way to Fr Peter Foley. Fr Jan Nowotnik, who arrived in 2003, is the present incumbent.

The cost of St Augustine's school building in 1937 was £6,000-7,000, the total debt for land and buildings met entirely by the parishioners. Considering the average manual weekly wage in 1937 in Stoke-on-Trent was no more than £3, this was a tremendous feat for the parishioners.

Father William Alfred Oddie died in 1998 aged 75, following 28 years at the church and school. In his funeral oration Monsignor Thomas Gavin said of his life long friend and his involvement in the infamous attempted school closure: *'..and of course he was always interested and involved with the Primary School, especially, when the topic of spare places was brought up by the Local Education Authority. He didn't mind them getting rid of spare places except if the Catholic education of God''s holy children was*

Father W.A.Oddie, parish priest
St Augustine's RC church, Meir.

involved. I shall always be grateful to him for his support when I was at the Schools' Commission. "Just tell me what you want and I'll do it." I never had to, but Alf must have smiled when he heard the reclassification of schools.'

Autumn held out prospects for a start on the Derby Link road. Called the A564 and running from Blythe Bridge to Uttoxeter it neatly by-passed all the Tean Valley villages at a stroke. Spokesman Joyce Plant said, 'It was wonderful news!' Ultimately made of concrete it was noisy to drive on. While it removed the nightmare of heavy lorries from winding country lanes, it assisted the Department of Transport's case for their 'Chalker Cut' plan for the A50. The pieces began to fall into place.

Sir Hugh Fraser's death in March 1984 closed the record on an exceptional life as a soldier and MP for the parliamentary constituency of Stone and Meir which had changed much since his election victory almost 40 years earlier. What would have the war hero Sir Hugh made of the actions of a former city schoolboy in the same

Father Jan Nowotnik, parish priest at St Augustine's RC church in Sandon Road, Meir, by the Presbytery steps.

year: Former Longton High School 6th form pupil Michael Bettany (leaving in 1968) was accused of spying and breaking the Official Secrets Act. He was prosecuted by Keele graduate Michael Mansfield QC. The verdict condemned Bettany on 10 charges to 23 years in jail. Sir Hugh would have probably had him shot.

In Meir, little by little, another development nibbled away the once expansive acres of Meir Airport: *'Plans were accepted to build on a public open space close to the Blythe Bridge by-pass in Meir. The site at Lysander road, between the roundabout junctions on Whittle Road and the by-pass was the location for the proposed Meir Motel.'*

Formerly the venue of celebrities from the world of entertainment during the 1970s, Jollees night-club, a mile from Meir and adjacent to the Empire theatre, went into receivership.

The proliferation of plans, proposals, counter proposals and blueprints for the redevelopment of the A50, bewildered Meir residents living along its route. The Derby Way through Meir abandoned in 1979 implied acceptance of the Southern By-pass. Thousands were bemused why in 1985 they were embroiled in the same rigmarole again. Despite Meir residents' intense opposition, the Department of Transport continued planning to build the latest version of the A50 slap bang through one of the most heavily populated areas of the city, Meir and Normacot. Summer 1985 confirmed Meir residents' worst nightmare:

'City Main Road Dual Carriageway' declared the Evening Sentinel. *'A scheme to upgrade the traffic choked A50 and turn it into a dual carriageway channelled through Meir in a cutting, has been prepared by Ministry of Transport officials. It is Transport Minister Lynda Chalker's 'alternative' route to the Stoke Southern By-pass and would provide the missing link between the M6 and Blythe Bridge By-pass. It is believed only four*

properties would be affected. Father Trevor Harvey (parish priest at Holy Trinity Church and born in the Meir) warned the scheme would mean the 'death' of Meir: 'Even in a cutting, the A50 would mean problems for schools, shops and the whole community. Until I have seen the scheme in black and white, it is impossible for me to comment! What I do object to is all the wishy washy comments, which have been made since 1971 just to keep us quiet!'

Staffordshire East Euro MP, George Stevenson added *'There was 'extreme concern' in the Meir area over the A50 being turned into a dual carriageway.'*

Despite huge opposition in Meir, the planners beavered away. The details were astounding: *'An underpass and dual carriageway through Meir are being designed to cater for 35,000 vehicles daily in 2004, almost 10 000 up on existing traffic flows.'*

For two Meir residents the outcome would be of secondary importance. They left for Manchester Airport, a couple of hours and a short flight to their destination. Unhappily for Paul Forrester 19, of Cobham Place and his 21 year old fiancée Amanda Reddin, of Leecroft Road they never arrived. Along with 54 people they perished in the inferno as a Boeing 737 caught fire on the runway at Manchester airport, seated at the back with the last two tickets for the flight. They were united in death buried at a joint funeral paid for by the airline company, the accident a sobering reminder of the fragility of human life.

Whilst for many the very idea of flying fills them with trepidation, others seem born to it: *'Air cadet Paul Withington has just fulfilled many a budding pilot's dream by taking the controls, of an aircraft over the Grand Canyon. Paul a member of 239 Squadron Air training Corps was among 250 cadets chosen worldwide for the annual exchange visit to foreign countries. He was flown to the International Air Cadet Exchange Centre in Frankfurt by the United States Air Force. Paul, along with eight other British cadets was selected for a two week visit to America. After an overnight stay in North Virginia he went on to Salt Lake City.*

The 19 year-old student presented the Mayor of Salt Lake City, Palmer de Paulis with a letter from the Mayor of Stoke-on-Trent, Mr John Birkin and a plaque of the city's crest. He then stayed for three days in St George, where he took the controls of a Cessna 127 over the Grand Canyon. "It was an absolutely fantastic experience!" he said. Cadet Warrant Officer Paul Withington of Cayley Place, Meir Park, a student at the City 6th Form College, now hopes to study for a degree in Geography.'

At Holy Trinity Church the parishioners and friends of Father Trevor Harvey gathered to wish him well on his appointment out of the district, one he modestly described as a minor canon at Windsor Castle. With his wife Eileen, sons Dominic and Richard they left in the Autumn of 1986 for a world far removed from that of Meir. An exceptional musician and organist, and known affectionately as "Trev the Rev", he frequently led the annual foray of an ad hoc band of 'church' singers around local pubs and clubs at Christmas to bolster church coffers and the fortunes of the disadvantaged. His gambit of 'bashing out' the opening bars of various carols inevitably succeeded in making their presence felt above the hubbub of the drinkers at the King's Arms. His versatility between playing the organ at Holy Trinity and accompanying the *'wandering carollers'* was remarkable. Rev Harvey was a staunch opponent of the A50 but could only watch and wonder from Windsor Castle. The clamour to finalise plans now reached a crescendo and push had come to shove:

'Public opinion in the Meir has forced the Department of Transport to revise the A50 plans. The original scheme, which included a single carriageway in a cutting, has been abandoned in favour of a "more acceptable road scheme" said Staffordshire County Council chairman, Mr Arthur Cholerton. Earlier Mr Roger Ibbs accused Mr George Stevenson and Stoke South MP Mr Jack Ashley of 'whipping up' opposition to the new proposals. He suggested that they should thank the government for agreeing to invest so much money in the area. Highways chairman Terry Dix claimed however that "without a public meeting last year the county might have been forced to accept an inferior scheme".'

The latest plans in 1986 chopped up Meir and Normacot more than the old Derby Way, realising for many their worst nightmare. In October 1986 Euro MP, George Stevenson voiced his disquiet. Following talks with county highway officials and the Department of Transport he admitted, *'I can see there are certain benefits for North Staffordshire and parts of Stoke-on-Trent, but I am worried about the effects the scheme will have on Meir and Normacot. But the Stoke Southern By Pass remains on the table and the real answer is to tackle the problem of through traffic!'* And the tantalising question remained, although the A50 route had become the Ministry's preferred choice, the Stoke Southern by-pass was still a viable alternative - would it ever be built?

Meir was the 'keyhole' once more. And George Stevenson's views were augmented by Britain's truck and bus operators who urged the Government to speed up by-pass work including 32 proposed schemes in Staffordshire and Cheshire.

By March 1988, Holy Trinity Church had a new priest, the widely travelled Rev David Tudor. His ministry, inescapably entwined with the A50 controversy, found him pitched in at the deep end. Forcibly at odds with the A50 Government Public Inquiry inspector in late 1990 over the impact of noise in tunnels, he was quick to point out it was something about which he had wide experience, should the Meir scheme be constructed. Apart from his ecclesiastical duties, Rev Tudor was an undoubted authority on trams, although after being featured in a local newspaper he said *'how easy it was to be labelled eccentric by such exposure':*

'Tram-driver priest, Father David Tudor is back in the Potteries after a working holiday at Glasgow's National Garden Festival. The bachelor clergyman, who is vicar of Holy Trinity Church has just spent a week training newly-recruited staff to drive tramcars on loan from the National Tramway Museum of Crich, Derbyshire, where he is honorary chief driving instructor. His skills were acquired during an earlier engineering career which included four years as an electrical technician in Cologne where he regularly tested trams. Father Tudor says that after unemployment projects helping churches in the area with building and landscape schemes, he's been very pleased to be able to repay the compliment by putting his skills to use in Glasgow.'

Whenever planners unveiled any ideas it seemed no matter what was proposed for Meir, hostile public opinion instantly railed against it. After so many years of opposition to wholly unsuitable road schemes it was a Pavlovian response. With the expansion of Meir Park on the Meir Airport site, the retailer Tesco drew the fire of one of the 'awkward squad', the redoubtable councillor Fred Ball, one of Stoke-on-Trent Council's more inspired members:

'Plans for a multi-million pound super store alongside a major trunk road were roundly attacked by a local Labour party group. The scheme, planned for a site off the A50 at Meir, was slammed on the grounds 'it would cause traffic problems' by Mr Fred Ball, the Labour party's prospective Meir Park candidate for the May local elections. He says the plan for a 67,000 sq. ft Tesco store would lead to 'serious traffic and safety problems'. The development would 'devastate' Meir and Longton shopping centres.'

The inquiry six days later, supported the case to build the store at Meir. It also meant that ratepayers faced a bill of about £100,000, the cost of Stoke-on-Trent City Council's fight at the public inquiry. (Not unusual - in a similar public enquiry in 1986 the costs to Melton Mowbray Council were £70,000)

Numbers were declining in Staffordshire schools in 1987; pupils leaving at 16 years numbered 16,012. By 1993, 6 years on, they would fall to 11,006 - a 31% drop. It indicated a city in decline as people haemorrhaged from a place that was looking sad and dated.

Rusty golf clubs, languishing in garages and outhouses in Meir received welcome attention with an announcement in spring 1989 that Park Hall Golf course would soon open. With the loss of Meir Golf Course in the 1960s a new course was long overdue. It had actually been built for three years:

'The first drive on the new Park Hall Golf Course should be hit around next autumn (1989). The course was constructed from a hill side that was a waste tip and part of our reclamation project. The course obviously needed a longer time to settle and an extra wait will have done it no harm, especially in a wet year. We have tendered for architects for a clubhouse and everything should be completed by the back end of this year.'

The buy out of Staffordshire Potteries by the Coloroll Group gave the Meir company new impetus. In new hands, part of the workers' car park was sold to Tesco to fund Coloroll's ambitious plans for expansion of the ceramics site on the former Meir Airport.

The old axiom *'constant change is here to stay'* seemed suited to the upheavals on the railways throughout the 1960s and 1970s. When Longton Chamber of Trade applied to get Meir station reopened and were refused, the outlook for Blythe Bridge station just down the line looked none too rosey. But fluttering hearts were quelled after John Heddle, MP was given a guarantee that *'Blythe Bridge railway station would not be axed'*, by Sir Robert Reid, British Railways Chairman.

True to his word the station did not close, but the building was demolished. Stirred by news of the demolition of the station, a group rallied by campaigner Ellis Bevan sought to have the order curtailed. To out-manoeuvre the protestors, bulldozers arrived at Blythe Bridge station at first light, reducing the Victorian brick and tiled waiting rooms to rubble. Its replacement, a 20th century plastic bus shelter, is a poor exchange unless passengers waiting on the platform number no more than half a dozen.

The 1980s had almost run their course. Industrial unrest was still apparent but in decline,. In Meir, in April, news that another piece of the road jigsaw puzzle was falling into place was viewed with dismay by the locals: *'Stage one of a multi million pound improvement scheme was approved by councillors which involves the link from Victoria Place to the proposed Longton Fenton by-pass. It incorporates a new roundabout in King*

Street along with a route to the A50 under the main Stoke to Derby railway line.'

Unfortunately by now each time Stoke-on-Trent featured on TV or radio it was the butt of negative comment, the proverbial 'Aunt Sally' and outright winner of the 'wooden spoon.' A Granada TV programme, *Out of Order* stirred up a hornet's nest by labelling Stoke-on-Trent the *'Dirtiest city in Britain'* - a sobriquet a trifle harsh after the giant strides both City and County councils had taken to reduce derelict land, clear slums and provide more green spaces.

The decline of traditional manufacturing industries, generally with well-paid jobs, increased. In the early 1950s, of 152,000 in employment, 62,000 (41%) worked in the potteries, 15,000 in coal mining, 6,000 in steel and 1,500 in producing 'light manufactured goods'. By the early 1980s, the number employed in potteries was just 28%. Colliery closures in England World Cup winning year, 1966, increased derelict land to 1,750 acres although prodigious efforts to reduce it followed in the next three years. The city still had over 7% of land within its boundaries derelict in 1970.

Proving that scouts as well as old soldiers never die but only fade away was Arthur Bennett of Sandon Road, aged 82, one of Meir's originals. He reminisced about times past at that 'happy land of fun', Kibblestone Boy Scout camp, 3 miles from Meir. A Meir resident for decades his father Luke had run a small business from the back of the old King's Arms Hotel in the early 1930s.

The City of Stoke has produced some very famous names.

Royal Doulton

Royal Doulton Tableware Limited,
Domesticware Sales Division, Hobson Street, Burslem, Stoke-on-Trent ST6 2AJ.

Coalmining, Iron and Steel, but foremostly Pottery, was what Stoke-on-Trent did well for 200 years. The area is home to many famous names.

Many surviving impressions of Meir in its formative years are due to Arthur Bennett's perspicacity and his 'Box' Brownie camera: *'I was a scout in the 1st Blythe Bridge Group at a time when the late C Marshall Amor initiated that historic opening on land at Kibblestone Hall once owned by the Copeland family.'*

He recalled the 3 scouts that joined them at the first camp - Ernest Downes, Alfred Johnson and Harry Watts from Longton. Arthur - waiting to welcome visitors on Daffodil Sunday at Kibblestone scout camp - is the sole survivor of the 5 pioneers who set up the first camp on the site in Easter 1927. Arthur Bennett has never lost his interest in scouting or affection for Kibblestone as the years have rolled by and he can still take you to the spot where that first Easter weekend scout camp was held.

The rise of hooliganism during the 1970s and 1980s meant that at many football grounds spectators were penned in during the match, barring access to the pitch and from each other. Whether it was a consequence of this or not, in April 1989 a disaster of immense proportions was unfolding across the wires of the news agencies as the afternoon wore on. The headlines appearing beggared belief:

95 DIE IN FA CUP CRUSH

A pleasant day out, full of promise, anticipation and excitement was to end in scenes of horror and carnage. Before the day ran its course, almost a hundred football fans at the Liverpool versus Nottingham Forest FA cup match at Hillsborough, Sheffield, lay dead. For one Meir family it was a personal disaster:

In the Monday editions, the Evening Sentinel solemnly announced:

'CITY BOY DIES IN CUP HORROR'

'Casualty of the Hillsborough tragedy Tony Murray lay injured in a hospital bed unaware his only son was among the 94 victims of Britain's worst sporting disaster. Mr Murray spent 11 hours agonising over the fate of soccer mad teenager before medics told him the grim news early yesterday (April 16). Birthday boy, Paul, 14 just three days before the trajedy, died when a human tidal wave swept across the terraces. His dad suffered severe bruising as he was also trampled to the ground in the chaos of football's blackest day. Mr Murray, detained in a Sheffield hospital, underwent Xrays to his ribs, legs, shoulders and arms. As he lay injured doctors confirmed his worst fears as a neighbour identified Paul at 2.30am. Mr Murray's heartbroken wife Edna, and close friends, were at his hospital bedside when the announcement was made. Today amateur football official Mr Murray was too upset to talk of the disaster as he recovered back at the family home in Harcourt Avenue, Meir. But Paul's mother told how the couple went to watch her son's Anfield idols after getting tickets to the FA cup tie two days earlier.

Mrs Murray said, "They travelled to the match with the Stoke branch of the Liverpool Supporters' Club on an organised trip which ran from Hanley Bus station. Paul was really excited about seeing his team - he was crazy about them. They were standing quite near to the back of the crowd when there was a sudden surge and everybody was pushed forward. Tony just lost him in the crush. It got to the stage where they didn't have any control over where they were going - they were just forced along with the crowd."

Prayers were said for Paul at Holy Trinity Church and neighbours spoke of the young football fan who had turned his bedroom into a shrine to his Liverpool heroes. Mrs Kay Howe, also of Harcourt Avenue, said *"He was a wonderful lad, extremely kind, who always had a smile on his face. What has happened is a terrible tragedy."*

Paul was a pupil at Sandon High School. An inscribed Book of Remembrance to those who lost their lives at Hillsborough resides in Liverpool Cathedral.

Paul Murray

Shops and housing in Uttoxeter Road, Normacot, demolished for the new A50 included the Post Office, Derek's Chip Shop and Warrilow's Upholstery (right). Looking towards Longton, the Station Hotel is seen to the extreme left. Taken from Bengry Road, December 1993.

Victorian terraced houses in Uttoxeter Road, Normacot, looking towards Hollinson's Corner and Meir. The Remploy Factory and Percy Withington's Garage stood opposite the large hoarding by the third car down. These Victorian houses, until just beyond the hoarding, were demolished for the A50.

Offices of Les Hart, Accountant, and the Meir Takeaway, at the bottom of Sandon Road. This building was once a pharmacy owned by the Co-op in the 1930s. It escaped demolition in 1990 after the Dept of Transport Inspector amended plans for the new A50.

An artist's impression of how the Meir town centre would look after the proposed new A50 had been built, including the elevated A520 from Sandon Road (left) to Weston Road (right), deleted by the Inquiry Inspector.

Seen from the 1960s Community Centre looking east, are left to right, Queensway Court, the King's Arms and the Methodist church.

Below: Weston Road April 1993, seen from the town centre. Traffic lights were removed and a roundabout put in again to speed traffic but this largely failed at certain times of day.

CHAPTER 12

"If you have enough meetings over a long enough period of time, the meetings become more important than the problems the meetings were intended to solve."
                                                                          Dr E.R. Hendrickson

Among the few large manufacturers relocated to the periphery of the old Meir Airport site fronting the A50 was Johnson Matthey. Its prestigious factory, occupying 40,000 sq metres, supplied the ceramic industry, locally and world wide, with glazes, colours and other ceramic materials. It was the United Kingdom's number one. The portents of its downfall were already evident for those who knew the pottery industry intimately. The number of people working in the industry had fallen and during the 1990s the trickle became a flood. Long established pottery firms diversified overseas or else ceased domestic production entirely. With wage levels abroad a fraction, the 'men in grey suits' shut local factories. A knock on effect reduced demand for Johnson Matthey's products, leading eventually in 2003 to its closure and demolition.

Looking eastward into Meir and the western portal of the A50 Meir tunnel, an artist's impression of how the scheme would look. Note no pavement appears on the right hand side of the main A50 carriageway.

With so much decline it was a moot point as to whether the City really needed the ambitious plans for a new road network that appeared with increasing monotony. An artist's impression of what the new A50 would mean for Meir appeared.

Public participation exercises sought to sell the idea to a suspicious and sceptical population. Normacot would be badly affected, so too Heron Cross but Meir especially so. Here the most incredible plans were proposed. In addition to a road tunnel beneath Meir crossroads, an elevated roadway carried traffic from Weston Road to Sandon Road. That it was connected on one side to a very narrow Victorian carriageway (Weston Road) seemed to have caught the planners 'asleep at the wheel'. Demolition for its construction meant a

Now deserted the former Johnson Matthey/Cookson factory at Meir is a reminder of the decline of the pottery industry in Britain and Stoke-on-Trent in particular. April 2004.

great swathe of the southern Potteries towns would vanish leaving only concrete, brick, railings and tarmac. Was the A50 being used for slum clearance?

Another action group was formed. From humble beginnings in the 1960s Community Centre, the Meir Action Group (MAG) had a dramatic effect on the outcome and design of the new A50 in Meir. Local accountant Clive Hulse became chairman and under his captaincy the group punched above its weight at local and in government circles. Pharmacist Jeremy Billington, former surveyor John Roberts, Councillor Fred Ball, Phil Ellis and Tom Corden were also part of a talented team who suggested in many cases better alternatives, which irked the professionals immensely.

Almost weekly meetings took place knowing time was short and the Highways Agency was determined to build the new A50 road at any price - a price many thought was astronomic. For a road of 6.91km (4¼miles) it was to make a hole in the Exchequer's purse to the tune of £130 million pounds at £35m a mile, four times as expensive as the newly completed 6-lane M40 motorway.

Meir Action Group discuss plans with A50 engineers from Scott Wilson & Kirkpatrick (SWK) of Chesterfield and the Highways Agency, 1993. L to R: Tom Corden, Phil Ellis, Fred Ball, Clive Hulse, Chairman MAG (behind), Mike Lodge, John Roberts with Ken Weir (SWK) holding plans. John Parkhouse, David Bass and John Hornagold, Highways Agency.

Other counter proposals abounded. *'George Ray's A50 plan'* left the A50 in Blythe Bridge, travelling in a fold in the landscape across country to the M6 at Knowl Wall, skirting the village of Barlaston. Another, the old Stoke Southern By-pass, went to the south of Stoke linking the Wedgwood factory at Barlaston to a high speed road link. Objectors and Highways Agency officials met and talked daily. Even during a working lunch at the King's Arms in Meir, between the two camps, alternative proposals were parried and counter-parried. Not a moment was wasted. By November 1990, the assembled 'pro' and 'anti' forces met in Stoke-on-Trent.

The A50 Public Inquiry, under inspector Brigadier J.M. Holden, was held in November 1990 in the King's Hall in Stoke-on-Trent. The enormity of the opponents' task was daunting - against them a battery of Highways Agency specialists, each an expert in their own respective field. It was like Manchester United playing Accrington Stanley.

The Inquiry finished in mid-December 1990. The Inspector's verdict and the recommendation in spring 1992 was to *'build the new A50'* but not with the elevated flyover section at Meir. City Council officials greeted it with relief, for as a trunk road they would not bear a penny of its cost. The unrelenting hard work of the Meir Action Group, its chairman Clive Hulse and many protestors, by their submission of a credible alternative had proved their case. The Inquiry Inspector said, *'I have concluded that the Meir Action Group alternative lay out is markedly superior to the published proposals for Meir; that the advantages of the alternative are substantial enough to outweigh clearly the disadvantages that its adoption would cause; that the Department's published proposals should not be adopted; and that the Department's scheme without the flyover and subways, should not be adopted. I conclude that the Meir Action Group's alternative should be adopted. I note that modifications to the Orders would be needed.'*

While the verdict condemned the Department of Transport's blueprints to the waste bin, many believed, wrongly, it was the end of the nightmare. Lives, 'on hold' for an eternity, restarted. Months later Meir residents were enraged and puzzled to learn that 'the recommendations of the Public Inquiry Inspector *'WOULD NOT BE IMPLEMENTED IN FULL.'* Many asked pertinently, *'What was the point of the 1990 Inquiry, if, when, the decision went against the Department of Transport, they intended following their own agenda as though nothing had happened?'* Behind the annoyance and disappointment, it indicated to Meir residents their views amounted to nothing and the whole 1990 A50 Inquiry was a sham. What else could they think?

The gargantuan £600,000 Box Lane bridge and its carbon fibre cable stays would straddle the landscape outside Holy Trinity church. Meir Tunnel would be the same length as in the defeated Department of Transport 1990 A50 plan and not be lengthened by 80 metres at the Meir church end as in the 'approved' MAG plans. But the flyover taking the A520 from Weston Road to Sandon Road had gone. Brigadier Holden's decision to abandon it uniting and annoying Labour and Tory factions of the City council who claimed the scrapping of a pedestrianised area in the Department's original plan was an *'opportunity lost'*. One even claimed delays caused by objections could lead to the scrapping of the whole Meir section of the £135 million A50 scheme. Incredibly one HA official declared retrospectively, *'We were never very happy with the flyover anyway'.* For the MAG it left a rump of dedicated die-hards to fight on. The Highways Agency went away yet again, regrouped, to draw up more plans for Meir.

With the A50 in a state of impasse, in nearby local villages its construction was seen as a double-edged sword. It was just what the planners didn't want to hear; *'Road will bring £135 million headache, villagers warned. Councillors fear a £135 million road to ease traffic problems in North Staffordshire will cause a major headache for villagers in Blythe Bridge. They believe the road linking Stoke and Meir will attract greater volumes of vehicles to the Blythe Bridge by-pass. The new road which links the by-pass includes a tunnel beneath the road surface at Meir and motorway style 3-lane carriageways. But members of Staffordshire Borough Council want compensation for the increased noise which causes misery for hundreds of families living in Blythe Bridge.'*

The A50 proposals meant not only that Holy Trinity's new parish priest, Rev Gordon Whitty had to keep his eye on matters ecclesiastical, but gauge also the effects of the scheme on the 100 year old parish and its parishioners. He and his wife Joy embraced the task wholeheartedly, showing enormous resolve.

The future was also uncertain for one of a diminishing number of Longton's historic buildings. The Empire, formerly the Queens theatre, a mile or so from Meir town centre, boasted a prestigious lineage and lengthy history. Almost a hundred years earlier, at Christmas and New Year January 1897, it had been a favourite haunt for Meir citizens during the 'season of goodwill': *'The Queen's Theatre: 'Cinderella' was performed and produced by Messrs Hardie and Van Leer Company. The 'Theatrograph', an exhibition of annotated pictures is a great attraction.'*

Fashions change, conversion to a cinema preceded a short ignominious and downward step to a bingo hall. Now, in the cheerless light of a January day in 1993, and the aftermath of a fire, the Empire stood forlorn. Bad though events were, its situation in Longton was not unique. In August 1927 it was reported that, *'A fire in Longton at the Alexandra Picture Palace had reduced the building to ashes. All performances have therefore been cancelled. Nobody was injured.'*

Now with the 20th century through and its legacy of notable old buildings already squandered, two more Longton churches and the Empire Theatre joined the ranks. Before the fire, Stoke Repertory Players had been keen to have the Empire as a base for its activities. Now at this eleventh hour it emerged behind the scenes efforts to rejuvenate it had been pursued:

'The Empire Theatre, extensively damaged in a fire in 1992 was sought by Save the Empire Action Group who wrote to owners Bass Breweries to seek a solution. Its chairman, Ellis Bevan said "I have written to Bass this week to ask them to name their price."'

The interior grace and elegance of Matcham's design, a reminder of times past was gone, ornate boxes for the privileged few, gilded swags and plaster work, a product of his genius, no more. A brave crusade to rescue the Empire failed and it was demolished, part of the site of the former auditorium later occupied by a supermarket. The Empire's destiny seemed like a contagious disease.

Next door neighbour, Jollees, and later the bus station - cruelly nicknamed Chaos House - on the ground floor of Jollees, closed. Boarded windows, peeling paint and dereliction now symbolised Longton's continuing decline. Minus one bus station, passengers flagged down buses from outside the old Co-op Emporium in Longton before a modern replacement in 2002, by the Tesco store, offered perhaps a glimpse of things to come?

Decay bedevilled Meir. Awaiting the outcome of the A50 Inquiry, many had done little property maintenance and the town acquired a more down at heel appearance than it warranted. Even the lampposts were going rusty. Stoke's famous picture postcard of grimy streets and smoking pottery chimneys was a fading recollection. Self-deprecating and risible comment on the Potteries was now wearing somewhat thin.

The Ad men saw it as valuable grist for their mill. But was it true? Stoke-on-Trent had changed dramatically during the 20th century in innumerable ways; housing, clean air and civic amenities were all shining illustrations. How galling now to have some ill-informed advertising 'Johnny' use Stoke as a pictorial punch-bag with another retrospective pastiche. It wasn't fair. Titled *'Springtime in Stoke-on-Trent'* the campaign provoked outrage by comparing the city, very badly, with that of Paris.

MAG members came under the cosh, this time from Councillor Roger Ibbs to *'acquiesce or risk losing the new A50 altogether'* - no matter what it looked like or whether it was right for the city. George Ray took up the cudgels in a broadside to the local newspaper about his unwelcome intervention.

The 1993 details of the latest A50 plans produced more criticism. The protestors, still fuming and incensed over the new A50 plans persisted in their opposition. Enormous swathes of land outside Holy Trinity church up to Broadway Court were included in new orders for the A50. So severe was the land take, Broadway Court residents would be forced to enter their apartments via wooden duck-boards strapped to scaffold poles with the entire pavement removed. Meetings raised more doubts: *'A showdown with planners and A50 protesters in Holy Trinity Church Institute, Meir, revealed bridges spanning the new A50 - there was to be no street level crossing - and they were to be fitted with 'spy cameras'. Deployment of these cameras, ostensibly to target criminal elements loitering on the footbridges across the proposed new road were ridiculed as 'ludicrous'. Clive Hulse, indicating these cameras would be viewed more than 5 miles away, at Unity House, Hanley, asked, "Security guards will only monitor the screens during working hours, so what good are they going to be?"'*

Fearing for public safety, the 'boys in blue' warned *'footbridges'* were *'a haven for muggers'* after revealing a report describing a similar bridge in Coventry had been demolished in the light of a serious sexual assault.

Mr Hulse called for a further petition to be presented to another Public Inquiry in June. The Meir Action Group would still insist on extending the Meir tunnel by 80 metres to eliminate the Box Lane footbridge, its attendant security problems and poor 'line of sight' visibility on the Box Lane access road heading west.

Longton Town Hall became the venue for the 1993 A50 inquiry Environmental aspects now began to play an even greater part. With the A50 now closer to domestic

Seen before roadworks began, this view looking up Sandon Road, Meir shows the clear and uninterrupted view across this busy junction which disappeared after A50 construction.

Rumoured as a candidate for demolition this elegant structure, the King's Arms is one of the few 'signature' buildings left in Meir post A50. Also shows the crossroads and the traffic lights which were removed at the beginning of the new A50 construction in 1993.

property, noise was a major worry. The Highways Agency insisted its impact was minimal, objectors proved it was substantial. *'Whispering asphalt'* was specified for the Meir tunnel section, something of a pyrrhic victory, its wearing out in just 6 years. But the A50 was given the green light, Armageddon lay around the next corner, setting in motion the massed ranks of contractors' vehicles and heavy machinery.

Throughout 1994, A50 preparatory work became part and parcel of the lives of Meir citizens. Amid the chaos many pondered how much worse it would get? A welter of criticism grew. Contractors countered complaints, implementing plans *'to centralise the rubbish'* which ensured the air became so thick with swirling dust, it was difficult to breathe. Before building started, old and worn out services, gas, water and sewage pipes were replaced, electricity and telephone cabling renewed. Some protested in more subtle ways. One, ingeniously simple, received city-wide coverage. A brilliant parody emerged overnight, alongside the A50 in Meir. Visible to all incoming motorists it

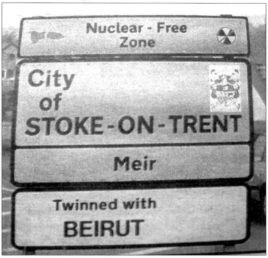

This 'Twinned-with-Beiruit road sign appeared during the A50 construction in Meir.

proclaimed, *'City of Stoke on Trent, Meir. Twinned with Beirut'*. The message provoked a wry smile, but residents feeling the full force of the Highways Agency's 'scorched earth policy', wanted their views addressed, quickly.

Meir Community Centre built during the 1960s had now gone - and a unique chance was lost. It would have been possible for Cllr Doris Robinson who opened the 1960s centre to officiate at its demolition!

Another worry made local residents uneasy. With a growing portfolio of empty properties, arson and more pertinently, the threat to public safety, was raised. The admirable Station Hotel in Uttoxeter Road, Normacot, was a remarkable red brick building loved by local drinkers. In its prime, it typified this leafy suburb, quiet and dignified. The pub, now isolated became the target of numerous attempts to set it alight. Boarded, bruised, battered and charred the contractors summoned the 'heavy brigade' to administer the 'coup de grace'. No more would amateur footballers use the cover of the Station's outbuildings to don their team's colours for local matches at the nearby Recreation Ground. A way of life had gone forever. After demolition the vulgar brickwork of the new highway retaining walls that replaced it, were, many agreed, *'reminiscent of those in a Victorian public lavatory'*.

The Waggon and Horses public house, on the Blythe Bridge side of Meir cross roads by the A50, lay abandoned for 5 weeks. The original Waggon, in a run of terraced housing in Uttoxeter Road, opposite, had been supplanted by a newer version with a hint of art deco, a style repeated in the Broadway cinema and in the designs of Clarice Cliff with her 'Bizarre' pottery range, which Wedgwood are reproducing in 2004. The 'new' Waggon, popular with

The Station Hotel, Normacot was another architectural gem.
It was demolished and replaced by a retaining wall.

American personnel from Cresswell during the Second World War, had now become the haunt of the two-wheeled motorbiking fraternity.

Predictably, it met its end in flames at dusk on September 13, 1994. Such was the ferocity, 50 firefighters battled the inferno, with 10 families living close by evacuated. Councillor Fred Ball re-stated Meir residents' fears of arson by vigorously chastising the Highways Agency for their lethargy in demolishing vacant property.

But yet again, in spite of this, more was to come:

'Hottest August since records began in 1952 at Keele,' said Mike Edge, Keele University Meteorological Officer as summer temperatures soared to 31C the day before. Dry weather forced a hosepipe ban as water supplies at Tittesworth reservoir shrivelled in the heat. As the new A50 racheted yard by yard across the city, the predicament of some residents became critical:

NEW DUST UP ON THE A50.

Families living in dust-laden streets near the new A50 construction site, are sitting indoors in 35C heat with windows closed and doors shut. Residents of Heron Cross who cannot open the windows because of the dust say it is intolerable. Filthy dust has been a problem for residents since the A50 construction started in Blurton Road, 18 months ago.

Nothing it seemed, short of emigration would bring relief, but some stoically suffered in silence. Landmarks were pulverised. The Meir headquarters of the Territorial Army (put up just before the Second World War) and the new Air Training Corps HQ fell victim. The TA relocation to Baskeyfield House, Adderley Green cost over £2 million.

As work continued in Meir, families fatigued by living their lives under siege, sold up and moved away. With more properties vacant, the threat of arson reappeared. In July 1995, a detached house, the former residence of Herbert Walley, a pioneer of Longton's first

Meir Community Centre, built in the 1960s, served Meir's needs for 25 years. It was opened by Clr Doris Robinson. Its splendid trees and lawns were a pleasure to see and a 'lung' to the west of Meir.
Mrs Robinson is seen left in another public role. It is interesting to think she opened the 1960s centre and was still alive when it closed.

The removal of the old Community Centre began shortly before the A50 roadworks started. Before it was torn down the new Community Centre was built behind it (see below), in Uttoxeter Road.

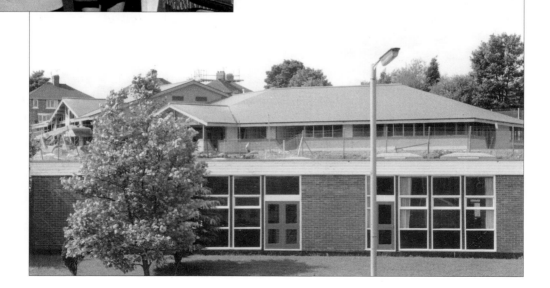

A Tompkinson and Betteley house in Eden Grove during the new A 50 works.

The Saracen's Head, Sandon Road was rebuilt in the mid 1930s to replace the earlier building at the crossroads.

The Longton Library and the
Sutherland Institute,
Longton, spared during the
demolition spree.

An old pottery, for many
decades the backdrop for tennis
players on the old Lightwood
Recreation Ground.

The remains of the water
pumping station on airport
level, Meir which is still in use.
Parts of the Victorian building
have been knocked down.

Early stages in the new A50 construction, outside Holy Trinity church.
The old A50 is seen behind the temporary fencing.

The original Longton High School (see p. 64) in the course of demolition in December 1993.
The 'new' Longton High, in Sandon Road, Meir, was built during the 1930s.

Meir Road looking eastwards in the 1920s.

Meir Road looking eastwards towards the British Legion Club in 2004. Little changed from 80 years before.

The 'Art Deco' Waggon and Horses, Uttoxeter Road, Meir, was built in the 1930s and replaced an earlier version on the opposite side of the road which was later the children's playgroup. The pub was the subject of an arson attack in September 1994 following which it was razed to the ground.

With the eastbound carriageway yet to be constructed all traffic used a single carriageway in passing through Meir along the 'airport level'. Seen from the Edenhurst Avenue footbridge looking towards the eastern portal of the tunnel where work is still underway.
(The price of unleaded petrol at the service station is 57.9p a litre (March 1997).

'Drop battle or face 10 years of road misery'

Press reaction to the opposition encountered at Meir to the new A50.

PARTS of Stoke-on-Trent face 10 years of roadworks misery unless an action group drops its opposition to a multi-million-pound road scheme, a councillor has warned.

Consider health of A50 residents

SIR, — News that there could be a two-year delay in the construction of the A50 (phase 2) in Meir should be used as a breathing space (no pun intended) to seriously consider the impact upon the health of those who will be living in the immediate area of what will be an urban motorway.

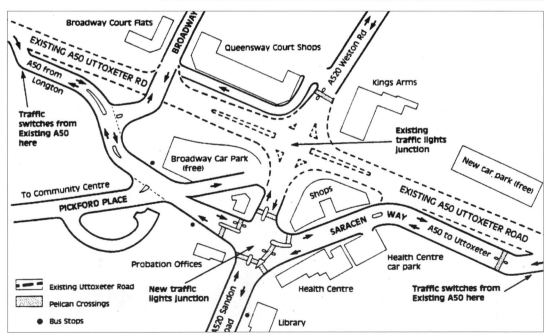

A schematic diagram of traffic management during Meir tunnel construction. Note the temporary road crossing the Broadway car park which cost in excess of £1 million. See overleaf for picture.

Meir's landmark, the King's Arms, beset by shuttering during A50 work.
Much of the famous bowling green was removed in the building of the tunnel.

A temporary road built over the old Broadway car park carried traffic through Meir during tunnel construction.

Two huge yellow cranes from Baldwin's of Chesterfield manoeuvre the 'A' frame of the £600,000 Box Lane bridge which straddles the A50 at Meir. The job took all night. September 1997.

Engineers carefully slide into position the decking of the Box Lane footbridge at Meir. The houses dimly seen in the background are in Kenilworth Avenue. September 1997.

Early stages in the construction of the tunnel seen from the Longton end and with the piling visible inside. Queensway Court in Meir centre is seen above.

A fire engine returning to Normacot along the old A50 in front of Holy Trinity church, while below the new A50 takes shape. The trees around the church were ultimately felled and the 'award-winning' churchyard dug up, to make way for the new road.

The construction of the Lightwood Road Recreation Ground in the 1920s
with the Sutherland Institute in the background. *Lovatt Collection.*

The westbound A50, running through the former Lightwood Road Recreation Ground, passes the Sutherland Institute, left, and the St James' church school, right, which the Composer William Havergal Brian attended.

George Avenue footbridge Meir straddling the A50.
Two white cottages, demolished for the works, once stood to the right.

The George Avenue footbridge. This ground level view looking west shows a variable road sign
informing motorists whether Meir tunnel is closed for maintenance.

supermarket, next door to Broadway Court, became the latest victim. Set alight at 7.30 pm the fire fighters took 2 hours to put out the flames. A residence once containing a doctor's surgery in the 1970s was demolished 2 days later.

Meir, Normacot, Longton and Heron Cross resembled a war zone. Both Salvation Army and Spiritualist Churches in the Strand were re-established in Longton. Amidst the mayhem it was not wholly unexpected that one or two of the contractors' best laid plans should go astray. With miles of new wiring and pipes on site it was not a matter of 'if' but 'when' some 'faux pas' would occur. It fell to hapless electrical contractors to be left with egg of their faces in laying new cables to houses in Coronation Avenue, Longton.

Enormous machines gobbled chunks out of the landscape. A million pounds was spent on a temporary road across the old Broadway car park during tunnel construction, a Meir Action Group strategy enabling the wheels of industry to turn, unhindered.

A 'cut and cover' method was selected in building the Meir Tunnel. A series of holes drilled downwards many metres into Meir's sandstone, reinforced with steel was surrounded by concrete, the method repeated opposite a few metres away. These piles formed two opposite tunnel walls. When hardened, a lid of concrete cast on top bridging the two sets of piles formed the tunnel roof. Earth beneath the hardened concrete roof was then excavated and removed; a difficult procedure performed over many months in trying circumstances. A new bridge to span the carriageway at Box Lane was installed. With immense skill two cranes from Baldwin's of Chesterfield lowered the huge 'A' frame into position. Three other bridges at Meir Road, George Avenue and Edenhurst Avenue of a more conventional design went up.

Phase 1B of the A50 diagonally bisected the enormous Lightwood Road Recreation Ground as it travelled east. It had been opened in May 1924: *'The Stone Road* (later Lightwood Road) *Recreation Ground was opened at 3 pm on 30th inst. by his Grace, the Duke of Sutherland. A musical accompaniment as performed by the band of the 5th North Staffs Regiment and to mark the occasion, school children in the area were given a half day's holiday.'*

Following the new carriageway, the game of crown green bowls once enjoyed with unhurried grace would now be played, uneasily, right up against the traffic, whilst those 'for tennis' could gaze out on a timber yard in Beaufort Road and over old pottery works.

But opportunities followed the new road. The second part of the 'Rec' fronting a boundary with Lightwood Road was sold eventually to a prosperous car dealership. On the other hand, financial hardship precipitated by the A50 upset many businesses and tradesmen. As the road neared conclusion, those blighted sought compensation for lost sales. Meir traders and shops, cut off more effectively than Stalingrad, were amongst the worst affected, some even featured on their own road signs.

Whilst many just staggered on, for one it was too much. One Meir carpet shop closed its premises, when an enormous pile of excavated earth was left by contractors across its doorway. They relocated to new premises in Weston Road.

Normacot shopkeepers were less fortunate. Whilst illegal immigrants were found working on the new A50, it appeared the future of legitimate, long established business concerns was of no consequence. They were told they would get *'no payments'* as *'it is your fault for assuming passing trade which once allowed their businesses to prosper would always be there.'*

By cutting the proverbial ribbon in 1996 County Council chairman Bill Austin opened part of the new A50. After suffering so much for so long, suddenly the A50 was becoming a reality. The city's motoring fraternity, who for decades had needed footwork to rival Tower ballroom organ maestro Reginald Dixon when driving along the old A50, could look forward to quicker journey times and lower blood pressure. But while acres of tarmac beckoned tantalisingly, behind the scenes many had worries. Fears of intimidation by gangs on the new bridges at Heron Cross became apparent. Old Age Pensioners dared not venture to cross the bridge at night fearing attack. Was this the price they had to pay for high-speed car travel?

Amid the confusion, inevitably acts of mindless vandalism went on, irreparably damaging the town's image and the City Council's efforts to improve life for Meir residents. For no apparent reason at a council depot in Normacot Grange Road arsonists set some petrol alight and several sit on mowers were destroyed. After the turmoil of the new A50, it was depressing; very depressing indeed!

The A50 seen from the George Avenue footbridge, looking towards the town centre.

The King's Arms and its outbuildings
are an important part of the skyline for
those living in Meir. May 2004.

A fine piece of 1930s' craftmanship,
The King's Arms is a surviving link to
Meir's 'golden age'.

The Alhambra in its heyday. *Lovatt Collection.*

The Alhambra cinema just before demolition for the A50 in December 1993.
The Alhambra in Normacot was owned by the Myatt brothers. Local historian Angie Stevenson faithfully numbered the bricks in the entire front facade and it now lies stored at Les Oakes' awaiting reconstruction.

CHAPTER 13

"Never check an interesting fact."   Howard Hughes, Film producer 1905-1976

In civvy street, Ernest Egerton worked at Staffordshire Potteries in the Meir as a lodgeman.   Now eighty years after his dauntless deed during the First World War, members of the local British Legion mustered to honour his memory.

Two inscribed plaques to honour him were dedicated, one at his old work place at Staffordshire Potteries in Meir (where is it now the works has been demolished?) and the other fastened to his home in Blythe Bridge, a perpetual reminder to passers-by of when the difference between life and death was a matter of great good fortune.

John McNeal, Secretary and Treasurer of the Blythe Bridge British Legion said *'It is particularly fitting these plaques should be unveiled exactly 80 years after Sgt Egerton's brave act.   We are all very proud of him.'* The plaque reads, *'Here lived Ernest Albert Egerton, born 1897, died 1966 who won the Victoria Cross at*

Mrs Margaret Porter, daughter of Ernest Albert Egerton VC, unveiling a plaque to commemorate her father's heroism in 1917 in the Great War. Blythe Bridge, September 1997.

Passchendale Ridge on September 20th, 1917 whilst serving with the Sherwood Foresters.' His medal now resides in the Sherwood Foresters' Regimental Museum.

By comparison the problems of residents embroiled with the A50 construction might seem to pale into insignificance. Dry weather turned the Meir area into a dust bowl yet again, thick clouds of swirling sand filled the air choking those nearby. They lambasted the hard-pressed contractors, who replied by spraying water over the entire area from a bowser. In July 1997 the newspapers blared, *'Asthma father says 'I'll sue over A50 dust.'* It was not an isolated incident. At the Grange Primary School, head teacher Nigel Johnson alerted education inspectors about the dust and soaring asthma attacks in the children under his care. He said *'Ten years ago we were getting two or three children in the whole school with asthma. Now it is an average of three per class - a twenty fold increase.'*

Parochialism is a feature of Potteries life. Many ridicule it but it is the social adhesive holding the city together at a personal level. This spirit of neighbourliness, never far away from the vast majority in Meir was the inspiration for organisers of local events. A charity Fair at the King's Arms on Saturday September 23 for cancer research, encouraged giving for the benefit of others less fortunate. Meir folk were historically warm-hearted and generous considering the town was often labelled, 'deprived.' Emulating the 'King's Arms' efforts, younger members of Meir pressed for a better future:

'Young people in a deprived area of Stoke- on-Trent have set up a campaigning body to fight for services and represent their views. A group of pupils from Sandon and Longton High Schools have formed Meir Youth Action - a lobby group intent on improving the lot of many people in the community. They have established with help from Meir in Action (MIA) a group of local housing, police and health experts, and teachers from the local schools. MIA coordinator, Marge Woodhead said, "We felt it was important not to tell the youngsters what they want, but to ask them. If they decide they do not have sufficient play areas for example, we will help guide them as to whom to put pressure on to do something about it.'

Although Meir's connection with the age of lighter-than-air machines was long past, through the development of housing on Meir Park, the names associated with aviation persisted; Brabazon, Canberra, Cobham, Lysander and Bleriot were examples.

By spring 1998, the A50 road works had lasted longer than the Second World War. Meir, around its centre, had been virtually redesigned, reassuring landmarks were gone and their modern replacements were less inspiring. Replaced by a broken-backed roundabout like an Alton Towers ride, the road was inexplicably now 18" higher than the original pavements outside Pizza Hut.

But Meir had acquired a splendid new Community Centre overlooking the town, sitting in the shadow of millions of gallons of water inside the Waterhead reservoir. Holy Trinity Church fared less well, cut off from Uttoxeter Road, its entry was in Box Lane, new railings adding to a sense of isolation.

Vast areas of walkways channelled pedestrians down concrete canyons. Only an Olympic pole vaulter would be able to cross the A50 other than by the bridges at Box Lane, Meir Road, George Avenue and Edenhurst Avenue.

Friendly, knockabout, slightly down-at-heel Meir had vanished. In May there was an announcement that a *'Carnival will mark the end of the Road'*. Contractor Scott Wilson planted trees and landscaped grassy banks lining the £150 million trunk road and a spokesman from the Highways Agency confirmed this was it!

'Along parts of the A50 between the postal depot in Normacot and Blythe Bridge there was programme of tree planting through the spring. This will be completed in the autumn and apart from that work, it is finished. A three day carnival at Longton High School, from Friday June 12, is planned to celebrate the end of five years work on the A50. Lord Mayor Kath Banks is hoping all schools in Meir and Longton will set off balloons at the same time on Friday and organise displays.'

Anti-road protestors predicted heavy congestion along the A50 when the road was completed in Derby toward the end of this year. Michael Wilmot, of the North Staffordshire Rail Promotion Group also warned, *'Once the 800 metres of the A50 are completed the road will become a high speed link between the M1 and the M6. It will mean motorway traffic being diverted through Stoke-on-Trent along the A50. We will have the crazy situation of motorway traffic being diverted through the heart of our city.'* (Defying all Highways

The new 1.02 million Meir Community Centre built by A.V. Shenton and vastly superior to the 1960s building it replaced. Walking visitors though need a sturdy pair of legs as it is on one of the highest points in Meir.

Agency predictions, traffic flow along the A50 in 2004 reached 70,000 vehicles a day. Michael Wilmot had been proved correct.)

The new millennium brought a renewed sense of purpose. Resolutions to improve Meir were profuse. The Meir Community Centre, at £1.02 million, was inspiring and impressive in operation. A youth centre/cafe was on the drawing board to complement wide-ranging plans to upgrade computer literacy, recalling Rev Charles Addenbrooke's efforts a century earlier at Holy Trinity Church. Opening in 2003, on a site below Meir library, the Community Centre's clean-cut and futuristic design was the precursor of far-reaching plans to restructure Meir which emerged at a public consultation exercise in February 2004.

Like an irritating relative, Stoke's undeserved notoriety for being *'an undesirable place to live'* continued to plague efforts to promote a better image. A newspaper article *'City's sad place in ranking of despair'* inflamed passions by asserting that *'certain parts of Stoke-on-Trent were amongst the most deprived in England.'* If it were true and you lived in Fenton, Burslem Grange, Tunstall North, Bentilee, Blurton and Longton South then you sat in the corner wearing the dunce's cap.

For once Meir eluded this invidious criticism due partly to the A50 makeover. It did have its uses after all! But the impression that everything in the garden was lovely was rudely shattered by battling Councillor Bill Austin, never one to hide his light under a bushel, who spoke forcefully for residents about a little 'local difficulty': *'Residents fear a pitched battle involving gangs armed with sticks and ornamental swords could mark the start of trouble on their troubled housing estate.'* Stoke-on-Trent City Council spent millions of pounds in renovating homes and demolishing others.

Ward Councillor Bill Austin said, *'We spent a lot of time and money on the situation in the early 90s. We got a lot of good response from the scheme to improve the lives of people of the estate - it's disgusting if that now has come to an end.'* An unnamed resident said, *'We had all this before about 2 or 3 years ago. It was all drug related. Then the council tidied the area and it all went quiet. It would be deeply depressing if it went back to that.'* Would Bill Austin's rhetoric do the trick? Many hoped so!

As A50 contractors' vehicles drove off into the sunset, a quick glance revealed that few distinctive buildings in Meir and nearby Normacot had escaped demolition or alteration during the past five years. For some it had been a close call.

In the 1980s the King's Arms public house, built by John Joule in 1935, was proposed for demolition for car parking space. It caused some anxious moments but it survived. However the Broadway cinema, straddling the junction of Sandon Road and Uttoxeter Road was not so fortunate. In the early 1970s a plea for a delay in its demolition by Alderman Russell Finney at a meeting of the Highways and Plans Committee was ignored. The committee recommended that the Broadway be purchased for £52,000, but hopes were dashed, it all came to naught and demolition followed, although its name lives on in the road, Broadway.

However a future for the facade of the Alhambra, Normacot, was enhanced due to huge efforts by a devoted enthusiast. In August 2000: *'The facade of the Alhambra Cinema may be restored 5 years after the cinema was demolished. Historian Angie Stevenson patiently numbered each block from the facade according to its position in the hope one day it could be restored to its former glory somewhere in North Staffs. Since then the bricks have been kept at collector Les Oakes' farm near Cheadle. Angie has received offers for the blocks but has turned them down. She thinks the new Arts Centre would be ideal which would blend in with the architecture of Leek. The Alhambra was run by the Myatt Brothers until they retired in 1975'*

As ambitious as the plan seemed, the situation was plausible, as former clients of the 'Red Lion' public house in Stoke town centre will testify after demolition in November 1973. The famous facade and its eponymous king of the beasts - in fact, a replica - was removed to be reinstated at the National Tramway Centre at Crich, Derbyshire. Could the same happen with the Alhambra?

It certainly would not happen with the Waterhead Hotel on Hillside estate which had long since gone to the knacker's yard. Beaufort Court, a Beth Johnson Housing Association enterprise now occupied the site. Did the same fate now await another of Meir's inns, The Tiger Moth, in Sandon Road, as it lay battened down following numerous incursions beyond bolted doors?

The original Saracen's Head was demolished in 1932, but rebuilt higher up Sandon Road, almost a mile from its original site in Meir, during the 1930s. It escaped the A50 works and remains as one of Meir's more outstanding and impressive buildings.

The Youth Cafe/Centre in Sandon Road, Meir opened its doors in 2003, its white facade throwing into sharp relief the dated design of Meir Library. Some of 'old Meir' obstinately remained - the Duncan Ross parade of shops, occupying the former site of the old Saracen's Head, marginalised during A50 work, after Herculean efforts returned to normality. Meir Post Office with postmasters Howard and Jenny Monks, Sue and Mum, Nora at Baggley's Newsagents, Peak Pharmacy (formerly Duncan Ross), Pizza Hut, Rogers Barber Shop, The Broadway Cafe plus Dr H.P. Borse's surgery, all in the front line during A50 construction, awoke, refreshed from their enforced slumber.

Opposite and uniquely alone at the junction of Sandon Road and Uttoxeter Road, Chung's Chinese Takeaway and the offices of Accountant, Les Hart evaded the demolition only to be embroiled in the A50 turmoil. Originally destined to be demolished, the scheme's redrawing in 1992/3 reprieved them, it must be said more by luck than good judgement, to add presence to a depleted inventory of businesses and shops on the newer side of Meir crossroads.

While the Uttoxeter Road, A50, had altered beyond recognition, the only concession Weston Road (A520) had made to the 21st century was a 'Tardis'-style public toilet.

But closer inspection showed time and money had been spent in modernisation in Meir. Typically, the Labour Party Offices in Stanton Road (Station Road in the steam age) which was now a ripe shade of green, helped constituents meet with their highly approachable representative, the former Euro MP and MP for Stoke-on-Trent (South), Mr George Stevenson, when he held his surgeries.

In Cornelious Street, Yorkshire-born optometrist Mike Lodge had practised since time immemorial; now Mr Razvi and his son carried on the practice. Whilst in former off-licence premises, The Meir's Beauty Box catered for the finer things in a lady's life.

By relocating in the 1970s from the Duncan Ross parade to Weston Road, Hyland's Electrical Store eliminated any disruption to their customers from A50 work - an inspired decision in the circumstances! From the top of Penfleet Avenue to the King's Arms the shops still contained the nucleus of Meir's shopping centre: Wright's Pies, numerous greengrocers, video shops, Parker's Butchers, Parks Pharmacy, Co-op Travel, Estate Agent Alan Dale plus a ladies' hairdressing salon with its sideways blast from Meir's past - 'Hair-o-drome'. A fine diversity for any township.

Frank Amison, a former member of Meir Golf Club, a well-known and respected member of the community in his tobacconist's shop, died in the late 1990s. His widow and daughter ensured it survived, but the gent's hairdresser operating from a small room at the back of the shop during the 1940s has long since disappeared. Many recall the appealing aroma of tobacco while waiting for a quick trim.

Newsagent Stephen Woolridge, born in Meir, carried on a family connection in a business run by his late father. An early-riser, Steve continued marshalling the newspaper boys/girls with fairness and military precision, Lynn Oakes deputising while Steve practised his tee shots on 'an away day'.

But while some absentees 'post-road' were down to the vagaries of construction, others were not and the result of their absence on the Meir community was profound. Meir and Stone are 5 miles apart with a similar population. Stone was blessed with five banks whilst Meir had a Trustee Savings Bank, Lloyds, and a branch of NatWest While Stone's banks stayed unchanged, rapid closures and relocations, meant Meir was suddenly bereft of any. A principal tenet of the TSB at its outset was its offering a service to local people with personal or works savings schemes, some squirrelling away as little as 'half a crown a week'. After demolition of its Meir office, locals were notified the bank had 'moved and improved' to Longton. As one of North Staffordshire's busiest offices it was a bitter blow. Many cursed and traipsed to the Britannia or the Staffordshire Building Society or took to

Prospect House, Penfleet Avenue (formerly The Avenue) where Florence Dayson and Meir Golf Course stalwart Reg Dearing lived in the 1920s and 30s. This house is now the Meir Dental Practice of Dr Louis Lotter and his colleagues.

The Meir Youth Centre and Cafe in Sandon Road which opened in 2003. A building of some style and a welcome addition to Meir.

Below: Early A50 construction outside Meir Methodist church meant businesses had their own road signs to assist customers to find them. The Kings Arms is seen in the background.

Modern day Weston Road, the A520, looking back to Victorian shops and Meir town centre, May 2004.

Meir Post Office and Baggley's newsagents in Sandon Road in the Duncan Ross parade of shops which have returned to use after the new A50 construction.

Broadway, Meir. This photo reproduces as far as possible the evocative view of the American
photographer William Blake, taken in the 1920s (see p. 18).
This shot in 2003 shows the 1935 Kings Arms and the Duncan Ross parade of shops, on the right.

Holy Trinity church and housing on the eastbound exit lane off the A50 alongside the Meir Tunnel.
In the foreground there is a cabinet housing air quality monitoring equipment.

With a Victorian terrace, 'Smith's Buildings', as a background, this 21st century 'Tardis' stands proudly at the corner of Weston Road in the centre of Meir. It replaced the old public 'convenience' in Uttoxeter Road by the side of the former Trustee Savings Bank.

Looking west from Meir town centre towards the Box Lane bridge at the western portal of the tunnel. Queensway Court is at the right side.

Looking to Meir centre from Sandon Road in 2004. Since 1935 the King's Arms has been a familiar landmark. See picture on p. 139.

The Meir Community Centre viewed from the town centre. Numerous shrubs have given the middle of Meir a more horticultural feel post the A50 construction. The roundabout has been reinstated but the Broadway site is still unused. May 2004.

Looking down Sandon Road from opposite Meir Library with Queensway Court in the distance.
Compare this with the 1920s Bennett Collection view.

Meir Takeaway and Les Hart's offices in April 2004. They escaped demolition in 1993/94, as did
Holy Trinity church, Queensway Court and Broadway Court, all seen in the background.
The Broadway site is still unused 30 years after its demolition.

The Co-op Late Shop and Meir's Beauty Box in Weston Road, May 2004.

armchair or Internet banking. When the Staffordshire Building Society, next door to Sportsland, closed its offices in what was Meir Villas, many felt short-changed again. Newcomers to Meir in 2003, Weigh and Save, soon filled the building society premises,

customers possibly swelled by savers unaware of the closure of the Society's offices.

Meir Villas sign above Weston Road shops showing the wartime obliterated 'Meir'.

Early in the Second World War, to confuse possible invading German paratroopers according to Alan Key, Meir Villas had the Meir part of the commemorative tablet, obliterated. Considering the German Army already had detailed maps of the area it would not have delayed them for very long. In any case Ewart Key, who worked at Shelton Iron and Steel in the 1920s, recalled a German firm installing a special furnace at Shelton in the 1930s and the Germans would therefore have known of Shelton anyway.

Some were not so lucky. Tommy and Maureen Cliff's Multicraft Supplies, reached through an entry to the left of King Kebab, after years of service to Meir's army of DIY aficionados, was no more. Their premises in one of Meir's oldest properties, attracted the interest of the City Museum in Hanley.

The 1990 A50 plan incorporated a flyover between 35 and 40 feet wide, taking the road (A520) from Sandon Road into Weston Road. It was deleted removing a severe blight on the run of shops from Lockett's to Wardles Travel. Knowing a broad pavement in Weston

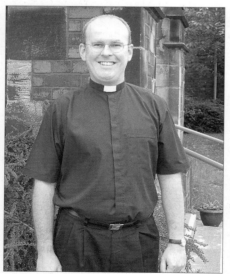

Rev John Foulds priest in charge Holy Trinity church, outside the side entrance to the church, May 2004.

Road would remain, encouraged Victoria Carpets and Tony Kemp of Cards and Gifts, to concentrate their efforts in this older, more homely part of town, the Weston Road side, relocating from Sandon Road.

Rev. John Foulds, priest in charge of Holy Trinity church stepped into the shoes of Rev Gordon Whitty. Fears on Rev. Whitty's arrival, that he would bring *'lots of smelly men with him'* to the Meir from his old church in Shelton were unfounded. His departure left Holy Trinity church physically enhanced by numerous changes to the church grounds; the car park, lawns and access and due to his determination that compensation should be ploughed back in.

At St Augustine's, the youthful and highly affable Fr. Jan Nowotnik, ordained in 1998, succeeded Fr Peter Foley.

An aerial view of Meir in 1945 produced for reconnaissance.

There were three Methodist churches in the Meir area, at Uttoxeter Road, next door to Swedish Car Parts, Normacot Methodist, opposite the British Legion in Meir Road, and in Sandon Old Road, formerly in 1939 a school. Consolidation to one site looked possible for Meir's Methodists under their priest Rev Andrew Baker.

With over 25,000 people living in and around Meir, professional health carers would never be short of work. In the refurbished Health Centre in Saracen Way, Dr H.P. Borse lightened the case load of stalwart Dr D.H. Ganapathy at Meir Health Centre, as he slipped into semi retirement on October 26, 2003 as the 'three score years and ten' approached.

Retirement of Dr D.H. Ganapathy (far left) at Meir Health Centre with Tony McGowan of the Primary Care Trust. His successor, Dr Harish Borse, is third from the left. Dr Prasad Rao is far right. *The Sentinel.*

A prediction to his father on leaving Mother India that *'he would only be away for a few years',* forty years later was somewhat wide of the mark, as he became a medical mainstay for his patients in Meir. Sadly his retirement was short-lived. He collapsed and died whilst on a visit to India in August 2004.

But his lengthy contribution is not unique. Dr Justin McCarthy who died in March 2003 was a GP for over 50 years, some of that in Meir. A devout Roman Catholic, with his Irish charm, he never failed to leave an impression on his patients. He joined the Longton practice of Dr. Ron Beer in the early 1950s. He married Anne, combining his Mayfield surgery, Trentham with the Weston Road, Meir surgery where she was working. Their two children, James and Mary are both doctors. Dr James McCarthy practices at the Meir Health Centre and has patients who *'were brought into the world by his father.'*

Dr Justin McCarthy

In the town some street names had gone, others refined. The Avenue was renamed Penfleet Avenue in a municipal shake up to eliminate duplication. Prospect House former home of one of Holy Trinity's early benefactors, became the Meir Dental Centre for South African Dr Louis Lotter, his wife and colleagues.

It was not just Meir's street names that had changed. The 1939 Longton High School in Sandon Road sculpted in landscaped grounds and approached by a tree lined drive, was now Sandon High School Business and Enterprise College. The mantle of responsibility had been handed down through the years from Mr M.V. Gregory, its original head teacher, to its present headteacher, Miss Hall. During those forty years the building's exterior had become weather stained. Panelling applied to the outside during the 1990s gave it a much needed facelift.

Longton High School, moving from Sandon Road to Box Lane in the early 1960s, enjoyed an elevated position with views to the Parkhall Hills and the former Meir Golf Course. Not as visually impressive as its earlier incarnation it is a well-kept school carrying on the proud heritage and name of Longton High and its motto 'Renascor' from the reign of King George III into the 21st century.

The modern face of what was once the second Longton High School.

The A50, completed in 1998, was graced with a fly past by a Spitfire, signifying a link to Meir's disappearing past. A new era of high speed transport had arrived at last, unfortunately not just for those living in Stoke-on-Trent. Although denied by the Highways Agency as an M1 to M6 link, the A50 now connected, except for a small section, the two motorways. Traffic wishing to avoid Birmingham would travel to the M6 at Hanchurch, use the A500 and A50 and go on to Derby and the M1. The road proved highly successful in bringing out-of-city traffic on to city roads. Vehicle numbers rapidly increased.

Throughout two years of use, doubts were raised about the safety of certain of its features. The accesses on and off the road drew unfavourable comment. The Box Lane westbound access was particularly dangerous, a spate of accidents followed and the west bound access road at Heron Cross to Stoke was extended, to improve 'line of sight'. A50 bus stops imperilled bus drivers and passengers alike endeavouring to pull in, pick up and drive off as traffic hurtled past. Their use was discontinued. Following discussions a bus stop by the Royal Mail depot in Bengry Road was added.

Doubts about the durability of the road rumbled on. Patrolling police cars found several 4m x 2m panels weighing several hundred kilograms from the Meir tunnel lining, lying in the carriageway. The entire tunnel was shut, stripped of panels, new bolts fitted and the old panels re-installed. More was to come. Sewage entered the footings of the

Weston Road shops.

Right: The Tiger Moth pub sign is a link with Meir's aeronautical past. The pub built in Sandon Road is now derelict.

Meir's future - retailing. Aldi supermarket, and below Tesco.

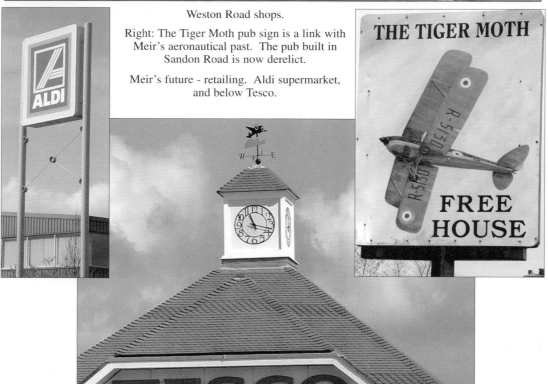

Above: The aeroplane weather vane on top of Tesco, and the plaque at B&Q both recognise the Retail Park's past.

Some of Meir Park's rolling acres are still for sale.

The new Longton High School in Box Lane, Meir, opened in the early 1960s.
It enjoys views across the old Meir Golf Course to Parkhall Hills.

tunnel with its corrosion threat to steel piling, and street lights seemed far from reliable, entire sections going out plunging motorists into darkness at a moment's notice. The road had acquired a life of its own.

During the Iraq war in 2003, the tragic death of Stephen Allbutt reinforced the risks the Armed Forces take in their daily round and the cost of maintaining stability in a world that at times appears to have gone mad. In Iraq the £4 million Challenger tank commanded by Corporal Allbutt of the Queen's Royal Lancers was hit by friendly fire killing him and teenager, Trooper David Clarke of Stafford.

Stephen's burial service at Holy Trinity church, held in pouring rain was a sombre day as the cortege silently drove up Broadway. Union flags lined the route. Hundreds braved the weather to pay their last respects to this 'quiet man' who had died in distant lands for his country. Stephen and his wife Debi were married at Holy Trinity Church by Rev Gordon Whitty years before. Now it was he who conducted the burial service, leading the mourners, amongst whom was the Rev Mavis Allbutt, vicar at Holy Trinity Church, and the mother of Stephen.

By 2004, 6 years after the opening of the A50, the carriageway from the Meir tunnel to Fenton was resurfaced with HAPAS, contractors working at night to install the new surface with little more difficulty than laying a new carpet.

However a far more fundamental problem emerged. Throughout the 1980s and 1990s the growth of traffic had been huge. The '500' in Stoke on Trent was prone to gridlock several times a day, traffic lights, installed to keep things moving, proved successful for a while. With the A50 and the A500 joined at Incinerator roundabout, the problem worsened overnight. The new A500 Pathfinder project was launched and in 2004 the work is ongoing. With exponential traffic growth, a Highways Agency Route Management Strategy (RMS) for the A50/A500 was launched in April 2004 to *'help make the best use of the existing road network rather than simply adding or widening roads.'* It brought into sharp focus whether the new A50 through Stoke-on-Trent in its present form was the correct decision in 1990/3. The Stoke Southern By-pass would have siphoned off huge amounts of A50/A500 inter-city traffic and was more cost effective. The possibility, unless rapid action was taken, was that the entire A50/A500, would on a day not too far away, just grind to a halt permanently. Would the Highways Agency finally be hoist with their own petard?

There is no one answer to the problem of traffic congestion other than not using the motor car. The appeal is the same now as it was in the 1930s, the dawn of mass motoring, of being able to go 'when and where' at a whim. Enormous strides have been made in the intervening 70 years. Through research, innovative car design, highway architecture and new materials, road deaths in 2004 are at a level of the 1930s, (3650 or 10 a day). But society today has been built around the car, out-of-town stores rely on customers being car owners; people travel distances unheard of a hundred years ago, to Derby and beyond, going to and from work on roads like the A50. The impact on towns like Meir has been immense, and the town's geography is vastly different from when Holy Trinity church welcomed its first worshipper. Whether the Highways Agency succeeds with their 2004 Strategy only time will tell. Many feel it is too late, the genie is out of the bottle. The smart money is on it failing.

Huge social and economic change in the 50 years from 1889 to 1939, transformed life for residents in Meir. The further period of 65 years, 1939 to 2004, continued this metamorphosis at a faster rate: the losses of Meir Airport, the Broadway and numerous houses and businesses; Meir Park with its retail outlets; Meir Golf Course; new schools, a library and a Youth Cafe and Community Centre, all added to by the upheavals caused by 5 years of devastating A50 road works. Anyone from the Meir of 1889 would fail to recognize it as the same town, although amazingly they did hazard a guess as to what it might be like.

On a sunny day towards the end of the 1890s, at Holy Trinity church, a series of tableaux or 'floats' portrayed scenes from history and legend. One called Life in 1999 was a prophecy of what future generations of Meir residents could expect a hundred years hence. Never in their wildest dreams could they have foreseen what would befall their Arcadia, its hedgerows, rolling acres, trees, wild flowers and birds. Now in 2004, awash in a sea of never-ending traffic it was beyond the bounds of human comprehension. But then who would go back to life a hundred years earlier?

Thankfully for the moment, Meir has deservedly settled back into period of tranquillity, sanity has returned. It is inevitable that will change given time. Time is a continuum - it never ends.

This was part of the Highways Agency literature advocating the new A50. Meir crossroads, although now with a roundabout, is often just as busy as this after the new A50 road has been built.

OPPOSITE:
A PAGE FROM THE 1912 *NEWCASTLE AND POTTERIES DIRECTORY* SHOWING THE OLD MEIR POPULATION.

Two old houses are all that remain of this part of old Meir.
The road bridge in the process of construction rises from the ground once occupied by Meir School built in the 1870s

Looking west from Meir town centre towards the Box Lane bridge at the western portal of the tunnel. Queensway Court is at the right side.

MEIR.

(Caverswall Parish.)

Local Members of Parish Council—G. Sherwin (chairman), H. Parkes, H. J. Sherratt.

Overseers—R. Mosley, John Jackson.

Postal Address—Meir, Longton.

Nearest Railway Station—Meir (N.S.R.).

ALPHABETICAL DIRECTORY.

Adams, Edgar, mining engineer, Weston Coyney-road

Adderley, Frank, commercial traveller, 77, Weston-road

Allen, Fredk. J., Waggon and Horses (B.H.), 51, Meir-lane

Amor, Arthur, 2, Charles-street

Amor, Arthur, Station-road

Aynsley, Jos., manufacturer, The Beeches, Weston-road, Meir-lane

Baker, William, 9, The Avenue

Ballance, George, draper, Weston-road, Meir-lane

Barlow, James Hy., estate agent, The Elms, Weston-road, Meir-lane

Bartlam, Wm., farmer, Waterloo Farm

Batt, A. A., Weston-road, Meir-lane

Beckett, Wm. Hy., builder, grocer, and beer retailer, 64, Weston-road, Meir-lane

Blackhurst and Bartlam, farmers, Cinderhill Farm, Weston Coyney

Blackhurst, Thos., manufacturer, 79, Weston-road

Blackmore, Wm. J., farmer, Caverswall Park

Blackmore, Wm. J. John, Catchem's Corner, 281, Meir-lane

Bowden, Arthur V., 3, Station-road

Bradbury, Thomas, Coal agent, 13, The Avenue

Bradley, C. W., draper, Weston-road, Meir-lane

Brassington, Charles T., tailor, &c., 65, Weston-road

Brassington, Jos., Weston Coyney-road

Brindley, Isaac, coal merchant, Weston Coyney-road

Brown, Thos. R., police constable, Police Station, Weston Coyney

Brookes, Andrew A., clerk in holy orders, 81, Weston-road

Burgess, Mary, 93, Station-road

Carter, Thomas Wm., farmer, Ivy Cottage

Cherry, A. B., 39, The Avenue

Clowes, Elizabeth, farmer, Little Weston Coyney

Collingwood, Chas., 35, The Avenue

Cooper, Ashley, manufacturer, Weston Coyney-road

Cooper, John, 89, Weston-road

Cornes, Thos., 43, Weston-road

Dayson, Hy., farmer

Deakin, George R., grocer, 74, Station-road

Ferneyhough, Thos., Weston Coyney-road

Ford, Thos., mechanic, 91, Station-road

Goodwin, Wm. farmer, Grove Farm, Weston Coyney

Green, George, farmer, Wood House Farm

Gunn, Edmund, 3, The Avenue

Hammond, Sarah, Weston Coyney-road

Harrison, John, chemist, Meir Ville, 141 Meir lane

Hart, Wm. G., and Davies, auctioneers, King's Arms Smithfield, Meir-lane

Heath, Frederick, sen., manufacturer, 1, The Avenue

Heath, Frederick H., jun., manufacturer, 91, Weston-road

Hey, John R., 25, The Avenue

Hill, John Edward, 201, Meir-lane

Hodkins, J., draper, 118, Station-road

Hodgkinson, J. J., 7, The Avenue

Hodgkinson, John, farmer, Meir-lane Farm

Holdsworth, Percy, 37, The Avenue

Holinson, William, 75, Station-road

Hood, Wm., farmer, Meir Farm, Meir-lane

Hughes, Elizabeth, farmer, Park Head Farm

Hughes, Walter G., farmer, Weston Coyney-rd.

Huise, Thomas, commission agent, Weston Coyney-road

Hunt, J. J., solicitor, 19, The Avenue

Hyatt, C., Weston-road, Meir-lane

Irving, Leonard, 79, Station-road

Jenkinson, Clement, beer retailer, 97, Meir-lane

Joliey, Alex., Weston-road, Meir-lane

Jones, A. C., manufacturer, Weston Coyney-rd.

Kelsall, Sidney E., 5, Station-road

Kent, George, 17, The Avenue

Kenworthy, George, 53, Weston-road

Lawton, The Avenue

Leese, Shadrach, King's Arms Hotel (F.L.), 1, Meir-lane

Lucas, Hy. John, farrier, Rose Cottage, 139, Meir-lane

Mackee, Thomas L., Weston-road, Meir-lane

Marson, Wm. B., farmer, The Sycamores, Little Weston Coyney

Massey, Henry, farmer, Calverhay Farm, Meir lane

Mear, Mrs. Alfred, The Limes, Weston-road, Meir-lane

Mear, Stephen, J.P., timber merchant, Weston Coyney House, Weston-road, Meir-lane

Meir Station (N.S.R.). Stationmaster, D. Walters

Middleton, E. Hy., grocer and beer retailer, 96, Weston-road, Meir-lane

Millington, John, schoolmaster, 11, The Avenue

Murray, George, 29, The Avenue

Newton, R. A., 31, The Avenue

Nixon, Wm., manufacturer, Weston Coyney-rd.

Oakley, Robert F., farmer, Lower Park Head, Weston Coyney

Parr, H., 7, Station-road

Pearson, Joseph, 33, The Avenue

Pemberton, Edward, grocer and beer retailer, Queen's Head, 27, Meir-lane

Phillips, J. M. schoolmaster, Weston-road, Meir-lane

Pickles, F. W. F., schoolmaster, School House, 125, Meir-lane

Poulson, Albert, 87, Weston-road

Rawlins, Martha, 77, Station-road

Rhodes, John, Weston-road, Meir-lane

Sherwin, George, butcher, 101, Meir-lane

Shenton, John H. commission agent, 21 The Aven

Siddall, John, 85, Weston-road

Sigley, Thomas, farmer, The Blythe, Little Weston Coyney

Slack, John, farmer The Blythe, Little Weston Coyney

Slack, Thos., and Sons, farmers, Bolton Gate, Little Weston Coyney

Smith, Albert, fruiterer, 67, Weston-road

Stanier, George, farmer, Weston Coyney-road

Stoddard, Elizabeth, grocer and beer retailer, 11, Meir-lane

Stonier, Jane, beer retailer, 261, Meir-lane

Swift, Ann, 99, Weston-road

Symcox, Fredk. Thomas, farmer, Small Brook, Little Weston Coyney

Taylor, Ernest H., 54, Charles-street

Taylor, Frank, schoolmaster, 15, The Avenue

Taylor, John W., schoolmaster, 5, The Avenue

Teggin, Jas., mechanic, 123, Meir-lane

Thorley, Jane, farmer, Meir Lane

Tunnicliffe, David, grocer, baker, and sub-postmaster, Post Office, 63, Weston-road

Upton, Mary E., 27, Weston-road

Upton, William, butcher, 20, Station-road

Wainwright, John, farmer, Wood Farm

Walters, D., stationmaster, Meir House

Watts, Margaret, 1, Station-road

Weaver, Jas. D., grocer and baker

Webb, F. C., The Avenue

Weston Coyney Brick and Marl Co., Brick Works, Weston Coyney

The England Boys' Golf Team in 1932. Ken Jones is seated in the front row wearing flamboyant socks!

A view to Parkhall Hills taken from the old Meir Golf Course in the 1930s.

MEIR GOLF CLUB
With acknowledgements to Ken Oakley

"All sports are silly, but golf, if you look at it dispassionately, goes to extremes."
Peter Alliss, Ryder Cup golfer

With monumental prizes resembling the gross domestic product of Third World countries, today's professional game is a great deal more than a chip and a putt away from the amateur game diligently played by enthusiastic dabblers a century ago at the Meir Golf Club.

By the mid-1930s residents in the Meir enjoyed ready access to numerous facilities on their doorstep. Tennis courts and bowling greens at Holy Trinity Church, and billiards at the Meir Institute were but a few and Meir Golf Club had resounded to cries of "fore" from the end of the 19th century. James Henry Barlow, a Longton estate agent had, along with other local businessmen, founded the Meir Golf Club in 1895, when the first ball had been struck in anger on the old Waterloo Course as it was known.

As well as his keen interest in golf, James Barlow, who lived at Beech House, Weston Road, wholeheartedly immersed himself in many aspects of the social and spiritual life of the Meir community: *'Mr J.H. Barlow has promised to give a handsome pulpit to the Meir Church, the only proviso is that sufficient money be collected for cleaning the church by the Harvest Festival. Holy Trinity is the daughter church of the mother parish of Caverswall.'*

His leadership qualities found a ready outlet during the Great War. A Justice of the Peace, his organising skills were apparent:

'The Meir is to have its own Civilian Training Corps. At a meeting in the church Institute presided over by Mr J.H. Barlow, Mr S.A. Griffiths, secretary of the Longton Corps, explained the movement and what had been done in other parts of England. The chairman said it was the duty of every man who was unable to join the Regulars or the Territorials to assist these forces as much as possible should the necessity arise, hence the Civilian Training Corps.'
and *'An enthusiastic interest has been displayed of late in the allotment movement and last week a food production society was formed in the village, a strong committee being appointed. Mr J.H. Barlow (from Holy Trinity Church) has been elected the first president. It has been arranged to hold a show during the present year.'*

He was Meir Golf Club captain for nigh on forty years, the rock upon which the club and its members relied. During its early days, Meir Golf Club was always on the lookout for prospective golfers. News of the official opening in the Staffordshire Advertiser:

'The Waterloo Golf Course, which is directly behind the Meir church and within three and seven minutes walk respectively of the Meir and Normacot stations, was opened for play on Thursday afternoon. This course is one of 9 holes: in good condition and from the configuration of the ground, it is claimed it is superior for beginners to any in North Staffordshire. A very pleasant game was enjoyed by the members, who at present number between 20 and 30. A considerable addition to the membership is looked for, now that the game is at the height of its popularity.' October 5th 1895

Being billed as one of the finest courses for beginners in North Staffordshire must have been greeted with mixed feelings by the parishioners at Holy Trinity church. The proximity of the first tee to the large stained glass windows of the church must have given rise to one or two anxious prayers from the faithful.

VERILY I SAY UNTO YOU ON THE WATERLOO GOLF COURSE...... TRY A 5 IRON NEXT TIME.

Having teed off and missed the church, the ball went out to the pin on the first green, which lay behind the line of the main road, near Meir crossroads. The next tee, the second according to Frank Amison, was at the rear of Smith's Buildings, Weston Road, and was by all accounts a difficult par 4 hole taking the golfers to new heights, technically and figuratively. Sited close to one of the highest vantage points in Meir, imaginatively called Tree Hill, the second green was over 700 feet above sea level. Golfers could take in breathtaking views over to Parkhall Hills and beyond.

The third tee took the players out to a point just shy of the heavily-wooded, Weston Sprink, as the fairways snaked behind the line of Weston Road. A few of the holes, like the third, ran exceedingly close to the houses. Towards the rear of Beech House - the Barlow family home-in Weston Road, Mr Barlow's son now took advantage of the situation - a small wicket gate built into his garden fence led straight on to the fairway - and with easy access, James Clarke Barlow, grandson of the founder *'would practise before breakfast'* taking *'a bag of balls to the top of the hill, playing them down to the green with a driver.'* His father, Mr Jimmy Barlow, would play them back again with a 4 or 5 iron.

The other six original greens were cleverly arranged so play was contained in a broadly square and grassy arena off Weston Road.

One facility members still lacked though, almost 10 years after formation, was a club house. So early in Edward VII's reign, the construction of this much needed addition must have been a welcome event. The Staffordshire Advertiser recorded this milestone.

'A new club house was opened on Saturday (October 30th 1904) Miss Edwards taking the principal part in the opening, and presenting the club with a cheque to meet expenses. Among those present were Mr W.A. Adderley, the Rev, the Hon LF Tyrwhitt and the Rev E and Mrs Wheeldon etc. After the opening ceremony, watched with great interest, an exhibition game between W Ulton (Trentham) and J Collins (Pipe Gate) took place.'

The Golf Club's wooden sectional club-house lay tucked away at the rear of the Church Institute, even appearing on a parish map of 1926. At a time of great hardship during the late 1920s and 1930s, the Club's annual membership fee for men and ladies stood around £2 to £3 with 'family membership' costing a shade more at a 'fiver'. Although substantially less, a boy's subscription of half a guinea, must have strained some family finances to breaking point.

Beginning as a 9 hole course, the Club was enlarged in the late 1920s to 14 holes; four holes played twice, so by the 1930s it boasted 18 holes. It was an enormous achievement for members to have created such a valuable asset. One particular facet of the course, making it popular perhaps above all others, was its easy accessibility. Lying so close to Meir town centre, devotees could practise at every available spare moment. Not surprisingly, several members became very accomplished, representing King and Country at international tournaments.

Ken Jones, a club stalwart, kept a golfing record of his performance - one in which he is unstinting in self-criticism - and whom he had played. These rough notes in a treasured leather bound diary, date from the early thirties:

KEN JONES' GOLFING DIARY

21st February, 1932: Ground very hard, putting difficult. Drove well. Approaching poor. Irons fair, lost no balls and beat George 9 up (40 shots) Out of bounds at the 3rd and over green with No? iron. Balls inclined to kick on landing on hard ground. Cold hands didn't improve play. (82 shots for a par 67 course)

22nd February 1932: Started badly but pulled up well. Only played 14 holes -very good score for these. Three putts on 9th. Beat Dr Nairn 1 up. Ought to have had a 4 at the eleventh. Played all clubs consistently well. Ground in good condition.

14th April 1932: Played a morning round by myself. Conditions perfect. Putts just stayed out of 4 and 5 and 15. 3 putts at the 6th. Approached very well especially coming home. (Score for the course 74). deserved a 5 at 18th but took 4 to get down from 80 yards.

20th April 1932 RECORD SCORE (71: out in 34, back in 37) Played very well. Drives uncertain, putting good. Bunkered at the 8th. Good drive over ridges at 18th but took a 6 owing to bad approaching. Beat Dr Nairn 5 and 4 and finished 7 up. Ground in good condition and weather good.

9th May 1932 Playing against Peter Roper. *MN score at 6th hole for a 2. Bad putt at 13th: should have had a 2. Played the last two poorly especially the 18th when had 3 putts. (Out in 34 back in 36)
(* MN = Mashie Niblick, a golf club)

Final entry, 4th January 1933. Playing against D.R. Morgan. Ground wet although perfect overhead. Sunk some very long putts and missed some very short ones. Drove with 'brassey' as no confidence in driver lately. Wasted strokes approaching 6th and 11th. Missed easy putt on 7th and 13th. Score card, hole number first. Total of 72 shots for the par 67 course

     1-3; 2-4; 3-4; 4-5; 5-4; 6-5; 7-4; 8-3; 9-4; (36 out)
     10-3; 11-5; 12-4; 13-4; 14-5; 15-3; 16-4; 17-3; 18-5 (back in 36)

The plan of the 'old' course, with additions, is derived from recollections of retired members and numerous contemporary sources. Although no distances for the various holes have been uncovered, the par for each hole for this early course are thought to be as shown.

HOLE 1	PAR 3	HOLE 10	PAR 4
HOLE 2	PAR 4 (Tree Hill)	HOLE 11	PAR 4
HOLE 3	PAR 3	HOLE 12	PAR 4?
HOLE 4	PAR 5	HOLE 13	PAR 4?
HOLE 5	PAR 4	HOLE 14	PAR 4?
HOLE 6	PAR 4	HOLE 15	PAR 3
HOLE 7	PAR 3	HOLE 16	PAR 4
HOLE 8	PAR 3	HOLE 17	PAR 3
HOLE 9	PAR 3	HOLE 18	PAR 5

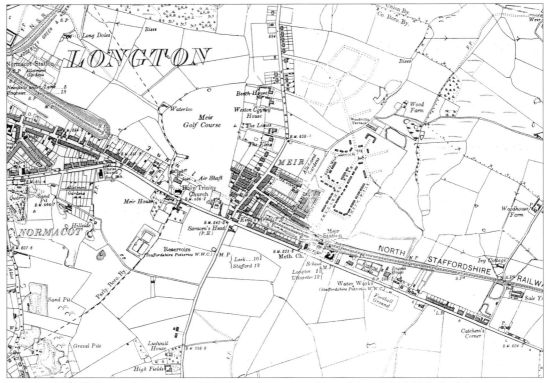

1925 Ordnance Survey map which shows the exact position of the original Meir Golf Course
and its proximity to houses in Weston Road.

Meir Golf Course, situated on agricultural land, was leased from Bartlam's farm, the farmer retaining 'grazing rights' for his stock. Meir had more than a passing interest in agriculture - a glance at a contemporary list confirms many coaxed a living from the soil.

Farmers: Bartlam, William, Waterloo Farm. the Meir.
              Blackhurst and Bartlam, Cinderhill Farm, Weston Coyney.
              Blackmore, William, Caveswall Park.
              Carter, Thomas William, Ivy Lodge.
              Clowes, Elizabeth, Little Weston Coyney.
              Dayson, Henry
              Goodwin, William, Grove Farm, Weston Coyney.
              Green, George, Woodhouse Farm.
              Hodgkinson John, Meir Lane Farm, the Meir.
              Hood, William, Meir farm, Meir Lane.
              Hughes, Elizabeth, Park Head Farm.
              Marson, William, The Sycamores, Little Weston Coyney.
              Oakley, Robert, Lower Park Head Farm, Weston Coyney.
              Slack, Thomas and Sons, Bolton Gate Farm, Weston Coyney.
              Thorley, Jane, Meir Lane, the Meir.
              Wainwright, John, Wood Farm, the Meir.

This rural location did have an unfortunate downside. To stop livestock nibbling the grass on the precious greens, the MGC members often resorted to barbed wire placed at

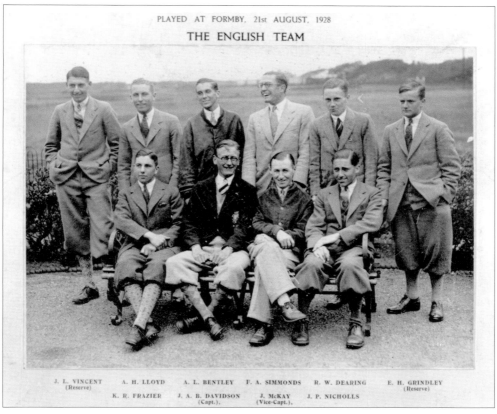

PLAYED AT FORMBY, 21st AUGUST, 1928

THE ENGLISH TEAM

| J. L. VINCENT (Reserve) | A. H. LLOYD | A. L. BENTLEY | F. A. SIMMONDS | R. W. DEARING | E. H. GRINDLEY (Reserve) |

K. R. FRAZIER   J. A. B. DAVIDSON (Capt.),   J. McKAY (Vice-Capt.),   J. P. NICHOLLS

The English Golf team in 1928 before their match against Scotland at Formby.
Meir Golf Club player Reg Dearing is seen back row, 2nd right.

Meir Golf club members during the 1950s. Bill Howells is 2nd row, 2nd from left.

strategic points. When livestock broke through on to the fairways, it was a case of 'all hands to the forks' to remove hoof marks before play could begin. In those days, the Professional/Greenkeeper, Charles Stanier, was assisted by George Bartlam, son of the farmer. In later years, Mr Bartlam *'did the decent thing in becoming permanent greenkeeper',* a position his son, Tom succeeded to in later years.

One old Meir golfer recalled, *'The greens were cut with a large hand mower pushed by either or both Charles and George with another local lad who was paid a few coppers to lend a hand.'* The larger fairways demanded a greater effort. They were kept in trim using a horse-drawn 'gang mower'. Even with this 'cutting-edge technology' it was quite a chore considering the size of the course. Mercifully during the 1930s *'...this four legged, one horse power unit was replaced by a 'very' second-hand Fordson tractor, bliss when George Bartlam could get it to start with the hand crank.'*

Meir railway station, opened in 1893, was on the main line from Crewe to Derby. The track at one point, directly beneath Meir Golf Course, ran through a long tunnel, the scene of an horrific accident shortly after the Golf course had been declared open; *'Yesterday a man was found in the Meir tunnel about 200 yards from the Normacot entrance. His head was shockingly injured. He proves to be Emmanual Shaw, for several years the manager of the Upper Bull's Head, Cheadle for Messrs J.Joule and Sons of Stone Brewery. His body was removed to the Cottage Hospital.'* At the inquest a week later, the verdict *'Suicide, while of unsound mind'* was brought in.

Engineers included a brick-lined steam vent which broke surface not too far from Holy Trinity church and the first hole of Meir Golf course, to the chagrin of its members. Many a good ball was lost down this air shaft never to be seen again.

Throughout 1937/1938 rumours circulated that Stoke-on-Trent City Council had plans for another housing development in Meir. It required land used by the Golf Club, which would undoubtedly severely curtail their activities. In 1920s Meir, new council estates at Leason Road (formerly Aynsley Road) and Harrowby Road had begun the cycle. Fifteen years later, the outcome was a compulsory purchase order (CPO) served on the MGC, which deprived the members of about one third of the course. For a less dedicated group, it would have sounded the death knell of their club but stoically the members failed to be cowed. They played on using the remainder of the original fourteen hole course they had so cherished.

The CPO meant relocation of the sectional Club House, something effected with good old elbow grease and a little ingenuity. Using a horse-drawn cart, the intrepid members trundled the various sections of the club house along the 14th fairway to its new position, resurrecting them at

Tom Bartlam teeing off at Meir Golf Course in the 1950s. The houses behind are in Broadway and are still standing

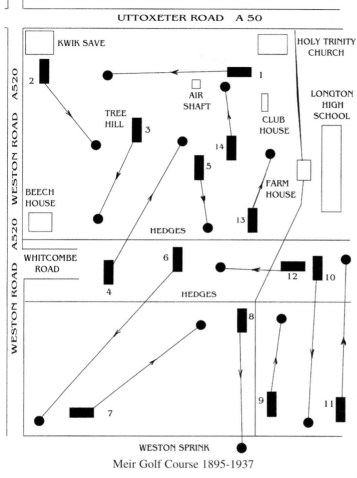

Meir Golf Course 1895-1937

the end of Greenfield (later Whitcombe) Road, off Weston Road. No mean feat - the Club House was quite large. One wing boasted a Ladies' Section with its own lounge, locker room and toilets with the Pro's shop, while the other, the Men's section, had a snooker room, locker room and toilets. The centre section had a mixed lounge/dining room with its own bar and kitchen at the rear.

With Neville Chamberlain's broadcast and the declaration of war, the pace of life at the club slackened, slipping into a state of suspended animation. Many wondered whether life in general let alone the Golf Club would ever be the same. By 1940, Meir Golf Club virtually closed down for 'the duration'. George Bartlam kept down the grass on the dormant course while attending to his own vital farm work. Charles Stanier, the professional had left after the purchase order.

At the end of the war, notice boards throughout many golf club houses declared that *'Players should pick up bomb and shell splinters from the fairways in order to save damage to the mower.'* This never troubled those playing the Meir Course. Their problems were more fundamental. Beset by monetary problems the Club soldiered on *'with a very much reduced membership'*, unable to raise revenue to renovate the course and the club house. In late 1946 its plight was desperate. In the event, the Club was rescued at the eleventh hour by local doctor, Dr C.W. Healey. Taking over the Club and its finances, his plan was to run it through a reduced members' committee. Members grasped this opportunity, believing this, the 'second' Meir Golf course, would usher in a new chapter in its chequered history.

The course, redesigned in 1947/8, under their captain Stanley Foster, would continue but with just 9 holes. To redress the loss of seven holes from the 'old' course, two additional fields beyond the far end of the original course were acquired by the club. Two new holes were laid out on this rough ground, which club members mischievously nicknamed 'Abyssinia'. This 'new' course, cleverly using some of the original greens would remain substantially unchanged for a decade.

The immediate outlook now looked more favourable. The Club appointed a new Professional, Mr Lovatt, assisted by George Bartlam. Tom Bartlam headed the ground staff, and Mr Stonier and Mr Stokes assisted when called upon, apparently unpaid, along with some local lads. Under them the course was entirely renovated during the next 2 to 3 years. The Club House, too, was spruced up, acquiring a new coat of paint. They enjoyed the culinary skills of a stewardess, Mrs Mellor, the memories of whose Saturday night suppers of *'gammon, double egg and chips, grilled tomato and peas, steak (3d extra), followed by pud and coffee for half a crown'*, remain undimmed for those who sampled them 50 years on.

MEIR GOLF CLUB COURSE 1947

HOLE 1	PAR 4
HOLE 2	PAR 4
HOLE 3	PAR 3
HOLE 4	PAR 3
HOLE 5	PAR 4
HOLE 6	PAR 4
HOLE 7	PAR 4
HOLE 8	PAR 5
HOLE 9	PAR 3

PAR for the course 34

James Clarke Barlow, grandson of the founder, was annual MGC captain around the end of the 1940s, and was succeeded by Stanley Foster, during whose term of office the revised and renovated course was inaugurated with an exhibition golf match. Among those taking part were Charlie Ward, the 'Pro' at Little Aston, who was a very well-regarded tournament professional; Geoff Mills (Harmil Bakeries), a member of Meir Golf Club and later member of Trentham Park Golf Club who captained Staffordshire, James Barlow, son of the founder, and Stanley Foster.

Having resurrected the Club from oblivion, members now learned of further wide ranging plans for their beloved course with utter disbelief. It would disappear finally if these new plans went unchallenged. With the growth of Meir many voiced an opinion that one of many amenities lacking was a park or open space for the children to play in. The wide open expanse of the Golf Course seemed an answer to their prayers. Meir residents were after blood. But then, just when all seemed lost, there appeared a ray of hope:

'The decision of the Minister of Town and Country Planning NOT to confirm a compulsory purchase order applied for by Stoke-on-Trent City Council in respect of the Meir Golf Course, was the subject of a protest meeting of local ratepayers at Meir Church Institute on Thursday night. The land, comprising 42.34 acres and including the Golf Club House and Waterloo Farm, was required for a public open space. At the meeting, which was well attended, the position was explained by the local representative of the City Council and a resolution was passed to the Minister to reconsider his decision and withdraw the cancellation of the Compulsory Purchase Order.

Mr A.E. Simcock, the proprietor of a grocer's shop in Weston Road, former president of the Meir Chamber of Commerce, told an "Advertiser" representative that a mistake had been made in asking for an Order in respect of an open space. The corporation, he suggested, should have specified 'a park and playing fields'. He believed that if the Minister

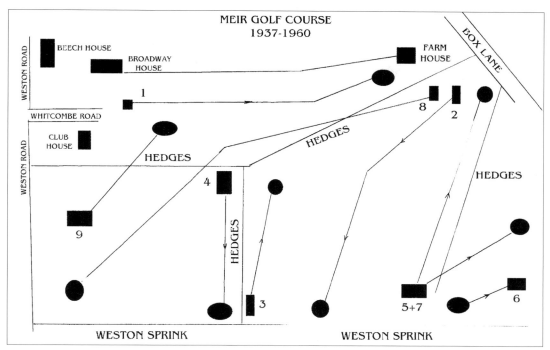

MEIR GOLF COURSE
1937-1960

had been aware of the real purpose of the Order he would have reached a different decision, as in the Meir district they had a population of about 30,000 people and if they had a park and playing fields, this would provide amenities for a further 10,000 living on the fringes of the area.'

As Meir Golf Club staggered into the 1950s, this chain of events did not auger well for its future. Many must have feared the worst. Dr CW Healey, who had offered succour following the Second World War, became a lay preacher on a permanent basis and this action precipitated the sale of the entire Golf Course and Club house. It was bought by Mr C Ball for £4,000.

In new ownership, Meir Golf Club gamely battled on for a year or more, but what next transpired meant that this time there would be no way out. Meir Golf Course was finally acquired as playing fields by Stoke-on-Trent City Council, the hallowed Club House finding favour once more as changing rooms for North Staffordshire Technical College football teams. Ken Oakley recalls:

'I played on the old pitches, once part of Meir Golf Course and on one occasion changed in the locker rooms, clearly remembering the wooden lockers and strange verandah at the front. I think it was around 1960. Sadly a couple of years later, it was set on fire. A man who lived on the side of Tree Hill, now Elms Way, with a panoramic view of the old course below, had seen the lad come out of the Club House with the place on fire. When the Fire Brigade arrived it was well and truly alight and beyond redemption.'

It was a dreadful finale to something that had promised so much. Just when more progressive councils were creating new golf courses to fulfil an increased demand for leisure activities, the reverse was true for Meir. On a site visit during the 1993 A50 Public Inquiry, recollections of another golfer, George Ray, who had played the greens of Meir Golf Course, came to light. Accompanying the Inquiry inspector, he pointed out, just behind the line of the A50, in a garden, *'the first fairway of the old Meir course'.* The Inspector humorously asked whether he *'could have green rights?'* - ie could he keep any 'lost golf balls' he found?

In its heyday, Meir Golf Club produced many very fine golfers. Several went on to international duty. Of those who drove and putted the fairways and greens on the old Meir course, the achievements of local hero Reginald Wagstaff Dearing are writ large in the annals of the club. However they are by no means unique.

REGINALD WAGSTAFF DEARING:

Harry Dearing, Reg's father, the Meir Golf Club secretary, won the club's silver hall-marked 'Fred Radford' trophy in 1924. At the tender age of fourteen and off a handicap of 12, Reginald Dearing carried on from where his father had left off. Winning another inscribed goblet for his sideboard in 1926, he beat a field of 24 opponents with a score of three up, with Eric Heath, second and George Ballance a well deserved third.

Reg Dearing was a friend of the late Frank Amison whose tobacconist's shop still trades in Weston Road, and Donald Bradley, with whom he was at Newcastle High School.

With Meir Golf Course a two minute stroll from Reg Dearing's Meir home in The Avenue (later Penfleet Avenue), it's easy to see why he was a frequent visitor and Reg's hours spent practising eventually paid off. His 'finest hour' came in 1928 at Formby in Lancashire when playing for England in the Eighth Annual Boys' Amateur Golf Championship against the 'auld enemy' Scotland. Given this was an international match, remarkably Reg had to cough up a guinea for the entrance fee to play and represent his country. Against A. Dobbie of the Inverness Club in the singles and again in the doubles, Reg turned in a low scoring card at this difficult seaside course.

The Honorary Secretary of the Meir Golf Club, Mr J.J. Fernyhough wrote to Reg Dearing to tell him that the Club's General Committee *'...were unanimous in their praise for your achievement at the International Match, England v Scotland and in your performance in reaching the 5th round. As a mark of our appreciation, it has been decided to elect you Honorary Member of the Meir Club until you are twenty one.'*

No. 78

EIGHTH ANNUAL
BOYS' AMATEUR GOLF CHAMPIONSHIP
at FORMBY GOLF CLUB during Week beginning 20th August 1928.

10th August, 1928

Received the sum of One Guinea, being Entrance Fee for the above Championship, for Master Reginald W. Dearing, The Avenue, Meir, Staffs.

Competitor's Badge is enclosed.   p. JOHN WESTON, Hon. Sec.

With Hon. Sec.'s Compliments and Thanks.

37 Castelnau,
Barnes, London, S.W.

£1 : 1s. stg.

The Club's own professional and greenkeeper, Charles Stanier, responsible for coaching Meir Golf Club's prodigy, briefly set aside his 5 iron and wrote in admiration and pride, *'May you never lift your head and miss a two yard putt.'*

In the mid-1930s, young Reg partnered the manager of Meir's new and prestigious Broadway cinema, Lawrence Plumpton on many occasions. Lawrence, an Aussie, was a

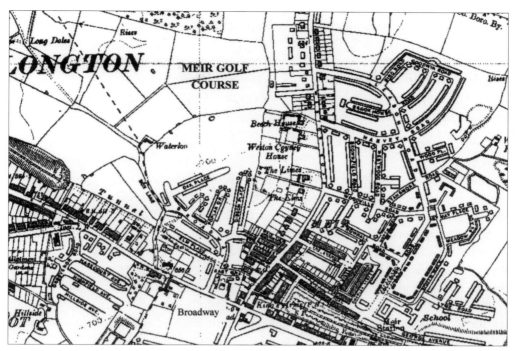

Ordnance Survey 1938, the effect of the CPO and new housing on Meir Golf Club's course can be seen.

Meir Golf Club Members at a tournament at the Club in 1952. Centre front: Staffordshire Professional Champion, Charlie Ward. Front, 2nd from left: Geoff Mills, Staffordshire Amateur Champion. Back row L-R: 2nd, Donald Bradley; 3rd, Charles Bradley, Club Secretary; Far right, Fred Shenton, President. Middle row, 2nd from right: Harold Lovatt, Meir Golf Club Professional.

captain of Rough Close cricket club, and invariably gave a good account of himself on the fairways. Winning the Birmingham and Midland Cinema Golf Club Tournament held in 1934, he followed it by pocketing the runners-up prize two years later.

Reg Dearing played on until family intervened. Called to active service in India and Burma with the Royal Engineers during the Second World War, he returned safe and sound in 1946 and died in 1993. His hallmarked trophies, now in the safe keeping of his daughter Pat, are proof of his deft touch and expertise on fairway and green.

KEN JONES

Ken Jones was another golfer of this 'MGC elite' and the second member of the club to grace the international stage. As a 16 year old Ken played in the English Boys Championship at the Royal Lytham course, an occasion when Donald Bradley caddied for him in a match against Scotland. Disappointingly, England were defeated. Ken, also a member of Trentham Golf Club, played for Staffordshire but left the area in 1941 for Leamington Spa. One of the first people he bumped into was Fred Bartlam, the former 'Pro' at Meir, who had his bags packed to leave for a club at Bognor Regis, where he ended his days.

Ken Jones, in his eighties now, plays golf at Copt Heath Golf Club, Solihull attaining the position of captain and president. As a former colleague recalls, *'he plays at least one round of golf a year to one less than his age gross, laying off a handicap of 12.'*

Other Meir Golf Club stalwarts include:

GEOFF MILLS: A fine golfer who went on to captain the Staffordshire team.

JAMES BARLOW SENIOR: Staffordshire player who won several trophies at Trentham. He was elected Captain of MGC holding office for 40 years.
CHARLIE JONES: A near scratch golfer who often partnered James Barlow Sr.

BILL SPARROW: Another 4 to 5 handicap golfer and James Barlow snr's partner for years. He owned a shop in Commerce Street Longton.

ERIC HEATH: Another near scratch whose sister, Marjorie was the best lady golfer at Meir.

DONALD AND CHARLES BRADLEY: Donald owned the Gent's outfitters close to the Dorothy Cafe, Longton, with Charles his older brother. He was MGC secretary for years. The Senior competition at Meir Golf Club, the Bradley Cup, was won by JC Barlow two years running before being defeated in the third year, when he was pipped at the last hole by Eric Heath. Donald Bradley died in 2004 and was buried in Llandudno.

AUBREY SHENTON: President of Meir Golf Club for some years after the war. A building contractor, who owned the sand pits in Star and Garter Road, Lightwood. His company, AV Shenton, built the Broadway cinema for Herbert Clewlow in 1936.

The Meir Club, far from being elitist, could boast members who represented a broad spectrum of occupations and professions. Amongst these were: Mr Hyland (Hyland's electrical shop); Mr S Brindley; Stephen Mear of Weston Road, a former JP; Mr Upton; Mr Frank Amison, tobacconist, Weston Road; Dr G.M. Toh, a GP who looked after the health of Meir for many years and whose son Charles M. Toh, a dentist for 40 years, still practises in

Weston Coyney Road in 2004; Mr Adamson, a dentist living in The Avenue; Mr C. Wild, pottery manufacturer; Mr. H. Oldham, teacher at Longton High School; George Ray; and Dr Zinck and Mr Bill Howells from The British Ceramic Research Association.

James Clarke Barlow, the grandson of the founder of Meir Golf Club, recalls vividly certain personal memories of the now departed Club:

'There was Bill Howells and his wife, Sheila. Doug Clarke joined the police force and was stationed at Longton before moving up the tree. Ron Lovatt became a bank manager. The man who kept us in order in Meir at the time, Police Sergeant Warburton, 6ft 4 ins, with waxed moustache and who walked like a guardsman, his truncheon swinging from his belt. The kids used to cross the road to avoid his beady eye. There was no vandalism on his patch and very little crime either.

In the early 1930s as an eight year old boy, my first recollection of Meir Golf Club was a large pool by Bartlam's farm where we had a 'seaworthy' oil drum raft which we sailed to the 'cockpit', a large hollow tree in the middle of the pool. From this vantage point, we watched the golfers playing the short 13th hole. 'Our Gang' included my cousin Michael Beswick, who practically lived at our house. We used to knock balls about on Meir Golf Course with cut-down hickory shafted clubs. Tragically Mike was critically injured when a land mine blew up his tank in the Normandy landings and died about two weeks later in a south coast hospital at the ripe old age of 19 years. RIP.

As a young teenager before the war, on Saturday afternoon, I was my father's partner versus Abe Bradbury and Meir vicar, Bobbie Bell, followed by teacakes and two rubbers of bridge - a satisfactory arrangement as neither the vicar or I played for money, and father and Abe did! I was allowed to play in the Sunday afternoon foursomes when I was fourteen year old.'

POSTSCRIPT

During the intervening years, the old Course was used for a variety of purposes. Today, in 2004, it is the haunt of the dog walking fraternity. Adjacent to the Whitcombe Road entrance lies the forlorn remains of Broadway House, a refuge for senior citizens now shuttered and closed. Sunday footballers pursue their boisterous hobby on a pitch in a corner nearest Whitcombe Road, and Longton High School, in Box Lane, use some of the rolling green acres for football and rugby pitches and a staff car park.

The panoramic views towards Park Hall Hills are much as they were in the 1930s except for a large housing estate nestling in a depression in the landscape. The air is still as fresh and the wind just as keen on cold days as it ever was. Even so, a careful glance reveals some of the features of the old course, reminders of what might have been jog the senses. In amongst meadow grass and weeds, a couple of tees linger. Although Meir Golf Club has long gone, its members scattered to the four winds, a lone golfer still uses the facility on rare occasions. With his clubs and a bucket of golf balls, Ken Oakley, no slouch with a sand wedge, practises his tee shots in a corner of the lofty old course.

But on a warm summer morning, if you're ever tempted to saunter over and see for yourself what remains of Meir's legendary course where so many enjoyed their golf, just for a moment stop, pause and listen. When the weather is fair and still, you may just hear a ghostly cry of 'fore' floating on the breeze across the forlorn and deserted fairways.

A very early photo of the inside of Holy Trinity church. *Dorothy Mear collection.*

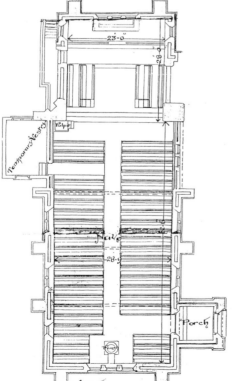

Taken from the original drawings made in March 1894, this plan shows the later additions to Holy Trinity Church, the Meir. They were made by Messrs. Scriveners of Hanley.

HOLY TRINITY CHURCH

Throughout history, the Staffordshire villages of Caverswall and the Meir, just 2 miles apart, had much in common; both small, isolated and with most of their population engaged in working the land. But whereas Caverswall possessed a church, St Peter's, the Meir did not; a state of affairs that lasted until the last quarter of the 19th century.

Until then, the 'faithful' in the Meir were faced with the unenviable prospect of a two mile jaunt to reach St Peters', where they and their forebears celebrated the liturgy on the same site for nigh on 800 years. During fair weather, a gentle stroll must have been very pleasant, especially when accompanied by fellow travellers, the conversation melting away the miles. However when it turned stormy, the same two miles must have seemed a long way home in pouring rain or whatever the seasons decreed. Those from the Meir who died were interred in Caverswall's 12th century churchyard, where the shadow of the castle, rebuilt around the time of the English Civil War by Matthew Craddock, daily marked the passing of eternity across the tombstones.

However after 1876, following its opening, Meir's worshippers began using a room at the Meir Board Schools in Meir Lane (later Uttoxeter Road), just beyond the 1905 building of Meir Methodist church. It was an arrangement which worked well for about 15 years:

'The Harvest Festival was held on Sunday 12th October 1890. At morning service, the Rev Thomas Heywood Masters preached the sermon and in the afternoon, the Rev J. Beckett of Dilhorn occupied the pulpit and in the evening the Rev J.G. Addenbrooke preached to a crowded congregation. The room was tastefully decorated and a large quantity of bread and vegetables was given to the poor. The anthem 'And God said let the earth' by Caleb Simper was well rendered by the mission choir. The offertories amounted to £8.7 shillings.'

Never mind that Meir folk had little of their own, it did not preclude them dipping into their own meagre supply to give to those less well blessed. The culture of 'giving' to the poor and other worthy causes was a philosophy running through Victorian society before the advent of the 'welfare services' safety net. Indeed in nearby Longton, charity for those poor devils bereft of a Christmas meal had become, over the years, a permanent annual event. A few months after the reported harvest festival (1890) the local press declared, *'On Christmas day 600 poor children were entertained to a feast of roast beef and plum pudding in the Town Hall. This was the eighth occasion on which a similar treat has been provided for those children whose poverty entreats compassionate consideration at this time.'*

During the long summer of 1890, Rev. J.G. Addenbrooke, vicar of Saint Peter's, Caverswall, had been approached by many people from the Meir congregation about their need for a church in the Meir village. Weeks later and convinced of their cause, he journeyed to Lichfield to present their petition to a higher level, the Bishop of the diocese. Shortly after their meeting his Grace acceded. There would be a new church for the Meir. With the first hurdle cleared there now remained the thorny question of where to build it. Was a suitable site in the Meir available?

For this isolated rural community as small, and it must be said in fairness, impoverished as it was, left to their own devices it would have been exceptionally difficult, if not nigh impossible to build a church of some substance. External funding was required. As with many causes in Victorian society, the patronage of well-connected and wealthy members of the local gentry was paramount. History at the time is littered with countless examples of benevolent worthies who saw it as their station in life to help the down-trodden and needy. The Meir was fortunate in having financial help from many benefactors. Sir Smith Child, who had helped finance a ward at nearby Longton Cottage Hospital, donated a huge sum of £500 which got the fund off to a flying start.

Another philanthropist was the Fourth Duke of Sutherland. Through the harsh winter weather of the late 1890s, with typical and unswerving generosity, he had kept alive 'half' the local population with gifts of meat, bacon and coal by the lorry load. His grace responded to the Meir parishioners, offering them a parcel of land off Meir Lane, for 'their new Jerusalem.' Needless to say they accepted it with open arms.

Whilst this was important, there would be many more occasions in the future when more grass roots monetary help would be needed. Into this category fell Eli Bowers, or more especially his wife and family. Living at Caverswall castle, Mrs Bowers' name runs like a thread through the enormous building programme the Meir church had planned, aided by the Meir congregation who lessened the burden of debt through their ingenuity and determination.

Bazaars and church fetes were, like today, a popular means of generating extra church income. One in May 1890 was in the style of an auction held by T.H. Griffiths, selling off those valuable and 'unwanted' items remaining from a bazaar held the previous day. A persuasive man, T.H. Griffiths sold all before him - when his gavel crashed down for the last time, £447, around 25% of the capital cost of the building had been raised.

With work on the church finally under way during the autumn of 1890, William Dalrymple, the Bishop of Lichfield, gave his permission for *'the performance of divine service in the said chapel'* on its completion. He did not consecrate the church because of *'legal difficulties',* and the ceremony went ahead without him:

'The opening and dedication of the new church at the Meir was performed by the Right Reverend, the Bishop of Shrewsbury. The consecration was to have been performed by the Lord Bishop of the Diocese, but the sacred rite had to be deferred as a consequence of 'certain formalities' of the handing over of the building to the commissioners not being completed in time. At present there is only a temporary chancel but when the church is completed it will accommodate about 400 people. It will then consist of a chancel, nave, north and south transepts, vestry and an organ chamber. The estimated total cost is about £2,000.

The church, which is in the Early English Style is constructed of red brick and stone facings. At present there is seating for about 260 people. The plans were prepared by Messrs Scriveners Limited and the contract executed by Messrs Inskip of Longton.

The opening ceremony was performed at four o'clock, the Bishop and the clergy assembling at the Meir House, the residence of Mr W. Webberley. A procession was formed and proceeded to the church headed by the surpliced choir who sang a processional hymn, No. 166 Ancient and Modern, "All people who on earth do dwell". The clergy who followed wearing the surplice and hood, were the Bishop of Shrewsbury, the Rural Dean (the Rev. H.C. Turner), the rector of Longton (the Rev G.F. Tamplin), the Reverends J.G.Addenbrooke (vicar of Caverswall), W.I. Smith (vicar of St. John's Longton) and S. Salt vicar of Dresden, J. Finch-Smith, T. Becket (Dilhorn), T.P. Forth (Forsbrook). There was a crowded congregation.

The opening prayers were recited by the Bishop and the lessons read by Rev G.F.Tamplin and Rev H.C. Turner and the subsequent prayers taken by Rev J.G. Addenbrooke and Rev T.H. Masters. An able sermon was preached by the Bishop from II Chronicles vi. 18, "But will God in very deed dwell with men on earth?"

At the conclusion of the service, a tea took place in a large marquee erected in the grounds and subsequently an entertainment of wax-works with live models was given by Mr R. Clive of Kidsgrove. The offertory at the dedication service, which was in aid of the building fund, amounted to £27 16s 10^1/2d.'

Celebrations at the Meir church continued unabated during the days after its opening:

'The services were continued yesterday (Friday 22nd May 1891), the special preacher, announced at evensong, being the Venerable Archdeacon of Stafford. Special services will also be held on Sunday and during the week, the preacher on Monday 25th May 1891 being the Venerable Archdeacon of Stoke:

'The dedication service continued with the new church at the Meir on Sunday and during the week. The preachers were as follows: Sunday morning (24th May) Rev W.I. Smith, vicar of St John's: afternoon Rev E.H. Spink, curate in charge of St Jude's, Stoke: evensong, Rev J.G. Addenbrooke (vicar of Caverswall). Monday, the Venerable Archdeacon of Stoke; Tuesday, Rev H.C. Turner Rural Dean, vicar of Fenton; Wednesday, Rev G.F.Tamplin, Rector of Longton and Thursday, Rev E.S. Carlos, the vicar of Cheadle. The total offertories which were in aid of the chancel fund amounted to £37.9s.1d'

The fact the Meir now had a new church would have been the signal for many to sit back and bask in the glow. Tremendous though it was, the vicar of Caverswall, Rev J.G. Addenbrooke still had other ideas dear to his heart no doubt to add the finishing touches.

Holy Trinity, as the Meir church was known, was a *'daughter to the mother church of St Peter's, Caverswall'* with no resident priest, Caverswall supplying the tireless clergy for the Meir parishioners. Many of these were musically talented, clever and well educated men, university graduates who held higher degrees when education was costly and limited. Their stipends or pay reflect how well paid they were for their vocation.

One, Rev. David E Bush was an organ scholar at St David's College Lampeter, moving to Lichfield to become a deacon at Caverswall in the autumn of 1894. Another, Rev. Hugh Nanney Smith, a BA graduate from Cambridge University in 1891, followed the same path becoming a priest a year later. At Caverswall as a curate in 1892, he left for Yorkshire and the parish of Walkley in 1894.

The mantle of 'eccentric' sits well on the shoulders of Rev Charles Addenbrooke MA, brother of John, vicar of Caverswall. Charles, instrumental in beginning 'classes for adults' - in effect adult literacy classes - for the Meir parishioners, was one of many clergy who sought to improve the education of the Meir parish. A popular man by all accounts throughout his time in the Meir, he eventually emigrated to New Zealand continuing his ministry. He

A snowy Meir church. The hawthorn hedge along with several hundred square yards of frontage and the entire 1900s Church Institute were removed to make way for the new A50.

Holy Trinity church in the early 1970s with Tom Sutton in the doorway.

Holy Trinity church in the 1990s.

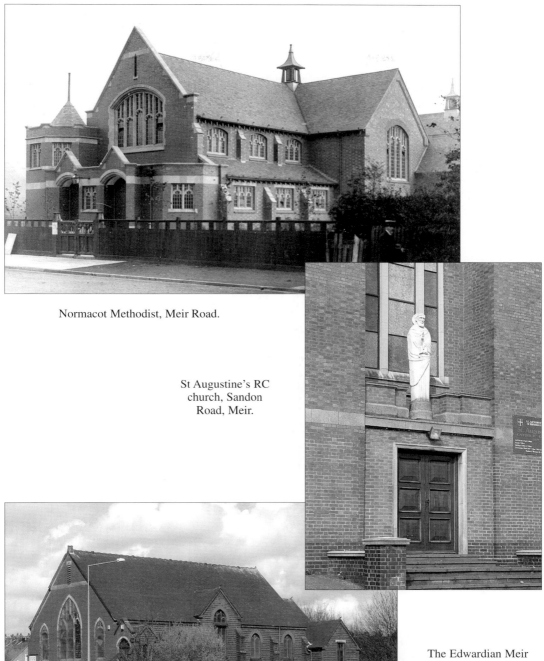

Normacot Methodist, Meir Road.

St Augustine's RC
church, Sandon
Road, Meir.

The Edwardian Meir
Methodist church in
Uttoxeter Road. Erected
in the early years of the
20th century, the architect
was T.P. Hulse. The
demolition to the right
was the site of two old
Meir cottages.

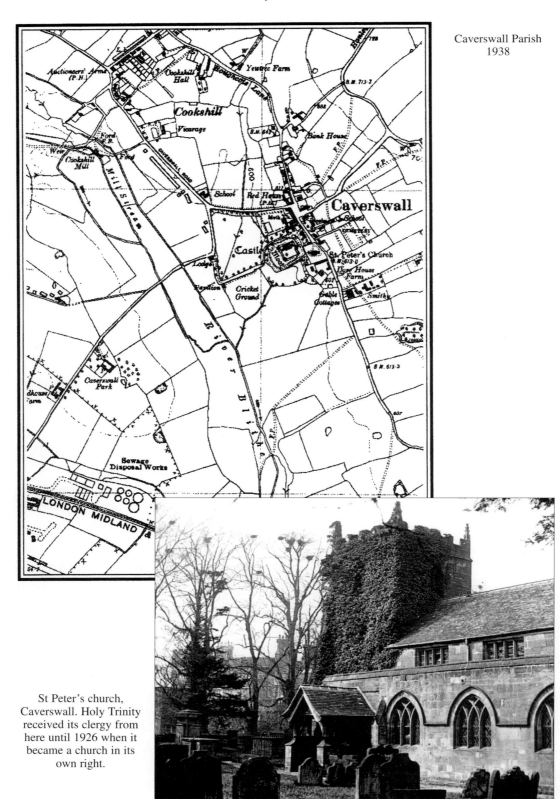

Caverswall Parish
1938

St Peter's church, Caverswall. Holy Trinity received its clergy from here until 1926 when it became a church in its own right.

never returned to England and died in the 1940s. His tenure as curate at Holy Trinity is marked by a handsomely inscribed brass plaque in the church's vestibule passageway.

Records of the clergy at Caverswall, many on parchment, stretch back beyond the Middle Ages. Putting to one side William de Fenton in 1284, a titled incumbent, Sir George Bowles and a member of the Sneyd family, Rev. Ralph Sneyd, who have no connection with Holy Trinity, one of the most conspicuous during the Meir church's formative years was Rev Thomas Heywood Masters MA, curate in charge between 1889-1893 and twice mentioned in dispatches during the Great War. He became Chaplain to the King from 1921 to 1939. He was responsible for the training of Havergal Brian to play the organ:

'Brian applied for the post of organist at Holy Trinity, the Meir and greatly to his relief succeeded in obtaining it. The church was small and recently built.'

The organist from Stoke parish church, Theophilus Hemmings, and Bertram Walker also played a major part in Brian's musical education. The organist at St Gregory's Roman Catholic church, Longton, Stoke-on-Trent, the knowledgeable Walker 'fine tuned' Brian's organ technique, once famously chiding him *'never to look at his feet if he wanted to be an organist.'* Brian held his tutor in such high esteem he inscribed the flyleaf of a book he gave him as a Christmas gift in 1892.

Brian continued his musical education whenever he could, eventually after many years becoming well known as a composer. A close friend of Edward (later Sir Edward) Elgar, controversy was a constant companion of Brian whether through his music or personal relationships. Unhappily after one disagreement with Elgar their friendship finally foundered, giving credence to Brian being labelled *'The Awkward Cuss.'*

During the 1960s, Brian was fortunate - given it needed the combined efforts of several massed choirs and orchestras and he was an old man - to hear and see his Gothic Symphony performed in London. As the last note died away to the acclaim of the audience, he got to his feet to acknowledge their appreciation.

He died in 1972 at Shoreham by Sea, Sussex just short of his 97th birthday:

Meanwhile at Holy Trinity Church, fundraising continued: *'On Tuesday and Wednesday a sale of work was held in the Meir Board Schools on behalf of the building fund of the Holy Trinity Church. The sale consisted of a quantity of useful and fancy articles left over from the Michaelmas fair and about 350 warm winter garments which were disposed at cost price to the mothers of the Sunday school children. The sale was opened by Mrs. W.E. Bowers of Caverswall Castle who was supported by the vicar of Caverswall (the Rev J.G. Addenbrooke),the curate in charge of the Meir church (the Rev Thomas Heywood Masters MA) Mr Henry Hill JP and others. The vicar in opening the proceedings, explained that the May Fair (not the bazaar) on behalf of the church building fund resulted in a clear profit of £368 8s 5d and the Michaelmas Fair (the postponed May Bazaar) a profit of £174.10s. They now required about £150 to complete the building of the chancel.*

The trustees thought if they could raise £50, they might commence the work in the Spring and it was with that object that the sale was held. Mrs Bowers had laid the foundation stone of the chancel in the figurative sense and had already collected from the ladies of the county a sum of £76. She said she had much pleasure in declaring the sale open.

She was very pleased to do what she could in assisting to complete the church and hoped the sale would be successful. On the motion of Mr Hill a vote of thanks was passed to Mrs Bowers for her kindness'.

At that point in its history the Meir had a close affinity with agriculture and animal husbandry. Celebration of the harvest had a greater significance in the calendar then than in later years, as locally, farming declined. The first service in the new Holy Trinity church lifted the celebration to something of a red letter day for the Meir congregation:

'The Harvest thanksgiving services were held on the 8th inst. and Sunday 11th. The new church was tastefully decorated. On the 8th, the vicar of Dresden (Rev S.Salt) was the preacher. On Sunday morning, the vicar of the parish (of Caverswall) J.G. Addenbrooke officiated. On Sunday afternoon the Rev. A.B. Standford, assistant curate of Holy Trinity, Hartshill addressed the school children and in the evening the Rev W.I. Smith preached to a crowded congregation a practical and earnest sermon taking his text from St Mark iv.28. 'The full corn in the ear.' The offertories amounted to £10.18s.'

While the newly opened Meir church was a great achievement, it was not the architect's finished design. Most noticeably, the north and south transepts had yet to be built and the chancel - the next goal for Rev. John Addenbrooke and the embattled Meir parishioners.

With few alternatives and outside distractions, social events in the Meir were well supported. They were fortunate to have access to rooms at Meir Board Schools for the occasional function: *'On Monday evening a concert was given in the Meir Board Schools, the vicar of Caverswall (the Rev. J.G. Addenbrooke) presiding and there was a large attendance. Among those who assisted were the Rev. Thomas H Masters and Mrs Masters, the Misses Storey, Barlow, Middleton, Jones and Pothecary and Mrs Martin, Bevington and F. Forth. Tableaux representing Pygmalion and Galatea, A Gipsy Scene, After tea in Japan, Florence Nightingale and Bluebeard and his 7 wives were cleverly performed.'*

To 20th century eyes, much of Victorian entertainment is incomprehensible. But the appeal of the annual local prize-giving, two weeks later, is understandable. An eager and responsive congregation would always turn up in droves to support their offspring. Or was it, perchance, that they might be the recipient of what would be a much valued piece of winter clothing, often lying outside the realms of a meagre family budget? Who can say?

'The annual distribution of prizes to the children attending the Holy Trinity Church School, the Meir took place on Monday evening at Meir Board Schools. The vicar of Caverswall, Rev J.G. Addenbrooke presided, being supported by the Rev T.H. Masters and there was about 250 scholars present, besides a large number of their parents and friends. The prizes were distributed by Mrs Stephen Mear in the absence, through illness, of Mrs J.G. Aynsley. An interesting entertainment was then given-songs being contributed by Miss Pothecary, the Rev J.L. Murray and Mrs H. Bevington. Pianoforte duets were given by the Misses Barlow and Middleton and several recitations given by the scholars. During the evening the vicar gave an address alluding with satisfaction to the prosperous state of the Sunday Schools. To the children especially, he gave much good advice. At the end of the evening each child received a parcel of warm clothing, the results of much hard work willingly given by the many friends interested in the new church at the Meir. It is intended that clothing shall be distributed annually as Christmas gifts.'

Several charities or doles existed whose sole purpose was ironing out life's 'ups and downs.' One, to support the elderly, bore the name of its founder, Henry Hill. It used a simple strategy to slip them a 'bob or two' should the need arise, which continued even after Henry Hill's death.

'The funeral procession left the deceased's (Henry Hill JP) residence, Beech House, the Meir shortly before 2 o'clock and was met by the choir of the Holy Trinity church, the Meir; the deceased being a prominent member of the congregation. The service was conducted by the vicar of Dresden (Rev S. Salt) and the curate-in-charge, the Meir Church, (Rev J.E.Carey). As the procession entered the church, Mr W. Brian, organist at Meir church, played Chopin's March Funebre and at the close the Dead March in Saul.'

Several years later the 'Henry Hill' soldiered on, scattering gifts for the needy in the local parishes. (1902)

'The Henry Hill charity for the benefit of the aged poor was distributed at the Court House on Monday (the birthday of the donor.) Each year, the annual interest on £1,000, less legacy duty, is divided in the proportion of 5 shillings to each person. On this occasion there were 198 recipients, the oldest of whom is 98. The Mayor made the distribution.'

The Hill charity was not unique. From amongst a variety of societies, which included the quaintly-named Pearson's Fresh Air Fund, two other doles or charities, the Webberley Dole and John Aynsley's Gift to the Poor existed: *'The charity left by the late Mr W.Webberley for the relief of the poor widows in St James' parish was distributed on St Thomas' day. There were 50 recipients among whom £15 was distributed.'* (1902)

'John Aynsley's (who celebrated his 80th birthday in December 1903) *'Gift to the Poor' charity disbursed the annual interest on £500 to 80 people giving them 5 shillings each.'*
(1904)

As these doles were perpetual, whatever became of these once large cash sums invested a century ago by these honourable gentlemen?

In the space of three months well over three quarters of the capital cost of the new chancel at the Meir church had been raised, an astonishing feat. Having the effervescent Mrs W.E. Bowers of Caverswall Castle, who made a career wringing huge sums of money out of people for charitable causes, was a bonus. With the bit firmly between their teeth, she, clergy and congregation, set their sights on building the new chancel.

'The congregation of the new church of the Holy Trinity, the Meir have decided to proceed with the erection of the chancel, the ceremony of cutting the first sod was performed on Monday (26th June) in the presence of the vicar of Caverswall (Rev J.G. Addenbrooke),the curate in charge (Rev T.H. Masters) and members of the Building Commissioners and a number of parishioners. The act of turning the first sod was performed by Mr E. Cartwright who has taken a deep and practical interest in the erection of the new church. The architects are Messrs Scriveners and Sons, Hanley and the builders Messrs Tompkinson and Bettelley, Longton and it is hoped that the work will be completed by the end of October. The sum of £250 is still required to complete and furnish the chancel.'   1st July 1893

On a Thursday in August, the great day finally arrived:

'The commissioners having decided to proceed with the erection of the chancel of

Holy Trinity church, The Meir, the foundation stone was laid on Thursday afternoon (16th August 1893) by Mrs W.E. Bowers of Caverswall castle, a lady who had taken a particular interest in the new and handsome church. The church, which was erected at a cost of over £2,000 on land given by the late Duke of Sutherland, was opened for public worship in May 1891 and there still has to be added to complete the edifice, a chancel, organ chamber, vestry and north and south transepts. At present it is proposed to proceed with the erection of the chancel only and for this, a sum of over £700 is required. Most of this money has already been subscribed, viz £415 10s.8d which including a balance on the church building fund and proceeds of sales of work amounts to £276 7s 8d; £76 from Mrs Bowers Ladies Fund, £50 from the Incorporated Building Society, £30 from the Diocesan Church Extension Society, £20 from Mrs J.G. Aynsley, £20 from Mr Bowers and other donations. The chancel will be constructed in the early decorated style in conformity with the nave and will be 28 feet in length and 23 feet in width, the height from the floor to the ridge being 42 feet. On the south side there will be an arch so as to admit the erection of the organ chamber and on the north side a doorway for communication for the vestry. The east window will have three lights and the floor and a portion of the inside walls will be paved with Minton's tiles. The chancel is to be completed by the end of October.

The ceremony of laying the stone was preceded by a short evensong the choir singing as a processional 'Onward Christian Soldiers', the service conducted by the Bishop of Shrewsbury.

The Bishop said he had been happily associated with the church at the Meir from its commencement and he was glad the time had arrived when there was a prospect of completing the church by the addition of what was the most sacred part of any church. The rest of the office was said by the Bishop and the stone was laid by Mrs Bowers who was presented with the inscribed silver trowel. The vicar announced the patron of the church (The Hon E.S. Parker-Jervis) had subscribed £150 and sent a further donation of £25 and he thanked Mrs Bowers for the kind and practical interest which she had manifested in the church, mentioning the fact that the fund she had collected was really the nucleus of the chancel fund. While the offertory was being made, the hymn "Christ is our corner stone" was sung; 'At the name of Jesus' being used as recessional hymn.'

It was a triumph for the vicar of Caverswall that shortly after the opening of Holy Trinity church, they were able to add such a large extension. This event would furnish the Meir with one of its more enduring and more inspired pieces of architecture.

CONSECRATION OF THE MEIR CHURCH

A new chancel having just been added to the new church of the Holy Trinity at the Meir at a cost of £700, the ceremony of the consecration of the church was performed on Monday (16th May) by the Bishop of Lichfield.

The foundation stone of the new chancel was laid in August last by Mrs WE Bowers of Caverswall Castle. In construction, the chancel follows closely the character of the nave having brick facings on the outside walls and stone dressings to the windows and angles. Inside, the dressings to the windows and walls are also of stone and the lower portion is faced with tiles. The chancel is fitted with a large three-light window in the east wall and single-light windows in the north and south walls.

Provision is also made for the addition in the future of an organ chamber and vestry. Towards the cost of the chancel the sum of £250 is still required.

The service of consecration was the first of a special series extending into May and there was a large congregation.

Amongst the clergy present were the Reverends J. G. Addenbrooke (vicar of Caverswall), J.E. Carey (curate in charge), H.V. Smith, W.I. Smith, T.P. Forth, D.H. Briggs and the Hon S.G.W. Maitland. The usual office for the consecration was used, the Registrar (Mr W. Hodson) reading the deed of consecration which was signed by the Bishop of Lichfield who ordered it to be enroled and preserved in the registry of the diocese. In the course of his address, the Bishop reminded the parishioners present of the deep responsibility which rested upon them and urged them to take an active part in the work of the church. A celebration of the Holy Communion followed. The organ has been presented to the church by Mrs Stephen Mear and the credence table has been purchased from the Lenten savings of the teachers and children of the Sunday School.'

21st May 1894

The church, began now to resemble Scriveners' blueprints, although still lacking two transepts. Five years passed before the organ chamber became a reality and the shape of the church was finally established as it is today.

'On Thursday afternoon, Miss Child of Stallington Hall laid the foundation stone of the new organ chamber at Holy Trinity church, the Meir which is estimated to have cost £205. The congregation have acquired the old organ of St John's church, Longton at the very moderate price of £20 and it is proposed to expend an additional £30 in effecting repairs and tuning.

This musical transplant would have left St John's, Longton without a church organ and the clergy and laity obviously had a replacement quickly lined up. By the end of the same month it had been plumbed in: its cost, a measure of the difference in the size of the congregation between the Meir and Longton.

The new organ at St John's was used for the first time at evensong on Christmas Eve, the organist Mr J.H. Bamber officiating. It has cost £400. The old organ has been sold to Holy Trinity, the Meir where an organ chamber is being built for its reception.'

30th December 1899

The long journey to the Meir, from St Peter's, Caverswall, was at an end. There now only remained the erection of the new Sunday School building. It would be a brave man or woman who dared get out the battered collecting tins for yet another fund raising foray. The necessity for the 'Meir Church Institute' was recognised a year earlier when secular events took place in rooms furnished by the Meir Board Schools. A specially designed structure close by the church was now top of the agenda. The financing of the scheme was left in the hands of Mrs Bowers of Caverswall Castle again, who graciously offered the Meir parishioners use of the castle grounds on one occasion. Judging by her earlier successful efforts, the result must have seemed a foregone conclusion:

'A garden party and Sale of Work took place on Thursday in the grounds of

Caverswall castle, by the kind permission of Mr and Mrs Bowers, the object being to assist the fund which has been inaugurated for the purposes of erecting a building to be used in connexion with Holy Trinity Church, the Meir as a Sunday School and Men's Institute as well as for holding Bible classes, concerts and various meetings. In view of the large and increasing population of the Meir, such a building has been found essential to the proper carrying on of church work and a fund has been opened to provide the necessary means. It is estimated that the building will cost about £1,300 towards which £600 has already been raised. The picturesque and pleasantly situated castle with its beautiful grounds made an ideal spot for a garden party affording as it did, pleasant shelter from the hot rays of the sun.

A marquee had been erected in the shelter of the trees just below the castle and in this, stalls had been arranged and with Miss Ethel Aynsley as Hon Sec. with other ladies having brought together a large assortment of goods.

The opening ceremony was performed by Mrs Jas.Heath and amongst those also present were the Rev.J.G. Addenbrooke (vicar of Caverswall) and Mrs Addenbrooke, J.G. Holford and Mrs and Miss Meakin. The Rev J.G. Addenbrooke, in introducing Mrs Heath, said they wished to give her a hearty reception. The Meir people had worked excellently in maintaining their church and all that belonged to the church's organisations in the parish and Mrs Heath was doing excellent work in coming down from London that day to open the sale. They very much regretted that Mr Jas. Heath MP was prevented from attending owing to illness.

The Rev C. Addenbrooke, in proposing a vote of thanks to Mrs Heath expressed their sincere thanks for her kindness with helping them with their sale and also signified their appreciation of the kindness of Mr and Mrs Bowers on throwing the grounds open on that occasion. Mr Bowers seconded the vote of thanks which was carried with acclamation. During the day the band of the 1st V.B North Staffs Regiment played a selection of music, courts were open for tennis and various amusements were provided, dancing taking place in the evening.'

As the year petered out, the worshippers at Holy Trinity could be excused a self congratulatory pat on the back. In the space of 11 years £4,500 had been raised to put up the main church, a chancel and organ chamber. On a spring day in 1902 the new Church Institute was officially begun, with all the pomp and ceremony it richly deserved. Tables groaned beneath plates of thinly-cut cucumber sandwiches, iced buns and tea. Optimism was in the air. The final enterprise by the intrepid Holy Trinity parishioners had begun.

'New Parish Institute at the Meir: The laying of the foundation stones of a Sunday School, Men's Institute and parish room for educational and parochial purposes in connexion with the Holy Trinity church, the Meir, took place on Thursday afternoon (15th May 1902). The scheme has been in hand for a number of years having received its first impetus from a legacy bequeathed by the late Mr Henry Hill. The sum has gradually grown by the aid of parochial concerts and while generous help was given by the Caverswall garden party, which realised £240 and the Duchess of Sutherland's entertainment at Stoke in December 1900, when from then proceeds of the splendid performance given on that

occasion, the Institute fund participated to the extent of £100.

The site has been given by the Duke of Sutherland and is on a plot of land that is contiguous to the church. The opening part of the ceremony took place in the church, the office being that for the laying of foundation stones of a parish building. The prayers were said by Rev Charles Addenbrooke, curate in charge and the venerable archdeacon Lane gave an address. The clergy, choir and congregation having proceeded to the site the stones were laid as follows.

South west corner by Mr W.R. Parker-Jervis of Meaford Hall and patron of Caverswall): the Henry Hill Memorial Stone in the central bay by Miss Ethel Aynsley (representing Mr John Aynsley of Blythe Bridge):South-east corner by Mrs J Warren of Belleview, Shrewsbury (formerly of the Meir); The Institute Library Corner Stone by Mrs Stephen Mear of Weston Coyney House. The builder's contract is for £1,200 and the furnishing will bring the cost up to £1,600; to make up, a further sum of £450 is required.'

Work on the new Institute progressed steadily. By spring of the next year it was complete. Meir church and its congregation were again, 'en fete', May 1903:

'The new Sunday School, Men's Institute and parish room for the Holy Trinity church, the Meir were formally opened on Thursday (2nd April 1903). The Institute scheme received its first impetus from a legacy of £225 bequeathed by the late Mr Henry Hill. The sum was gradually increased by the aid of parochial concerts etc while generous help was given by the garden party at Caverswall which realised £240 and the Duchess of Sutherland's entertainment at Stoke Theatre on that occasion, the institute fund participated to the extent of £100. The site was a gift from the Duke of Sutherland that is contiguous to the church. The foundation stones were laid in May last year by Mr W.R. Parker-Jervis, patron of the mother church of Caverswall, Miss Ethel Aynsley (representing Mr John Aynsley), Mrs J Warren (formerly of the Meir) and Mr Stephen Mear.

The opening ceremonies were performed on Thursday by Mrs Manningham-Buller and the Mayor of Longton (Alderman G. Bennion). In the course of the proceedings, the Rev Charles Addenbrooke, curate-in-charge, stated that the building had involved an outlay of £1,600, towards which, £1,280 had been raised. During the proceedings, further donations of 5 guineas were announced from Lady Manningham-Buller and the Mayor. The building has been erected by Mr Bagnall of Fenton from designs by Mr Thomas Tindal, architect of Longton.'

Throughout the long and bitter years of the Great War, those back home at Holy Trinity did not sit idly by wringing their hands in despair. In a rural environment like the Meir, it was natural local farmers make a determined effort to raise cash for 'our brave lads overseas' during 1915. From amongst many local charities two especially sought to raise money for victims of the War. One, the Silk Nursing Association sold flags raising £46 9s 9d for the treatment of the injured and wounded. Another, the Longton Prisoners of War Society bought parcels with money they collected which were shipped over to Prisoners of War. Nineteen local Longton men were at this time held in prisoner of War camps in Germany. One, Corporal Horace Woods, *'who before joining the army in 1915 had been for several years a member of the Stoke-on-Trent Borough Police Force stationed in the town'* was reported missing in action before later news he had been taken prisoner announced in the pages of the local press. *'Corporal Woods has written to his wife, who resides at the Meir that he is now at an internment camp in Germany.'* Chin up Horace.

For others, news was life changing. The death of one of Caverswall's more notable sons shattered the tranquillity of this hushed country village:

'Lieutenant W. Aubrey Bowers, son of the late Mr and Mrs Bowers (1st) died from wounds received the following day in the great battle in France, July 1916. Lieut. Bowers joined the 5th North Staffs Territorial regiment in April 1915 and went to France early in the present year. He was the only son of the late William Bowers, the 'squire of Caverswall'. He was born at Barlaston Hall a little more than 29 years ago and educated at Manchester and New College Oxford. He married Miss Vera Annie Latham, 3 years ago. Mrs Bowers was staying in Eastbourne with her one infant daughter when the sad news was communicated to her from Caverswall Castle'

A memorial to Aubrey Bowers was commissioned for Caverswall church, not far from the castle and amongst the winding lanes where he had spent so many pleasureable sunny afternoons:

'Choir stalls of oak with a brass mural tablet to the memory of 2nd Lieutenant William Aubrey Bowers of the North Staffs Regiment who died from wounds in action on July 2nd 1916 were dedicated by the Bishop of Lichfield (Dr Kempthorne) at Caverswall Church on the 13th inst. The tablet bears the following inscription, 'To the Glory of God and in ever loving memory of William Aubrey Bowers of the North Staffordshire Regiment, Caverswall Castle. Born January 22nd 1887. Died July 2nd 1916 of wounds received in action at Gommecourt, France on July 1st. This tablet and choir stalls in the chancel are erected by his widow.' The inscription goes on, 'And whosoever will lose his life for my sake, shall find it.'

Churchwardens Mr Stephen Mear and Mr J Barlow from Holy Trinity Church, the Meir were present as was Rev. H.M. Fowler, now of Holy Trinity, Hereford - formerly vicar of Caverswall for 13 years, Rev F. Barton Horspool, vicar of Caverswall and the Reverends Maurice Davies and T. Caleb.'   22nd September 1917

The comings and goings of the local clergy were usually chronicled in minute detail. Odd, therefore, little was written of what the congregation of Holy Trinity thought about their priest, Rev Theophilus Caleb. Church registers record his presence during his ministry (save for one Christmas Day when he was ill), but the most notable incident colouring his whole incumbency was the famous strike of 1916 which resulted in Holy Trinity's choir picketing the church.

The petulant inscriptions in the register indicate something slightly more than 'a local difficulty'. Rev Caleb wrote, *'Holy Trinity church abstained ....owing to my appointment as curate in charge....'* The situation soon spiralled out of control after lads stationed outside Holy Trinity Church told worshippers, *'...not to go in. Please Miss, don't go in that church!'*

Tempers cooled by September, although forgiveness appeared very far away, and Rev Caleb countered with a salvo in his own hand in the registers. *'Choir strike finished. Most unsatisfactory. It would have been better had they never come back.'* Adding: *The peace of God's church was broken at the Meir and much offence given to the children of the church. An absolute fresh start would have been better.*

But six years later the acrimony was forgotten. 'Evidence of the regard in which he was held by his parishioners was forthcoming on Sunday, when the Rev T Caleb, curate-in-charge for the past six years of the Holy Trinity church, Meir, bade goodbye to his friends. A crowded congregation on Sunday evening heard Mr Caleb's farewell sermon and there was also a large attendance at a farewell meeting in the Sunday schools over which Mr G.C.V. Cant presided. Mr Cant said they were gathered together to bade farewell to Mr Caleb and to offer him their hearty congratulations on his preferment to the village of Norman's Heath. He paid a tribute to Mr Caleb's ministrations at the Meir and expressed the hope he would have happiness and success in his new sphere of work. A series of presentations were made to the departing minister during the evening.

Until now, the lights or windows above the main altar in Holy Trinity had been plain glass. In October 1925, through a generous act by a former member of the congregation, Holy Trinity church was left with one of its most notable and enduring features.

'The stained glass memorial light in the east window of Holy Trinity Church, to perpetuate the fondly remembered services of the late Mr Frederick Henry Heath, was unveiled at a simple little ceremony on Saturday afternoon. The late Mr Heath, whose death took place in 1914, had been a chorister at Meir church from the time it was opened for public worship up to the time of his death. In later years he took up the duties of choirmaster and also served as churchwarden. Apart from his church work he was widely connected with public and social organisations. The ceremony attracted a large congregation, in addition to the members of the family, including a host of persons who had been associated with him in his various public and social interests:

'There were present a representative gathering of the Etruscan lodge of Freemasons and also the Longton China Manufacturers Association. The Rev H.C. Sheldon priest in charge of Meir church conducted the service, assisted by the Rev R.O. Walker of Sleaford, Lincs, who was formerly priest in charge. Following the hymn by the church and congregation, Mr F.H. Heath, son of the deceased, unveiled and formally handed over the gift to the church. The gift was accepted by the churchwarden (Mr J.H. Barlow) and dedicated by the priest in charge.

The address was delivered by the Rev R.O. Walker who said that although 11 years had passed since Mr Heath's death, his memory was still as fresh as though he was still with them. He was one of the very first worshippers of the church and he laboured ungrudgingly for 25 years to serve it. It was mainly through Mr Heath's work that the church at the Meir was founded and it was fitting that it should be adorned by something which was meant to keep his memory fragrant. In coming back to the Potteries he (Rev Walker) was confronted by a picture of grime, soot and squalor, but beneath it all was hidden wondrous beauty of kind hearts such as the late Mr Heath possessed. The late Mr Heath's life, he concluded remained as a lasting memorial and as an example to those who followed. The light which has been given by the widow, is one of the highest quality glass which considerably enhances its beauty. It occupies the central position in the east window and represents, "Christ knocking at the door of the human Heart." The panel is surrounded by a rich architectural canopy of the 14th century style empanelled with figures and angels, one of *which is holding the inscription.' The window is a faithful reproduction of William Holman Hunt's masterpiece, 'The Light of the World'.'*

While the church continued to improve, it was noticeable that the lot of Rev Harry Christie Sheldon at Holy Trinity had not. Curates had lived in Weston Road for years with a local Meir vicarage well down the list of priorities. All that changed in November 1925:

'The annual sale of work in connection with the Holy Trinity church, Meir was opened on the 10th inst. by Mr Edwards, when the proceedings went towards the funds for the erection of the new vicarage. The opening ceremony was presided over by the vicar (the Rev H.C. Sheldon) who was supported by Mr J.H. Barlow (people's warden, Mr T. Hull (secretary) and the Rev E.W. Bridgwood (vicar of Forsbrook) and many prominent church workers. The hall had been artistically arranged and the efforts of those responsible were amply rewarded.'

The year 1926 was a watershed. Up until this time, the church had been merely 'a daughter from the mother church of Caverswall' and the latter had supplied all the curates for the Meir. The term 'conv. distr.' meaning a conventional district appears frequently in legal documentation from about 1919 (for example in the CV of Rev T Caleb). When a town begins to grow rapidly, due to new housing perhaps, then as a precursor of creating a new parish, that town or area may be termed a "conventional district". It is an agreement between the bishop and the clergy of the parishes concerned. By doing this, the town or area is removed from the incumbent's charge, the bishop licensing a 'curate in charge' who works towards a legal separation from the 'mother' parish. The legal position of the parishioners is unaffected and the obligations to marriage, burial etc are unaltered. The area or town, now on its own, can organise itself into a complete parochial unit which has its own PCC (Parochial Church Council) and electoral roll.

An agreement as to the right of presentation to the living had been made previously by deed dated 16th July 1925 in which the incumbent of Caverswall, who was previously entitled to appoint the minister at Meir, with the agreement of William Parker-Jervis, the patron of Caverswall, conceded the patronage should transfer to the Bishop of Lichfield.

When Rev H.C. Sheldon succeeded Rev Theophilus Caleb in 1923 his CV included that same terminology. In 1926 the official documentation proclaiming the Meir church's claim to be a parish on its own was presented on June 28th at Court at Buckingham Palace.

Holy Trinity had come of age, loftily perched on the hill out of Normacot was a church in its own right with its own vicar, Rev Harry Christie Sheldon. A series of official church documents, released at the time of the 'making of Holy Trinity' parish illustrate the boundaries of the new parish.

The most noticeable feature of the map are the acres of open space, later to be used for housing. Although the estate off Broadway was still years from construction, behind the Institute and church, the Meir Golf Club House had already been relocated, the scattering of large and imposing houses of James Barlow and Stephen Mear would continue to impress travellers journeying to Leek along Weston Road for decades. In Kelly's Directory for 1936 Meir is described as an *'An ecclesiastical parish formed in June 1926 from the parish of Caverswall and part of Normacot. It has a station on the London, Midland and Scottish Railway. The living is a perpetual curacy (without residence) net yearly value*

£350 in the gift of the Bishop of Lichfield has been held by Rev Harry Christie Sheldon BA of St David's College, Lampeter since 1926.'

During 1936, Rev Harry Christie Sheldon departed, succeeded by Rev William R Bell, known as 'Bobby' Bell. On his shoulders rested the responsibility of taking Holy Trinity church, its congregation and people throughout the whole of the Second World War. He and several clergy ministered to the members of the forces stationed in the Meir and services were held at the aerodrome and the TA Drill Hall, Rev Edward Fenton Woodward MA and Rev Bernard Paton Jones appearing in the registers.

With the war over Rev Bell left Holy Trinity, and his curate, Rev H. Vivian Woodward was made parish priest. The late 1940s and early 1950s was a period of austerity, money scarce and rewards few. It is to his great credit the church went from strength to strength - that is except for the church's transitory and celebrated wooden floor. Throughout the 1950s Meir continued to expand becoming the subject of an 'in depth' article by Bernard Sandall of the Evening Sentinel, HVW being pictured outside the still-unbuilt transept of Holy Trinity Church with his mother, Kate.

By the 1960s William A Richards had taken over from Rev Woodward. A scholarly man with degrees from Oxford he arrived with missionary zeal but left in 1964 for Warmington with Shotteswell staying for 11 years. His departure heralded the arrival of Rev Frederick W Osborn, a 'spiritual man' from contemporary accounts. With more emphasis placed on the spiritual, the fabric of one or two of the church's assets had declined markedly by his departure in 1976. He oversaw the sale of the land at the rear of the church on which the tennis courts were once laid out, sold off for housing.

It is often said you should 'never go back' but in accepting the incumbency of Holy Trinity, Rev Trevor Harvey was doing just that. Educated at Longton High School in Sandon Road and later Sheffield University he had travelled via Kingswinford and Upper Gornal to return to his roots. It was a tempestuous period with The Derby Way road scheme threatening to devastate much of the church's rolling lawns, trees and front pavement access into Uttoxeter Road. The road was never built but ever-present proposals to construct a wider road outside the church pervaded his ministry in Meir.

Attention paid to the spiritual rather than structural side of the church during Rev Osborn's ministry finally led to a decision to demolish the Church Institute in 1977. A difficult call to make after the trials and tribulations of those determined Edwardian parishioners who had built it. But in 75 years times had changed; more modern facilities were required, the large rooms in the Institute were no longer needed.

Throughout the early 1980s, Rev Harvey consolidated the position of the Meir church in the Meir community. The church was regularly decorated and it was not unusual to see Meir's parish priest 10 to 15 feet up a ladder with a plasterer's trowel and hawk in his hands. Well-deserved accolades over the magnificent lawns and outstanding churchyard are well documented. In 1986 he accepted a position at Windsor Castle, a post he held until 1999 when he moved to Ellesmere College in Shropshire.

His successor at Holy Trinity, Rev David Tudor, was a cultured and well educated man whose knowledge encompassed many interests. A priest for 12 years before coming to Meir, his ready wit and observations enlivened many discussions. He spoke German fluently and had wide experience of public transport, something he put to good use in the 1990 A50 Inquiry. His affection for trams was legendary. In 1991 he left Meir Parish to take up an appointment as chaplain at Nottingham City Hospital, a post he relished.

His shoes were eventually filled by Rev Gordon Whitty with his affable Black Country accent. He too was thrust into the maelstrom of the A50 and attended the A50 Inquiry in 1993 in Longton. The church during the road works was encircled, but inspite of incredible problems, he and his wife Joy brought an infectious and optimistic air to the spiritual and social side of the church's life. They relished the wide expanse of the lawns and having their own large garden after the somewhat smaller one at Shelton. With the road completed, he opted for quieter time at Hanbury, near Burton on Trent where he still lives, the rural serenity in marked contrast to the non-stop turmoil of Meir.

In 1999 Rev Mavis Allbutt became Holy Trinity's first woman priest. With Rev Whitty's departure, the 'interregnum' imposed on the Meir church ended with the appointment of Rev John Foulds, a graduate of Lancaster and Southampton Universities, from which he obtained a degree in Theology. He remains in post in May 2004.

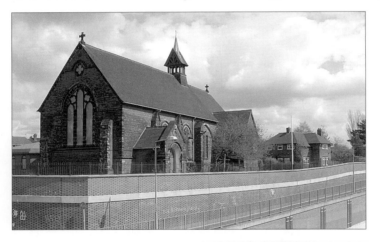

Cut off from any access to Uttoxeter Road, Holy Trinity has coped well with the indignities heaped upon it by unsympathetic civil engineering, thanks to a fine congregation and clergy.

Headstones at St Peter's, Caverswall (June 1993) showing the close links with Meir. Residents of Meir (Mear) were often buried here.

MEIR AIRPORT
STOKE-ON-TRENT'S MUNICIPAL AERODROME AT THE MEIR

When Orville and Wilbur Wright briefly coaxed their fragile flying machine into the air at Kitty Hawk, North Carolina it heralded the start of the aviation age. Locally Gustav Hamel, emulated their feat by flying a little farther from England to Germany. Now he thrilled the public with his airborne antics - for which he received £200 - at Queen's Park, Longton around Whitsuntide in May 1913.

But a farsighted few realised the aeroplane was becoming not only essential in the transport field but in aerial combat. The Royal Air Force had emerged from the ashes of its predecessor, The Royal Flying Corps and the Royal Naval Air Service, on April 1, 1918 at the end of the First World War. To survive the vagaries of those temperamental early planes was a major achievement in itself. Flying was regarded as the refuge of the map-cap few and the stout-hearted. The airmen who flew and fought in these contraptions were regarded with awe. But in the 'string and fabric' era at the end of the Great War, fliers were on the verge of becoming an endangered species when their lives were measured in days not weeks. The Meir was privileged in having its own champion in that small elite band of 'magnificent men in their flying machines': *'It has been announced that Mr Kenneth J Wolfe Dennitts, younger son of Mr and Mrs L. Dennitts of the King's Arms Hotel, the Meir has been awarded a commission in the Royal Air Force.'*

Given three years earlier his elder brother had lost his life in France, his joining the colours was an act of selfless gallantry. And although few realised it in 1918, it was to signal the emergence of the Meir's love affair with flying, lasting for over fifty years into the age of supersonic flight.

With the armistice in 1918, the world moved on. During the 'Roaring Twenties' air transport became ever more important. The first solo crossing of the Atlantic from the United States to Paris by Charles Lindbergh in his Ryan monoplane, The Spirit of St Louis and locally the Flying Circus's of Sir Alan Cobham and his 'Barnstormers' at the Meir aerodrome, elevated the aeroplane in the public's perception. From this age came many of the famous names that would be inextricably linked with aviation - AV Roe, de Havilland and Supermarine were prime examples.

One, the Supermarine Company, had on its books in 1920 the brilliant designer, Reginald J. Mitchell. Born in Congleton Road, Butt Lane, Stoke-on-Trent, the family moved to 87 Chaplin Road, Normacot, Longton shortly after his birth in 1895. From an early age and during student days, R.J. Mitchell's flair for aeronautical engineering soon became apparent. His name, inscribed amongst the alumni on the Roll of Honour at Stoke-on-Trent Technical School, is a testimonial to his prowess.

During a relatively brief career with Supermarine, later Vickers Supermarine, Mitchell led design teams producing a total of 24 different aircraft from bombers, light aircraft and flying boats. It brought him a deserved notoriety:

'The Supermarine monoplane designed by Reginald J. Mitchell has won a prize for

Enlargement of an aerial view of Meir in 1945 showing the airport.

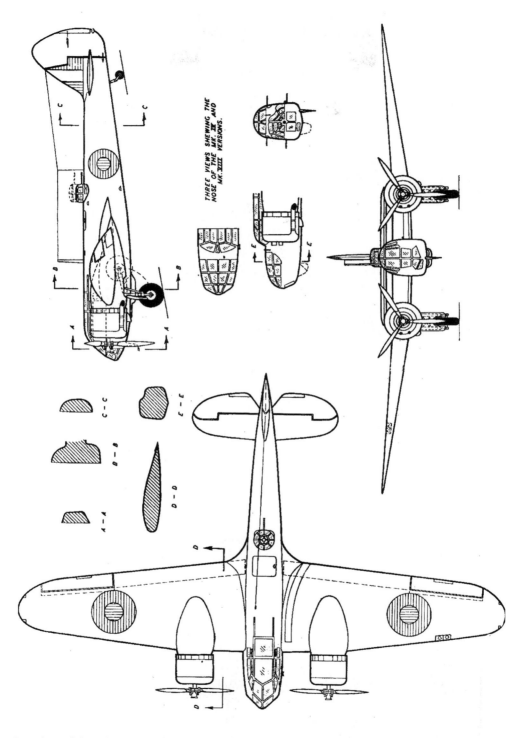

Drawings of the Bristol Blenheim, some of which were built at Meir's shadow factory during WW2.

the firm of £8,000 by designing an amphibious flying boat. The Supermarine monoplane will be flown by Captain C.H. Baird, who won the cup in 1922.'

This exceptional design, epitomising Mitchell's flair, was successful in winning the Schneider Trophy Races of the late 1920s and early 1930s and in setting a new World Air Speed Record for Great Britain.

The 'Schneider seaplanes' became the flying platform from which evolved the Supermarine Spitfire. With monocoque construction, revolutionary aerodynamics and its Rolls Royce Merlin engine, the Spitfire was a decisive element in tilting the balance in favour of the Royal Air Force during the Battle of Britain over southern England in 1940.

With Britain taking a prominent role throughout the early 1930s, allied to an upsurge of interest in aviation, many local authorities looked at involvement. Among their number was Stoke-on-Trent Corporation: 'Representatives of the National Flying Services arrived on Wednesday January 22nd to discuss with the City Surveyor's Department, who will survey 180 acres. The first planes should be using the aerodrome next spring.'

Discussions concerning the viability of Meir aerodrome continued during 1930. In early summer 1931, its proposers resorted to whatever means they had at their disposal to win over a sceptical public: *'An exhibition of gliding at Meir aerodrome has been given by Professor CH Lowe-Wylde and attracted visitors from as far away as Wrexham, Manchester and Nottingham.'*

The first airport in Staffordshire, Meir Aerodrome opened on May 18, 1934 with a basic small grass-landing strip, one hangar and a clubhouse. It was the HQ of the North Staffs Aero Club since 1925. In late January 1935, Mr G.B. Rogers, a vitriolic opponent of the aerodrome from the outset, declared the entire project had cost £29,180 plus other sundry expenditure of £2,632 10s 10d whilst the modest income was £243 16s 6d.

At any other time, the opponents might have won their case but did the bellicose warnings from Hitler's Germany, with the need for the country to have at its disposal the semblance of an airborne defence, sway the decision? Would it, in fact, have closed in 1935 had not the war intervened? What swiftly became apparent was that Stoke-on-Trent, then numbering a quarter of a million souls, should have its own airport or fall behind:

'The City of Stoke on Trent has gained control of the lease for £150 of Meir Aerodrome which was bought from National Flying Services. At a meeting of the council the future of the aerodrome was debated. "It was right that a city with a population of close to 300,000

should not be left out of the air ring," stated the Deputy Lord Mayor, Alderman A Hollins. Countering, Mr G.B. Rogers said he thought it should be converted to a building site, seeing the Corporation would have to spend from between £40,000- £50,000 before it could be made available for the purpose for which it was intended. Agreeing, Mr J Mooney added that he believed that somewhere about £32,000 had already been spent on the aerodrome.'

In the light of these developments, Reg Bishop, an employee at Meir aerodrome received a letter from the Town Clerk of Stoke on Trent. It read:

'Dear Sir, I have to inform you that at the last meeting of the Aerodrome Committee, it was decided that you be appointed for service at the Aerodrome for a probationary period of 6 months at 9/-a week. On being taken over by the Corporation, you will cease to be employed by North Staffs Airplanes Limited,   Yours faithfully,...'

Whilst politicians wrangled, more were finding access to the City Aerodrome, a gateway to and from Stoke-on-Trent, beneficial. The Potteries' own favourite swimmer, Norman Wainwright boarded a plane at Meir in October 1935 for his journey to Belfast, part of a service offered by Railway Air Services to Manchester and Birmingham from the Aerodrome. A celebrated visitor to the Meir during 1935, gave Alderman Hollins cause the veritable Royal Seal of approval to boot. *'Prince George arrived and left from Meir aerodrome on his tour of social service centres in Staffordshire.'*

But despite the to-ing and fro-ing at Meir, many remained unconvinced. The open wound within the city council over its fate, was polarising opinion.

'The proposed visit to the Stoke-on-Trent Municipal Airport at Meir of a squadron of the Royal Air Force on Empire Day (May 25th) was hotly debated by a meeting of the Stoke-on-Trent City Council on Thursday. The whole incident was not unanimous, because the RAF were proposing to bring their biggest bombers, bombs and machine guns - which did not meet with universal approval by the members.'

Arguments over permission for the RAF to visit Meir were not all negative. It did have its champions. Mr A.J. Hewitt spoke out and didn't mince his words: *'I have never heard so much bosh talked as I have in the last half hour. The country today owes everything to the Army, Navy and Air Force.'*

But the opponents won the day. The RAF's visit was cancelled. Even in defeat and as something of a 'two fingered gesture', a prophetic letter from the Secretary of the Air League of the British Empire reiterated *'an opportunity of strengthening the North Staffs Aero Club will have to be lost!'*

The aerodrome's supporters might have momentarily been put to flight but were some way from running up the white flag. The case to close Meir Aerodrome was weakened a few weeks later when another distinguished visitor disembarked at Meir. How Meir's supporters must have cheered. Close on the heels of his Royal Highness, Prince George, the Prime Minister of the Dominion of Australia. the Right Hon. J.A. Lyons and his wife landed at the airport in May 1935, fulfilling a promise to open a garden party for St Gregory's RC church, Longton, in Longton Town Hall. Travelling from London by air they were met on arrival at Meir aerodrome by Lord Mayor, Alderman A.C. Harvey. Afterwards the couple were presented with a tea service at a luncheon in Stoke Town Hall by the

Corporation. Mr Lyons, warmly applauded by Deputy Lord Mayor Alderman A Hollins, Sir Francis Joseph CBE, Alderman C Austin chairman of the Aerodrome Committee and others present, *'expressed his great delight of becoming possessed of British pottery, famed throughout the world,'* highlighting the need for greater trading links between Australia and the Mother country. Hear hear!

The case for Meir Aerodrome, now in the ascendance, was bolstered in August when, 'local dignitaries' Mr Harry Taylor, the Town Clerk and Miss F Farmer became the first passengers from Meir to London, when a Railway Services de Havilland Dragon Rapide touched down on its way south from Scotland. These aircraft landed at Meir at 11.50 for Manchester, Liverpool, Belfast and Glasgow after the stationmaster at Meir LMS station had contacted the pilot by short wave radio, as he flew over Tunstall. If passengers were waiting, a member of the LMS station staff, Arthur Rogers, crossed Uttoxeter Road to the airport and *'weighed them in.'* To supplement this, a rail link for those journeying to the continent was also available while at Manchester, the service also connected with the Manx Airway Section of Railway Air Services. The fare for the London to Isle of Man route was set at £ 4. 1s. whilst from the same departure point, the journey north of the Border to Glasgow was £6.11s.

In fairness, not all arrived and departed with such grace and elegance. Aircraft were notoriously unreliable, mishaps uncomfortably common. Viscountess Ednam of the Harrowby dynasty was to forfeit her life in a plane crash. Most of those whose fell to earth did so accompanied by the strains of rending metal, tearing fabric and broken bones:

'An aeroplane crash which had fatal consequences occurred at the Stoke-on-Trent Municipal Aerodrome, at Meir on Sunday afternoon when a 90 hp Miles Hawk piloted by Miss Dorothy Clive, the daughter of Col.and Mrs Harry Clive of Willoughbridge, Pipe Gate, who had with her as passenger her cousin, Mr Roger David Clive aged 21, of Hyde Park Street London, struck a tree and was wrecked. Miss Clive suffered from minor injuries and severe shock but unhappily, her passenger sustained very severe injuries to which he succumbed on Monday morning at the Longton Cottage Hospital. Miss Clive who was a qualified pilot and experienced airwoman was flying in the vicinity of the aerodrome when she was overtaken by the severe snowstorm which North Staffordshire experienced on Sunday afternoon. She tried to make a landing but falling snow made visibility limited and added to this the wind changed suddenly while her goggles were blurred with snow. Finding it impossible to make a safe landing, she decided to rise again and keep above the storm but the aeroplane struck a high tree about 200 yards from the aerodrome boundary. As the aeroplane fell to the ground, Miss Clive was thrown clear.'

But there were many happier times. Mrs Harrison of Maer Hall was often flown from Meir aerodrome to the Races in an aircraft owned by Major Anson. And in 1938 a DH Rapide registration G-AEWR landed outside the hangar on whose roof the legend announced, City Aerodrome. The arrival of Christmas meant, for children, toys and presents and of course Father Christmas. Given that many in the City council thought little of Meir's aerodrome, the news that Santa Claus was only too happy to use it when he arrived in Stoke-on-Trent must have been infuriating. Bah humbug! *'Father Christmas Comes by Air'* the advertisement said, *'Arrives at Meir by aeroplane - 10.20 am.'*

But as war approached more serious times lay ahead. Reg Bishop, an apprentice aircraft engineer, often flew from Meir, even when he would rather have not done so. After repairing an aircraft Reg would be 'invited' by the pilot to join him on board. Twice weekly, for 6 months they flew a triangular route in a Miles Magister from Meir to Trentham and Newcastle to give novice searchlight crews some practice.

Meir aerodrome played host to more famous visitors. One was Amy Johnson. Born in Hull, England in 1903, the year of the Wright Brothers first flight, she graduated from Sheffield University with a Bachelor of Arts degree in the mid 1920s. Leaving Yorkshire to work as a secretary to a London solicitor, she learned to fly at the London Aeroplane Club in the winter of 1928-29. A passionate believer that *'women were just as competent as men'* she illustrated her dictat by pursuing a career in aviation and demonstrating her prowess in what was still a male dominated preserve.

Amy Johnson

Following an agreement between Lord Wakefield and Amy's father, each stumped up £300 for a secondhand de Havilland Gypsy Moth (G-AAAH) she named Jason. On May 5, 1930, Amy set off alone on her epic 11,000 mile flight from Croydon, near London landing 19 days later in Darwin, in the Northern Territories of Australia, beating the record previously held by Bert Hinkler. Imbued by her success, in July 1931, piloting a de Havilland Puss Moth with Jack Humphreys, she flew from England to Japan in record time - the first occasion any pilot had reached Moscow from London in one day. Her achievements seemed endless. July 1932 saw her fly from England to Capetown, cutting the flight time by over 10 hours, setting another solo record in her Puss Moth 'Desert Cloud'. During 1933, accompanied by husband Jim Mollison, she flew her de Havilland Dragon non-stop from Pendine Sands, Wales, to the United States, followed in 1934 by another non-stop record to India in a de Havilland Comet Racer during the England to Australia MacRoberston Air Race. In 1936, her last long distance flight, she reprised her previous London-Capetown journey four years earlier in a Percival Mew Gull, in a faster time.

With war declared in 1939 her commercial flying career ended. Amy Johnson joined the Air Transport Auxiliary, a group of pilots who delivered or 'ferried' aircraft from 'shadow factories' like that at Meir, to RAF bases. Bill Rushton, then the landlord of the Station Hotel in Meir often had Amy and Jim Mollison stay as paying guests overnight. Both Amy and her former husband Jim Mollison - they were divorced in 1938 - flew aircraft as 'ferry pilots' out of Meir.

Tragically Amy Johnson died while ferrying aircraft on January 5, 1941, crashing into the Thames estuary. But her fortitude, ability and personality will always ensure the vivid memories of her pioneering long distance flights will live long in aviation lore.

Running counter to the business side of aviation was a sporting aspect where men and women in their tiny machines diced with the all too real prospect of sudden death. Autumn 1937 saw just such an event as the Meir, elevated to celebrity status, became a turning point in an air race. Meir, where was it? Readers the length and breadth of the country as one, pawed over countless maps to pinpoint this almost unheard of town as the news broke.

'It has been announced that Meir airport is to be the "turning point" in the King's Cup Air Race to take place on Friday and Saturday, 10th and 11th September 1937. The North Staffs Aero Club were anxious for Meir to assume importance as a control point. In the Coronation year, the Royal Aero Club had decided the race shall take the form of a circuit of Britain. Taking off from Hatfield, Herts, turning at Cambridge, Skegness, York, Scarborough and Whitby via Newcastle-on-Tyne to Aberdeen, the course then lies south west over Perthshire to the Glasgow control and from then on to Newtonards in Northern Ireland, finishing at Phoenix Park Dublin, where they will spend the night. Those who succeed this 780 mile eliminating contest, will leave Dublin the next day to Newtonards and fly round a "turning point" at Carlisle, St Bees Head and then Stanley Park Aerodrome, Blackpool. The machines will pass over "MEIR", another "turning point" 369 miles along the course from Dublin. The next "turning point" will be Leicester and then on to Cardiff before crossing the line at Hatfield.'

But the threat to life and liberty from rapidly moving political events in Germany and Europe had already rung alarm bells in London. No 28 Elementary and Reserve Training School, operational at Meir aerodrome from 1938 taught pupils the rudimentary principles of flight. Using the outdated de Havilland Tiger Moth and Hawker Hart, dinosaur biplanes from another age, the country's air defences were on a rapid learning curve. In February 1939 the Air Ministry, never without its critics, responded decisively about new plans in store for Meir. Colonel P Birch made the *'Royal Air Force Volunteer Reserve stationed at Meir Aerodrome'* the subject of his address to the well fed ranks of the Stoke-on-Trent Rotary Club.

'The total establishment of the school at Meir would be about 213 and present requirements were for another 70 pilots, 37 observers and 75 wireless operators. Recruiting for the Ground Section had not yet begun. He dealt with the training of entrants and said 'after each satisfactory year of service' a pilot received a training fee of £25; in other sections the fee was £20. Recruits he said were being drawn from Cheshire, Staffordshire and Shropshire. In the event of war, recruits would not be sent to fight at once. They would be assessed and be sent as occasion demanded, to advanced service training schools.'

Empire Day, later in 1939, appeared increasingly more relevant. It was to the Royal Air Force - in its 21st year and coming of age - that many now looked to as their hope of salvation. Detractors of the RAF's peacetime visits to Meir aerodrome during past years suddenly became strangely silent: 'The admission to the Empire Day Display on May 20th 1939 would be 1 shilling for adults and 3d for children. There would be 78 aerodromes in the UK including 63 RAF stations, 11 civil aerodromes, whose personnel are being trained by the Royal Air Force, the Auxiliary Air Force and the Royal Air Force Volunteer Reserve.'

With war declared, the gloves were off and well formulated plans for Meir aerodrome were put into immediate effect. One minute after Britain's declaration, a Bristol Blenheim IV of 139 Squadron flew the first of the RAF's many wartime sorties, a photo reconnaissance mission. The following day, based on that information, RAF Bomber Command attacked enemy warships. The Bristol Blenheim from 139 Squadron, would be just one of several aircraft types made and assembled at Meir during the next 6 years from within its 'shadow factory'.

When, in 1940, Winston Churchill became leader of the coalition wartime government, one of his first appointments was the enigmatic Canadian, William Aitken, Lord Beaverbrook. His position, as Minister for Aircraft Production, was not by all accounts a popular one, particularly with the Air Ministry 'top brass'. Fighter and Bomber Commands often complained bitterly that Beaverbrook leaned towards increasing fighter production at the expense of bombers, which were then thought of as 'attack aircraft'. But the underlying principle behind Beaverbrook's strategy was sound. Mobilisation of a credible defence force of fighter aircraft, ensured bomber production scattered over many sites, could continue with little or no disruption. It proved to be a revelation.

The 'shadow factories' concept was not new, their formation due to Wilfrid Freeman. Formerly Commanding officer 10th Army Wing of the Royal Flying Corps during the First World War, the genial Freeman also championed the, as then unproven, Chain Home Radar System, strengthening the odds of the RAF winning the Battle of Britain. Freeman's groundwork during the immediate pre-war years creating alternative or 'shadow factories' now bore fruit. But despite every endeavour, their production record was abysmal; by the summer of 1940, the Spitfire 'shadow factory' at Castle Bromwich Birmingham had not turned out a single aircraft! Beaverbrook instructed Vickers Supermarine, manufacturers of the Spitfire, 'to take over the Castle Bromwich factory from the Nuffield Organisation' and *'jolly things along'*. He turned next to the United States. Not content with upsetting the apple cart at home, he sought out the automotive moguls to boost war production.

Henry Ford was approached with a view to building Rolls Royce Merlin engines needed for the Spitfire, under licence, something he refused point blank. *'Britain had enough automotive manufacturers to construct the damn engines themselves.'* Beaverbrook pressed on undaunted and achieved a breakthrough when Packard agreed to build the Merlin engines in America, but only after a promise of a generous purse to enlarge the factory.

The 'ferry system' of delivering aircraft during the Second World War was another of Beaverbrook's suggestions. Aircraft, built in Canada, far from Hitler's Luftwaffe, were flown across the Atlantic to Britain. Typically it was set 'in train' without any cabinet approval, over which Churchill and Beaverbrook had a 'few quiet words'. Until March 1941, only one 'ferry' aircraft was lost out of 160 aircraft; by any stretch of the imagination Beaverbrook had put his critics to flight.

The Meir 'shadow factory', a small but vital cog in a much larger scheme of things was built under government instructions at Blythe Bridge and Meir. A taxiway, later added to the main airfield at Meir plus a short runway, enabled ground crews to iron out aircraft technical problems preceding their despatch. Work at Meir started in December 1941 on the Bristol Blenheim, its production having been transferred from the Rootes factory at Speke,

Women pilots in the Civil Air Guard who became part of the Air Transport Auxiliary Services.

Liverpool. The Speke factory turned its attention to manufacturing the Halifax bomber, a superb aircraft viewed by many RAF and Allied aircrew as a *'very solid aeroplane'*.

Like several aircraft of that era, the Bristol type 142 derived from a private design, flying in 1935. Over 150 aircraft were ordered straight from the drawing board, the first prototype Blenheim lifting off in June 1936. Although 1130 Mk I Blenheims were built, with a top speed of only 266 mph they were always too slow to fend off enemy fighters. Some were used as night fighters and on reconnaissance and long range fighter missions.

Development of the Blenheim was so rapid that by 1939 virtually all the RAF's Mk I models in service had been superseded by the superior Mk.IV Blenheim. Offering greater pilot visibility and better crew comfort, it also carried improved armour plating against fighter and flak damage. In the absence of an alternative, and suffering high losses, RAF Bomber Command had little option but using it during 1940/1 in daylight operations as its standard light bomber. In addition to those built at Meir, over 4,400 were also constructed by Fairchild Aviation in Canada. These, known as the Bolingbrokes, were used on Atlantic and Pacific coast reconnaissance.

The Blenheim Mk IV carried a crew of three. With a wing span of 56 feet and 40 feet long it could carry four 250 lb bombs 1,900 miles at an operational ceiling of 32,000 feet. In the Far East, Middle east and North Africa they saw service with 771, 780, 772 and 787 squadrons, having the distinction of being the aircraft in which airborne radar was pioneered.

The Bristol Beaufighter was another famous wartime aircraft manufactured in Meir. The Type 156 Beaufighter first flew in July 1939. Because of the RAF's need for a long range fighter and lack of time, the Beaufighter was largely constructed using the wings, rear fuselage and tail already proven in the Bristol Beaufort. Conceived by Leslie Frise of Bristol Aviation, the Mk 1F joined 25 Squadron in September 1940. The winter of 1940-41 saw it used as a long range strike aircraft by Coastal Command and a night fighter; the radar equipped versions took a heavy toll of enemy night bombers. When production ceased in 1945 over 5,500 Beaufighters had been built, 260 from the production lines at Meir.

With 2 aircrew, the Beaufighter V and its variants had a top speed of 330 mph and ceiling of 29,000 feet, it was a fearsome adversary with an awesome array of firepower. Four 20 mm cannons in the aircraft's belly and 6 x.303 Browning machine guns in the wings were augmented by 8 x 3" rockets AND either a 1,600lb torpedo OR a 1,000 lb bomb load. Flown by the Royal Australian Air Force in the Pacific it was nicknamed "whispering death" by the Japanese, because of its almost noiseless Bristol Hercules engines . Incredibly the Bristol Beaufighter carried on flying in service until the early 1960s.

As well as the Blenheim and Beaufighter, over 2,100 Havards and Mustangs, shipped in kit form from the United States, were assembled in Meir. But perhaps the largest aircraft ever to grace the runways at Meir was not produced at Meir. The Consolidated Liberator was by any stretch of the imagination an enormous bomber, twice the wingspan of the Mk IV Blenheim. Many might credibly argue that it could never have landed at Meir. It did. Several airfields in Staffordshire were photographed extensively, and one set from August 1945 shows Meir Aerodrome. Under magnification, the large four engine bombers, Liberators, can be seen parked just off the main runway. Flown in to Meir usually with just one 'ferry pilot' aboard they landed 'uphill' for obvious reasons.

According to Eric Clutton, the Liberators were *'ex Coastal Command, presumably from St Eval in Cornwall.'* After converting to freighters *'they were flown to Lichfield where they were carefully looked after - until they were scrapped!'*

Over 18,000, Consolidated Liberator or B-24 bombers were built during its lifetime, more than the other famous and perhaps more widely known US Bomber, the B-17 Flying Fortress. Flying first in December 1939, Liberators were ordered by the United Kingdom and France to address glaring shortages in their own air forces. When France fell to the German advance, Liberators on order were diverted to the UK for use ostensibly for coastal command reconnaissance patrol aircraft, because of their enormous flying range. Built in the United States at Fort Worth, Dallas, Tulsa, San Diego and Willow Run, Liberator production, starting in 1939, ceased with the 'M' variant as 'VE' day passed. Such was its reliability Winston Churchill's private war time transport aircraft was often a Liberator.

Although heavily armed, early raids over Europe due to lack of a credible fighter escort led to huge losses. In August 1943, 59 were shot down over the German ball bearing factory at Schweinfurt followed by a similar loss later in October. Later, with long-range fighter escort in 1944, Liberators and B-17s pounded Berlin in the first daytime raids, carrying the war into the enemy's backyard. Unhappily the Liberator was the aircraft flown by the son of Joseph Kennedy Senior, Joe Jr, which, while on active service in 1944, blew up killing the entire crew, a tragedy that opened the way, ultimately, for John F Kennedy to become the 35th US President in 1960.

At almost 70 feet long with a wing span of 110 feet, Liberators dropped 650,000 tons of bombs during the Second World War while thousands of enemy fighters fell victim to its guns. Although capable of a possible 300 mph, operational cruising speed was 215 mph, enabled the Liberator to carry an 8,800 pound bomb load 3,700 miles. Probably very few recall B24 Liberators landing at Meir aerodrome in 1945 but seeing one of these giant aircraft touch down must have been breathtaking.

Although the Luftwaffe knew of Meir aerodrome, as a map of the time showed, it was never bombed and Meir's 'shadow factory', employing over 5000 people at its height, produced an uninterrupted supply of essential war materials until 1945; due to careful planning and a committed work force of local Meir people.

No 1 Flying Practice School, early in the War, and later No 5 Elementary Flying Training School based at Meir aerodrome, were created primarily to polish the skills of allied pilots before being pitched into aerial combat. As such, the schools were equipped with the RAF's main training aircraft, the Miles Magister, where student and instructor sat in tandem. Many Canadian pilots flew in Magister, known as the 'Maggies', while training. One from many of the aircrew stationed at Meir, ultimately received the Distinguished Flying Cross (DFC) for his bravery. Born in Ottawa, Canada on September 14, 1915, Alfred Keith Ogilvie, nicknamed Skeets, signed on for a Short Service Commission on 11 August 1939 in the Royal Air Force (RAF) after unsuccessfully trying to enlist in the Royal Canadian Air Force (RCAF). After training courses at Hatfield and Hullavington he was posted to No 1 Flying Practice Unit, Meir on May 1, 1940. .

Flying Officer Keith Ogilvie, later Flt Lt RAF. This Canadian pilot was a Battle of Britain ace and then an internee of the infamous Stalag Luft 3 prison camp.
Courtesy Ottawa Citizen

September in the same year saw him in action over the capital. After a German Dornier Do 17 of the Luftwaffe bombed Buckingham Palace, P/O Keith Ogilvie 'finished him off', sending the stricken aircraft crashing into Victoria railway Station, London. Queen Wilhelmina of the Netherlands, in exile in London, had seen the entire episode. Her aide, on her behalf, wrote to the Air Ministry asking the identity of the pilot of the British aircraft. The letter said, *"I am commanded by Her Majesty Queen Wilhelmina of the Netherlands to convey to you Her Majesty was most gratified to see from her London house a German bomber shot down by an 8 gun fighter during the air battle on the morning of 15th September. Her Majesty would be pleased if her congratulations could be conveyed to the squadron concerned in this battle and to the pilot who shot down the German aircraft."* Signed Major General de Jenge Van Ellemeet, September 18th 1940.

P/O Keith Ogilvie's actions resulted in his receiving this 'letter of thanks' from Queen Wilhelmina. It remains in safe-keeping, a poignant memory of his consummate skill and gallantry during those desperate days. He *'shared the Dornier kill'* with another aircraft.

A few months later saw him in action on July 4th, 1941 escorting 12 Blenheims - of the type made at Meir's shadow factory - attacking the Kuhlman chemical works and power station at Chocques when his aircraft was damaged by a Me 109. Wounded, in the arm and shoulder, he baled out, landing in a field.

His personal account of the incident reads:

'About noon on July 4th we took off in absolute silence as close escort to the bombers

doing Lille, Sailor Malan leading the Wing, Michael Robinson our Squadron, Paul Richey leading the flight, I the other. Over North Foreland the bombers crawled in beneath us and wings of the fighters formed up ahead, behind and on either side - an inspiring spectacle, and I never lost the thrill of being a part of the show. Far below we could see the white streaks as the air-sea rescue launches put out from Dover and Ramsgate. On crossing the Channel and progressing inland we were greeted by 'ack-ack', first at Dunkirk, then St. Omer. Away to the side tiny specks represented the wary Hun climbing so as to be above and behind us when we turned down-sun for home... We had already started when about fifteen 109s floated over us, breaking up into fours, then pairs.

A pair came down to attack the bombers and I had turned in to attack them when there was one hell of a "pow" and I was smacked into the dashboard, my port aileron floated away and a great rib appeared up my wing... There was blood all over and I felt sick, so I blew my hood off and turned the oxygen full on to keep awake. If I could reach the Channel I'd bale out, because I could not land the kite as it was. But I must have passed out because suddenly everything was quiet and through a haze I could see my prop sticking straight up, and smoke coming from under my cowling. I figured, "this is where I leave", and let go of the stick..... Sometime later I came to in a field, surrounded by sympathetic Frenchies who tried to get me up and away, but I could not make it. I had been hit twice in the arm, once in the shoulder, and had lost too much blood. A little while later a sad-eyed German "sanitar" informed me, " For you the war is over" - and he was not kidding.'

Ogilvie was in hospital in Lille and Brussels for nine months before being sent to Stalag Luft III, Sagan. Ironically he had been due for some well earned leave a few days after his capture, having flown on every operation since June. He now had an extensive leave, unfortunately as a guest of the Germans. The boys at '609' did not know of his fate until Lord Haw-Haw broadcast the fact on July 4. The Germans regarded F/O Ogilvie as quite a catch.

After his enforced hospital stay - *'The Jerry docs fixed my arm up really well, though I can still tell when rain is in the offing'* - he eventually reached the notorious RAF camp, Stalag Luft III. It was during his captivity here that he was awarded the Distinguished Flying Cross on July 11, 1941 with the following citation appearing in the London Gazette.

'This officer has displayed great keenness and determination in his efforts to seek and destroy the enemy. He has shot down at least five hostile aircraft.'

He was promoted Flight Lieutenant on May 25 1942.

Chosen as one of 74 prisoners to take part in the 'Great Escape' under the leadership of Roger Bushell, Ogilvie was the last to get free of the tunnel before it was discovered. Captured two days later he was sent to a Gestapo prison at Gorlitz, Czechoslovakia. During repeated interrogations he said *'I stuck to my story that I was a career officer. This must have registered with the Teutonic mind, because I was one of eight returned to camp - the others, as you know, were shot.'*

The murder by the Gestapo of 50 British and American Officers, prisoners of war, breached the Geneva Convention and horrified not only those in this country but also the officers and men of the Luftwaffe. After the war those responsible were brought to trial; 13

were hanged at Hamelin jail, Hamburg in 1948 by the British executioner Albert Pierrepoint.

But how did Squadron Leader Keith Ogilvie, as he later became, get the nickname Skeets? It is a mystery even to his widow, Irene. She said *'Keith didn't know for sure how or when it all started but all his men had called him Skeets for a very long time.'* What did he feel about the movie, *The Great Escape*? *'One thing he pointed out was that there were no Americans involved at all in the real escape from Stalag Luft 3, but the details of how the fake documents, paper and official looking rubber stamps and inks were made were very accurate.'*

In 1963 the saga was made into a movie, The Great Escape, directed and produced by John Sturgess. Steve McQueen's motor-cycling exploits have since passed into movie history. But although 'Skeets' Ogilvie's story is true, events told in the movie were subject to 'artistic licence'. The Ottawa Citizen of March 21, 2004 printed *'The Real Story of The Great Escape'* to set the record straight. This edited version is reproduced by kind permission of the editor:

They called it 'The Great Escape' as well they might. It was one of the best of half dozen or so of those Second World War epics that 'carved the River Kwai bridge, George Patton and Private Ryan into the soul of a generation. But somewhere along the

Steve McQueen in the film of *The Great Escape*.

scripting they usually skipped over the Canadian content. So forget Steve McQueen and his stolen German motorbike; forget Charles Bronson, Richard Attenborough, James Garner, James Coburn and Donald Pleasance. They made a heck of a movie but the real life version, featuring a bunch of Canadian boys from places like Spearhill, Manitoba and Kirkland Lake Ontario is a pretty good yarn in itself.

The story of the virtually unknown Canadian heroes of the extraordinary events - at the German PoW camp Stalag Luft 3 is told with the 60th anniversary showing of The Great Escape. The sheer bravado and ingenuity of tunnelling out of a German camp on the Polish border - 10 metres underground and 120 metres long -- make it almost an epic engineering feat, given the circumstances. But what the movie completely ignored was the huge role Canadians played in the daring exploit. 'It's yet another story appropriated by the Americans,' says Ottawa film maker Don Young. It's happened before and it'll happen again, but it's important to set the record straight while there are few of the guys who remembered those days still around. If you watch the movie, you're given the impression that it was mostly Americans who dug the tunnels out of Stalag Luft 3. In truth, it was populated by Brits, South Africans and Canadians. In fact there was only one American in the camp, a guy called George Harsh, who was flying with the RCAF.'

The driving force behind the escape was Roger Bushell, the 'Richard Attenborough' character in the movie, who arrived at the camp with a long reputation for escapes and a burning hatred of the Nazis. He organized 600 detainees digging the three tunnels for a full year right under the noses of the. German guards. The man who did the engineering - Charles Bronson in the movie - was Toronto born, Ottawa Valley-bred, Wally Floody, a mining engineer in Sudbury before the war. In a bizarre twist of fate, he was transferred just before the breakout and so escaped the fate of most of the escapees. Henry 'Big Train' Birkland, 'a Canadian prairie boy who mined gold, busted broncos and played lacrosse before the war and spent his days as a Spitfire pilot, shared the digging duties with Mr Floody.

And it was Keith 'Skeets' Ogilvie from Ottawa who stole the wallet from a hapless German guard named Werner, providing invaluable originals for the prisoners' document forgers and was the last person out of the tunnel on the night of the escape '

Fifty escapees were shot on Hitler's direct orders, including six Canadians who were selected for execution by top SS investigator Arthur Nebe. Of the nine Canadians who squirmed through the tunnel to short lived freedom, only three survived - Alfred 'Tommy' Thompson, William Cameron and Keith Ogilvie.

Flight Lieutenant Ogilvie returned to duty with the Royal Canadian Air Force, retiring on September 14, 1962. The woman later to be his wife, Irene was resident in England from 1934 to 1946, the last 10 years spent in London. A photographer in the WD (Women's Division) of the Royal Canadian Air Force she first met Keith in London in 1940. They met several times during the war but only tied the knot in 1946 on returning to Canada, remaining together until his death 52 years later.

He is fondly remembered by one of the men he later commanded in the RCAF, Peter Sutherland of Ottawa, Ontario: *'I did know Skeets, as he served at RCAF Downsview whilst I was on squadron. He was Operations Officer. RCAF Downsview was a normal airforce base with an airfield and one permanent force squadron, 436 Transport and two reserve force flying squadrons, 400 and 401, and numerous other units. It was housed just north of Toronto. I attended his retirement party and I believe he did retire here in Ottawa.'*

After his death in 1998 Keith Ogilvie was cremated and his ashes scattered at RAF Biggin Hill, Kent, England, in the yellow rose garden by the chapel, and at a new cemetery in Ottawa, Canada. As is typical of so many combatants, his wife says he was always reticent about his war time contribution *'although he revealed more to local school children when they rang him up'* when pursuing school history projects.

With the end of the war, one problem out of many confronting the Board of Trade was to find a peace time use for all of its 20 former 'shadow factories' like the one in Meir. These government factories released for civilian use would give a total available floor space approaching nearly 20 million square feet, employing 200,000 nationwide.

In August 1945 plans for Meir had been drafted. The main thrust was to be directed in making colliery equipment and refrigerators. After the devastation caused by bombing, many factories in cities were either non-existent or in pretty poor shape. Meir's 'shadow factory' had escaped to produce something tangible, whilst giving work to over 2,000 local people.

Although as Eric Clutton says, around this time *'Meir was dead'*, Staffordshire Gliding Club, then using a Tiger Moth as a towing aircraft, operated out of Meir along with 632 Squadron Air Training Corps. This ATC connection with Meir aerodrome continued for another 20 years with 1037 squadron ATC training cadets training in the rudiments of flight, meteorology and marksmanship.

Throughout the austere 1950s, Meir aerodrome was still used for flying by local businesses. One, Staffordshire Potteries - with a factory close by - had a de Havilland Dove to fly their managers whenever needed. The City Corporation granted Dragon Airways of Liverpool a licence in 1955 to fly a regular service to the Isle of Man, re-inventing a route flown by Railway Air Services in the 1930s. But the Dragon Airways service closed a year later due to the worsening condition of the runway.

Concurrent with commercial interests, amateur private pilots still used the aerodrome flying small single engine aircraft. Fred Holdcroft, a local Staffordshire businessman was one. Another, Eric Clutton, constructed his own aircraft 'Fred', towing it in a trailer behind his car before launching it and himself into the *'wide blue yonder.'* Incredibly 'Fred' still flies today in the blue skies over Tennessee in the United States.

Gliders continued at Meir aerodrome into the 1970s. It was a common sight to see the pilot at the controls, silently skimming over the roof tops before crossing Sandon Road, Meir and returning to the sanctuary of the airfield.

Now itself in 'free fall' the airfield resumed its downward spiral until it closed. The gliding fraternity left, moving to a site outside Leek to continue their hobby, never to return.

The Air Training Corps, 1037 Squadron, based on Meir Aerodrome, relocated to new premises at the TA Centre site, Uttoxeter Road, next door to the Broadway. Deteriorating conditions inside the old RAF huts had made use impractical; rain water percolated through the roof and the electrical wiring was positively lethal. The ATC detachment - now renumbered 239 squadron - quickly settled into surroundings that were dry, warm and comfortable and less vulnerable to vandalism. Following many false dawns, the new HQ opened by Mr E.M. Breeze, promised a fresh start. Unhappily it proved too optimistic. A newly installed Stephenson Screen weather station within the 'secure perimeter', purchased with funds donated by a local committee, was wrecked by hooligans. In despair it was removed.

The Territorial Army site at Meir continued in use until 1994/5 before it was compulsorily purchased and demolished for the A50 improvements. The TA and ATC detachments left Meir - its logical and historical home for over 60 years and re-established in new £2m headquarters at Adderley Green, a mile away.

The perennial question whether Meir aerodrome could have been commercially feasible has been discussed ad nauseam. With an enormous population living a short distance of the airfield, customers would not have been a problem. Paignton airport, Devon, far smaller than Meir, operates a regular schedule from its tiny airfield. Withybush near Haverfordwest, West Wales is another good example of 'small is beautiful'. Meir could have been in the same league; commercial aircraft flying today land in far shorter distances than the cumbersome Liberators of the 1940s. The benefits for Stoke-on-Trent would have been enormous. Had it survived it would have put paid to bleary-eyed journeys at the crack of dawn to Manchester or Birmingham for that bargain holiday flight.

Meir, like the City itself seems destined to adopt the role of a 'might have been'. With more municipal foresight, less intransigence and rivalry, Stoke-on-Trent would have been well placed to play a part in the country's air network.

Now in 2004, with car use booming and railway journey times greater than a coach and four, the case of Meir aerodrome would have been strong. Commercial manufacturing concerns, relocated to the airfield site in the 1960s and 1970s have already been demolished in 2004, leaving piles of rubble and an eerie reminder of the 1930s.

But retail outlets have prospered on the airfield site; B&Q and Tesco with Aldi in April 2004. Are Meir Aerodrome's rolling acres destined to be just another anodyne retail park? Thoughtfully, two enterprises have given a 'tip of the hat' to Meir's former airfield. B&Q have a brass plaque indicating the site was a wartime airfield while Tesco have incorporated an aircraft on their weather vane above the store - a reminder of past glories and what might have been. In 2003 the BP petrol station in Uttoxeter Road opposite the old airfield was still referred to as the Airport filling station on a sign, but with a recent upgrade sadly that has now gone.

Arguments rage as to whether Stoke-on-Trent could have had its own airport at Meir. The recent development of Coventry airport is a lesson that proves a point. Has the failure of the 'City Aerodrome' at Meir doomed Stoke-on-Trent to be an also-ran in the transport league?

Amy Johnson and Jim Mollison, two
of the celebrities of the air travel
romance of the 1920s and 1930s
that Meir shared in.

Meir town centre crossroads and the Broadway cinema seen from the Uttoxeter Road looking west.
The cinema dominated the centre from 1936 to 1973.

Probably taken in the late 1940s/early1950s, the Broadway cinema, with the traffic island on the right,
at a strangely deserted Meir crossroads, with Holy Trinity church in the background.

THE BROADWAY AT MEIR
THE POTTERIES FAVOURITE CINEMA

Of all Potteries cinemas, perhaps none is as well-known or loved as the former Broadway at Meir, its construction heralding in a new age in cinema entertainment.

In the late 1920s the invention of the 'talkies' - movies with sound - led to an explosion of picture houses or cinemas. The popularity of music halls - vaudeville - waned almost at the same rate as movies gained overall acceptance. The outcome was inevitable. Old music halls, however unsuitable, were quickly and often tastelessly converted to show the new 'talking pictures'. On close inspection evidence of this metamorphosis showed through hastily applied paint. The age of towering ceilings, swags of fruit and cherubs adorning auditorium walls and cavernous opera style boxes was no more, their time gone forever

One local former 'live' theatre later converted to a cinema, and a brisk walk from the Meir was the Empire at Longton. As the Queen's Theatre and built in 1888 for £8,000, it was redecorated and reupholstered in 1890 at a cost of £4,000, only to be reduced to ashes in a calamitous fire in September 1894. Its rebirth 2 years later saddled its unfortunate owners with debts of £17,000. As long ago as January 1897, residents from the Meir, then a tiny rural community, walked to Longton to see many of their perennial favourites at this popular venue: *'The Queen's Theatre: Cinderella was performed and produced by Messrs Hardie and Van Leer Company. The 'Theatrograph', an exhibition of annotated pictures, is a great attraction.' 'The pantomime at the 'Queen's Theatre' was 'Sir Richard Whittington and his cat' which is produced by Messrs George B Philips and Company'.*

It was closed through 1917 to reopen on Christmas Eve with an appreciative audience seated in a sumptuously appointed blue and gold auditorium: The Empire Theatre has been acquired by Mr Leon Salberg of the Alexandra Theatre, Birmingham. The present theatre, formerly known as the Queen's Theatre, was built following a disastrous fire which destroyed an earlier building in 1894. It was designed by Mr Frank Matcham, a leading theatrical architect of the day and built by Mr Peter Bennion at a cost of about £20,000. The original opening took place on the 18th May 1896, when Miss Fortescue a popular actress of the time supported by a powerful company appeared in Pygmalion and Galatea by the late WS Gilbert.

But the advent of moving pictures and sound forced a change to its lifestyle. Amongst the new facilities that came to Meir in the 1930s was the popular cinema, the Broadway. Such was its fame, the junction of Uttoxeter Road and Sandon Road, on which this period picture house stood, was and still is referred to as Broadway by locals and visitors alike.

During October 1935, proposals for a purpose-built local cinema in Meir reached the newspapers. As yet unnamed, it would incorporate all the 'cutting edge' technology. It was a safe bet that nobody would shed a tear for the demise of tiring bus rides from Meir to visit other cinemas in an evening. The Evening Sentinel carried the official announcement. Cliff Perrin, husband of Dot Clewlow, the daughter of Herbert Clewlow, one of the founders, recalls it well. Given that huge amount of competition already in Stoke-on-Trent, building a new 'picture theatre' was a huge financial risk for all concerned costing £ 26,000. The relief a year later, in 1936, when the Broadway finally threw open its doors, must have been immense.

Proudly proclaiming *'NEW CINEMA ENTERPRISE AT MEIR'* it went on: *'The Broadway is to seat over a thousand people'*. Its actual capacity exceeded that figure and was close to eleven hundred. The newspaper continuing with its fulsome praise including an allusion to the fact the Broadway was close to the City Aerodrome at Meir.

A composite picture from the Commemorative Programme for the opening of the Broadway in 1936.

One of the numerous unusual features at the Broadway, its cafe and lounge, meant cinema patrons could buy anything from a cup of coffee to a full meal before or after the show, something the older converted theatres could not hope to match. Many patrons recount fondly sipping Earl Grey tea whilst gazing through the 3 large first floor windows towards the City Aerodrome down the road.

Although few owned a car in the 1930s, in a move typical of the management's foresight, those with cars leaving the warmth and comfort of the Broadway on a wet and windswept night didn't have to go far. To minimise their 'discomfort', a large car park at the rear of the cinema had been built and with an eye to the future, a proposal was made to build a large garage on the opposite corner of Meir crossroads, near the new King's Arms Hotel so that *'a full service would be at the disposal of patrons.'*

The cinema achieved prominence for its chrome plated fittings and zig-zag Art Deco design. It also became famous, or notorious, for its unique 'double seats' in the auditorium. One bleary-eyed patron recounted, *'For many, it was the beginning of the permissive society'*. The souvenir programme from that opening night, now a treasured possession, reveals details about every nut and bolt:

The development of Meir as a "bedroom" suburb of Stoke-on-Trent, particularly of Longton, has proceeded rapidly and large scale housing both by the Corporation and by private enterprise has resulted in a satellite town springing up.

The new population, forsaking the gloom of the older towns for the clearer atmosphere of the immediate countryside have found among the obvious advantages of the location of their homes certain minor disadvantages, one of the chief of these being the definite handicap of the journey back to the city for an evening's entertainment. The older residents of the district in considerable number, have likewise suffered under the disadvantage, and it is to supply a need which is felt by new and old alike that the erection of the Broadway cinema has been undertaken.

It is hoped by the directors, that in every way this cinema will be found to afford complete satisfaction and that it will contribute in no mean manner to the social and artistic life of the Meir. It was realised by the directors with their intimate business knowledge of the Potteries that here was a magnificent and commanding site on a main crossroads, in a district which will grow in importance with the inevitable progress and development of the City Aerodrome.'

The programme went on to introduce the directors, the courageous men who had ploughed an enormous amount of cash and time into the venture:

'Herbert E. Clewlow is a native of Hanley and a partner of the firm Charles Knight and Sons, removal contractors and former bus proprietors. For a number of years he was connected with the Roxy Cinema Hanley of which he was also a director. He has always been actively engaged in the removal business of Charles Knight and Sons and was greatly responsible for the construction of the Broadway being built. Served during the war with the Northumberland Fusiliers and King's Own Yorkshire Light Infantry and was awarded the Military Medal.

G. Harold Wright is also of the removal business of Charles Knight and Sons of which he is a partner. A native of Hanley and was formerly in the 'bus business and greatly responsible for the erection of the Broadway. Served during the war with the 1/5th Lincolns.

Lawrence AV Plumpton originally from Melbourne, Australia, has resided in this country for many years. He has been in the cinema trade since 1919 in which he is well-known. He was the manager of the Oxford Picture House, Manchester during the time of the famous Symphony Orchestra of 42 performers, afterwards at the Playhouse, Chelsea and the Premier Picture House, Widnes. At present is the lessee of the Royal Picture House, Longton. At the outbreak of war was with the fleet at Scapa, joined the army in September 1914, commissioned in 1915, served overseas with the Lancashire Fusiliers and wounded at the Somme.

J. Mee joined the City of London Fusiliers in August 1914, eventually being transferred to the Royal Artillery as Sergeant-instructor of Signalling. Had service in France, was gassed, finishing his services in 1919 with the rank of acting Sergeant-major.'

The architect, responsible for putting their dreams into reality, was Mr A. Glynn Sherwin:

'In his capacity of architect and surveyor for Housing schemes in the vicinity he was quick to realise the importance of the crossroads site for shops and business premises in addition to the Broadway cinema. Mr Sherwin has an extensive practice with head offices in Newcastle under Lyme and has been responsible since the termination of the war in carrying through in all parts of this and the surrounding districts, a number of large and interesting schemes including housing estate work on a large scale. He has been responsible moreover for the alteration and modernisation of important licensed premises and is an exponent of modern design as applied to shop and business premises.'

A local firm Messrs A.V. Shenton of Longton were engaged as building contractors for the Broadway cinema:

'They are an old established firm and the completion of this cinema is a further example of the services which they render. The finest British manufacturers are represented in the body of the building and fine British craftsmanship is also here displayed. The building itself, standing across from the recently rebuilt King's Arms gave the town a lasting trademark. Nothing could demonstrate the success of the architectural conception better than the happy and natural manner in which the building rises to view on this corner site. It gives the impression of having grown into position and its external appearance to traffic approaching the city from the direction of Derby and the east is both dignified and welcoming.

The main structure is framed in British steelwork to the specification and design of the consultant engineer, Mr GW Costain, Neville House, Waterloo Street, Birmingham 2 and the whole of the building conforms to fire-resisting regulations and to the By-Laws of the City Surveyor and ensures the absolute safety of staff and patrons alike. The floors are of solid concrete reinforced by Hy-rib.

The steel roof trusses to the main spans carry below an expanded steel ceiling and above a protected steel decking covered with asphalt; a walking space between ceiling and roof is provided for access to lighting features and for periodic inspection.

The main staircases are reinforced artificial stone covered with Terrazzo; the staircases to the projection suite are of no-slip artificial stone. In addition there is a steel escape stair on the north side of the balcony.

Lovers of statistics will be interested to learn that a quarter of a million bricks have been used in the main walls, that the Main Balcony girder of 60 feet span weighs 25 tons and that the total weight of the steel framing amounts to 200 tons.

Fine quality brickwork of subdued and harmonious tone with a plinth of contrasting shades and terra cotta dressings are used to mark the terminal features-the broad circular pylons of the entrance front-and also to give the long Uttoxeter Road frontage by day the horizontal emphasis which is produced at night by the lines of the Neon lighting.

The richness of the entrance front, the shelter provided by the sweeping curves of the marquise, the large floodlit windows relieved by the delicately figured etching of the plate glass, the shining Staybrite Entrance doorways, the glowing signs reflected by the glaze of the Terra Cotta all combine to give an air of gaiety of warmth and hospitality which reflects the comfort of the interior and the welcome that awaits within.'

But the appeal of the cinema lay inside:

> *'The auditorium has been designed cleanly and without fuss giving a calm restful atmosphere without adventitious ornament or finicky detail. We have a cinema interior which has made a clean break with tradition in order to fulfil the new requirements of the Talking Film..*
>
> *The main body of the auditorium is divided into Front Stalls and Back Stalls, each division having its own exits to both streets allowing the hall to be emptied rapidly and without discomfort. The Balcony access is so designed as to render the Cafe 'en suite'. Lavatory and cloakroom accommodation is conveniently disposed to serve all parts of the building.*
>
> *Extreme care has been taken to afford easy raking of the balcony and to afford easy sight lines from every seat, each of which is luxuriously upholstered in contrasting pastel shades.*
>
> *A most interesting and unique feature is the series of mural paintings by a local artist, Mr H Tittensor RI, well known for his charming Academy water colours as for his local industrial design. These panels occur at frieze level on the side walls and form a most refreshing, if not daring, alternative to the usual stock feature.'*

Even the lighting was special:

> *The lighting of the main hall is bound up with the internal decorative effect; in fact the lighting to a large degree becomes the decoration. The stage lighting is on a comprehensive scale and it is possible to provide numberless colour changes of every conceivable hue and never until recently has progress in artificial lighting made possible and fascinating effects of an ever changing sea of colour which here floods the Proscenium curtains.'*

During its lifetime of 35 years the Broadway only had one manager, Lawrence Plumpton *'..who,'* the programme went on:

> *'....with this experience at the Royal, Longton he has been able to study the requirements of the amusement going public of the Town and District. Mr Plumpton is an Australian and apart from the years spent in the Great War, his career has been devoted to the entertainment business in one form or another. A keen sportsman, it is only natural being an Australian, that he is very keen on cricket and has for the past two seasons been Captain of the Rough Close Cricket Club. At golf he won the Birmingham and Midland Cinema Trade Golf Tournament in 1934 and was runner-up in 1936. Mr Plumpton's appointment is to use his own words "A dream come true" and patrons can rest assured that their entertainment is in safe and capable hands. It is not widely known in later years that when Lawrence Plumpton used to carry the week's cinema takings to the bank, he carried a loaded service revolver in his pocket...just in case. He never had course to use it in anger.'*

Being a purpose built cinema, the Broadway was equipped with a cafe, something many others lacked:

> *'A special reference should be allowed to the Cafe where a leisurely half hour for afternoon tea or for supper may well be enjoyed. An excellent kitchen well lit and ventilated with Electrical Cooking Equipment is installed and it is intended to furnish light meals of an attractive nature.'*

The opening programme in the presence of Alderman J.A. Dale and the Lady Mayoress of Stoke in December 1936 began with the National Anthem. The British Movietone Newsreel then preceded a showing of *Java Seas* with Charles Bickford, Elizabeth Young and Leslie Fenton. A cartoon followed after which *Limelight* with Anna Neagle and *The Street Singer* (Arthur Tracey) completed the evening's entertainment.

The prices of admission (including Tax) were to the Matinees at 3.30 pm: Stalls 4d and 6d. Circle 9d (Bank Holidays excepted) and Evenings: Front Stalls 6d. Back Stalls 9d. Back Circle 1/- and Front Circle 1/3d, but the car park was free.

The Broadway screened many memorable films amongst which was the historical classic, *The Adventures of Robin Hood*. Directed by Michael Curtiz and William Keighley starring Errol Flynn as the eponymous rogue, it featured Olivia De Havilland as Lady Marian, Basil Rathbone as Guy of Gisborne and Claude Rains as King John. With his flamboyant musical score, Czech emigre Erich Wolfgang Korngold masterfully complemented the action and pageantry of this wonderful film, shot entirely in Technicolor, for which it received one of its 5 Oscars.

Shortly after the Broadway's opening, news reached the papers that a new 'army' building would be built next door the cinema. As signs of war with Nazi Germany increased, Meir became a temporary home to many military personnel.

'As a result of the changeover from an infantry to a mechanical searchlight unit attached to an anti-aircraft branch of the Territorial Army, the War Office has issued instructions for the erection of three new Drill Halls to meet the changed requirements. These new halls are to be built at Burslem, Cross Heath and Meir, Longton. In the planning of the new buildings, the comfort and scientific training of the men is to be specially studied. There will be classrooms for technical instruction, writing rooms and many recreational facilities, which were unknown under the old order of things.'

During the war years, the Broadway was a meeting place for those stationed in and around Meir, and amongst the Royal Air Force and Army personnel were American military staff. The reality was stark and unforgiving, for those trained in the Drill Hall and the Central Flying School on Meir aerodrome might soon be called on to lay their lives on the line. It was something that many were only too ready to put aside in the cinema's plush and reassuring comfort. For now, its soporific warmth provided an interlude, however short, between them and the horrors of the battle.

But as well as a film fayre at the Broadway light-hearted occasions were not infrequent. As Dot Clewlow (now Dot Perrin) recounted.

'We also had personal appearances at the Broadway over the years by famous people and once during the war we had the fortune teller, Gypsy Petulengo who told my dad he would live till he was seventy five years old. Unfortunately, my father died just a few years later at the age of sixty seven.'

Germany's surrender in May 1945 'brought down the curtain' on hostilities in mainland Europe. The next task was therefore to rebuild and set in place new horizons and goals. It was to the political arena voters now looked, as they chose their MP in the first General Election for ten years. Parliament was dissolved following Winston Churchill's resignation on May 23, and with it came the date of Polling Day, July 5, 1945.

Sir Joseph Quinton Lamb, the MP for the Stone ward (which in those days included the Meir) for 23 years, was not seeking re-election. The prospective candidates were Major the Hon. Hugh Fraser (Con), Major John Wedgwood (Lib) and the hopelessly outranked, Mr W Simcock (Lab) who at the end, was only two thousand odd votes short of victory. Major Wedgwood, a director at Josiah Wedgwood and Sons, began the campaign speaking at a meeting in Cheadle Town Hall on June 5. Not to be outflanked, Mr Simcock, countered, at Colclough Road Schools, Meir.

Hugh Fraser, in Newcastle, fielded friendly questions at the Westlands Sports Pavilion. After his wartime service in the SAS, he had, by 1945, packed more into 10 years than many could hope to possibly achieve in two whole lifetimes. On the hustings in a 'baptism of fire' at the Broadway cinema he invoked the wrath of the assorted electors at an extraordinary meeting. Accompanied by former Home Secretary, Sir Donald Somervell, he took the stage. The audience though had other ideas, the result being the platform party were caught up in a non-stop barrage of cat calling and interruptions from a group of truculent miners. Even the Home Secretary was booed.

Hugh Fraser shouted to the hecklers *'to come around later and talk over the problem'* in a vain attempt to restore order. He was unsuccessful and the furore continued. The chairman of the meeting, Sir Ernest Johnson (president of the British China Manufacturers Federation) pitched into the fray, warning one awkward so and so 'to be quiet'. Pandemonium reigned, many minutes elapsing before order could be restored.

At the back of the Broadway, a young American, watching the melee was taking notes. His ancestors, originally from County Wexford in Ireland had emigrated to the United States in the 1840s. The family were now rich and enjoyed a privileged existence, spending the long summers at Hyannis Port, on Cape Cod in Massachusetts.

With the end of the war, he found himself working as a journalist for Hurst newspapers. During the early summer of 1945 whilst covering the United Nations conference in San Francisco, he had submitted an article on the forthcoming General Election in England for printing in the New York *American*, *'British election seen vital to us.'* Now, leaving the USA, he embarked for England to cover the parliamentary upheavals at closer quarters. Coming from a Catholic family it was not wholly unexpected that this young man should choose to spend the two days he had available in the company of Hugh Fraser, both being firm friends and sharing the same Christian faith.

The next article written by this American journalist *'Churchill may lose Election'*, printed on June 24, 1945, was submitted to the newspapers whilst in England during the Election campaign and it was one of several he wrote on the subject. A further despatch followed, again in the New York *American*, under the banner headline *'England facing critical period'*. Within the month three more articles were submitted on July 27, 1945, an indication of his deep interest in politics. The first of the trio, *'Labor landslide surprises even happy victors'* appeared in the Boston *American,* followed by "*Majority over Churchill stuns Liberates'* in the New York *American*. The final article written and appearing in the New York *Mirror* was scripted *'British Labor victory viewed as reaction against war hardships'*.

Despite information to the contrary he never wrote under his own name for the New York Times. Of him, speaking much later, Hugh Fraser said: *'Jack had a memory which after years could be sparked into almost instant recall. In 1945 he had done a report on the British election for the New York Times. He stayed a couple of nights with me in Staffordshire and attended an adoption meeting. A neighbouring Tory candidate had been quoted as boldly saying that striking miners should be shot, so at our packed meeting on the edge of Stoke on Trent, 500 hundred miners just allowed me a hearing, but howled down the Conservative Home Secretary. The proceedings were more hilarious than riotous. In my turn I attended some of Jack's public meetings in Boston, when he was fighting Cabot Lodge for the Senate. Certainly compared to our meeting at the Meir, they were immemorably tame and boring.'*

That meeting at the Meir had indeed left an indelible mark. Incredibly Jack was John Fitzgerald Kennedy, in time the 35th President of the United States in 1961 to whom Sir Hugh wrote regularly. Sadly they met for the last time, on a flight to a US Air Force passing out parade in Colorado in 1963.

Sir Hugh remembered: *'After 18 years, he (JFK) reeled off in his flat New England voice, his description of my election meeting, the shouting, the discomfited Home Secretary but above all my chairman, whom he made the pivot of his argument, imitating accent, mannerisms and voice of the long forgotten declaration as to how lucky the audience were to have me, Hugh Fraser, as their candidate.'*

A picture of President Jack Kennedy that appeared in an advert after his death

During the war many institutions had not received the care and maintenance they required. The Broadway was no exception. Its external neon lighting, switched off during the war, was in 1946 in a parlous state, and never returned to its former glory.

Whilst the appearance of the first UK commercial TV station in the mid-1950s was for many a blessing, the outcome for cinemas was diametrically opposite. Why should cinema patrons go out to see 'movies' when they could see them in the comfort of their own home for free? The abundance of films formerly enjoyed in the Potteries quickly slimmed down to barely a handful. Cinema patronage in the 1960s declined rapidly, and smaller audiences created other problems - The Broadway was plagued by vandals.

Cliff Perrin recalls: *'We had to check each row to make sure they hadn't tried to start a fire in the cinema which would set alight after we'd closed.'* This behaviour was not an isolated occurrence as *'sometimes gangs of lads would rip out whole rows of seats and then disappear into the auditorium.'*

To remain solvent many cinemas changed tack, as they had done in the late 1930s, now becoming bingo halls and these often enormous barn-like cinemas rang to their patrons shouting 'House'. The Broadway soldiered on and was bought by 'Tudor Bingo' but never had the indignity of becoming a bingo hall. Several plans for its future included transforming the auditorium into a nightclub with a much reduced cinema. None of the schemes were viable and at 10.07 pm on June 19, 1971, with the end of a showing of *Performance* starring Mick Jagger, the Broadway closed. The glamour and razzmatazz were gone. Deserted, boarded up and left to decay, the Broadway stoically awaited its fate.

The sound of the wrecking ball hurtling into the brickwork on the Sunday morning of May 13, 1973 was the first many knew of its death throes. Holes in the building soon appeared, exposing the screen and proscenium arch. For so long a landmark, it was quickly reduced to rubble. A cluster of churchgoers returning home were stunned as falling masonry buried those famous Broadway front steps. Thirty five years of Meir cinema history disappeared. Had the appetite of the motor car for bigger and wider roads ultimately sealed the fate of the Broadway? Paradoxically, one of many features mentioned in favour of its being built in 1935/6, was its strategic position at one of the major traffic routes into Stoke-on-Trent. Now straddling the path of the 1970s Derby Way road scheme, it was doomed, even though the road plans were later abandoned.

Many examples of old cinemas being transformed to uses beyond their original remit exist: J.D. Wetherspoon's conversion of the former Palace cinema in Stafford for example. The Broadway was denied even this. Seen in isolation, its demolition might be thought of as unfortunate in an architectural wilderness like Stoke-on-Trent. But it strengthens the argument of visitors to Stoke-on-Trent that 'perhaps its acquisition of the dubious accolade of *'The Worst City in England in which to live',* might have some substance after all.

By 1999 the Broadway and A50 road works had gone. The former cinema site found a new use as a windswept car park for shoppers. How many knew of its brief and chequered history as they drive away? By 2003, the wheel had come full circle since 1935 when plans for its construction were published. Now a whole human lifetime away, were it not for the memories, photographs and souvenirs, it might appear the Broadway never existed at all.

1950s Meir showing how compact the town centre was then, with the
TA Centre in the middle ground and tree-lined roads. The Broadway cinema is on the left.

One of Reginald Mitchell's famous Vickers Supermarine Spitfires on display in the City Museum, Stoke on Trent.

The roll of Honour at Stoke on Trent Technical College shows the name of R.J. Mitchell in 1918. *Lovatt Collection*

SOME PROMINENT MEIR CITIZENS

ERNEST ALBERT EGERTON: Soldier and Victoria Cross Holder

Born in Longton in 1897, Ernest Albert Egerton or 'Ernie' as he was known to his friends, was an inspector for the Potteries Motor Traction Company during the 1930s. He was probably a driver before this, according to his old pal Norman Tudor.

'He was a modest man who wouldn't talk about his wartime experiences. Ernie was perfect gentleman, probably one of the best inspectors on the PMT in those days. He had a daughter in a wheelchair and I remember an occasion we took her to Cheadle Guildhall on a bus to give her a night out.'

The account of his deed reads,

'On Sept 1917 south-east of Ypres, Belgium, during an attack, visibility was bad owing to fog and smoke. As a result the two leading waves of the attack passed over certain hostile dug-outs without clearing them and enemy rifles and machine guns from these dug-outs were inflicting severe casualties. Corporal Egerton at once responded to a call for volunteers to help in clearing up the situation and he dashed for the dug-outs under heavy fire at short range. He shot a rifleman, a bomber and a gunner, by which time support had arrived and 29 of the enemy surrendered.'

After winning the Victoria Cross, Corporal Egerton (later promoted sergeant) returned home to a hero's welcome in the Potteries, touring the Longton area of Stoke on

The Royal British Legion march through Blythe Bridge to the home of Ernest Albert Egerton VC, where a service was held before the plaque was unveiled by Mr Egerton's daughter Mrs Margaret Porter. 1997.

Trent in an open car. An entry, in the pages of the Register of Burials at St Peter's, Forsbrook proclaims a local fondness and pride for the old soldier. Originally written as 'Ernest Albert Egerton' along with the day of his death, it has been amended later with a different coloured ink, the initials 'V.C.' (Victoria Cross) added after his name. His moment of heroism almost half a century before had followed him to the grave.

FLORENCE DAYSON:
Headteacher and wife of Reginald J. Mitchell, Spitfire designer

Long before the game of tennis had become altered by big money prizes, it was enjoyed by millions who liked nothing more than to knock a ball about on local courts. During the formative years of Holy Trinity church in the first quarter of the 20th century tennis courts were laid out for local sportsmen and women behind the Institute. One of many who perfected their game on these courts was the young Florence Dayson.

The Staffordshire Advertiser reported,

'The Tennis Club in connection with the Meir Church Institute was opened for the season by Lady Meredith, mother of the Rev. R. Creed-Meredith, curate-in-charge. The opening games were played by the Rev H.M. Fowler (Vicar of Caverswall) and Miss F. Dayson versus Mr Guy Murray and Miss A Radford. There was a large gathering and the company was entertained to tea, after which a hearty vote of thanks was passed to Lady Meredith for her presence.'

'Mr J.H. Barlow observed that at the Meir they were out for all that tended to further the social interests of the people, which he considered true Christianity. The church council had, by a loan, originally financed by the Tennis Club, layed out a bowling green which he hoped to see in use very shortly.'   24th May 1913

Towards the end of the Great War, R.J. Mitchell, only a year out of his apprenticeship, married Florence Dayson who was 11 years his senior. They had one son, Gordon, later Dr. Gordon Mitchell. Headmistress of an Infants' school in Lower Belgrave Road, Dresden, Stoke on Trent, Florence tied the knot with Reginald at 'the Meir church' - Holy Trinity - where she had spent so many happy days.

Elderly residents often told of seeing 'RJ' getting off the train at Meir station on a Friday night, and his Rolls Royce car was occasionally parked in the Avenue, now Penfleet Avenue, outside the home of Florence Dayson.

JOSEPH LEESE RN:
With Capt. Scott's *Terra Nova* expedition to Antarctica 1910-1912

Joseph Leese was born in Burslem, Stoke on Trent in 1884 and his connection with Captain Scott's *Terra Nova* expedition to Antarctica was purely fortuitous.

When *Terra Nova* sailed south from the United Kingdom in 1910, Joseph Leese (like Captain Scott) was not aboard but engaged in surveying as an able seaman in the Royal Navy off the Cape of Good Hope. This activity is detailed in a news item in the Staffordshire Advertiser some twenty years later.

During the first leg of its journey to South Africa, two members of *Terra Nova*'s crew came down with bronchopneumonia. With no facilities to treat them, Edward Wilson, the chief of the Scientific Staff, who was also a doctor, had them put ashore in South Africa.

One of the replacements for the two sick seamen chosen by Wilson was AB Joseph Leese, whose name in the *Terra Nova* signing-on register reveals his former ship as *HMS Mutine* and the signing-on port as Simon's Town (Cape Town) South Africa.

It is interesting to note in the book *The Diary of the Terra Nova Expedition 1910-1912*, (Blandford 1972) - the edited diary of Edward Adrian Wilson - he ascribes another ship , *Pandora*, a cruiser, anchored alongside *Mutine* in Simon's Town as the source of the two new replacement crew members. This is not so.

Able seaman Joseph Leese RN. Seconded by Captain Scott, he joined *Terra Nova* at Simonstown, S. Africa, sailing on to the Antarctic. It was on this 1910-1913 expedition that Scott and four colleagues perished.

With Leese safely aboard *Terra Nova* it sailed south, via Australia and New Zealand. After battling mountainous seas and almost capsizing, the ship finally reached McMurdo Sound in Antarctica, in January 1911. The stores and supplies were then brought ashore at Cape Evans by all the hands.

Joseph Leese is mentioned by Captain Scott in his actual journals (Scott's Last Expedition: Smith Elder and Company 1913) published posthumously. He writes,

'Rennick and Bruce are working gallantly at the discharge of stores on board. Williamson and Leese load the sledges and are getting very clever and expeditious. Evans (seaman) is generally superintending the sledging camp outfit. Forde, Keohane and Abbott are regularly assisting the carpenter, whilst Day, Lashly, Lillie and others give intermittent help.'

After unloading, *Terra Nova* and AB Leese returned to New Zealand later in 1911. Following the disastrous entrapment of Discovery in pack ice in Scott's previous expedition, *Terra Nova* was sent north to avoid a similar occurrence. During the summer Leese was engaged on surveying work around N.Z. coastal waters returning to Antarctica to resupply Scott's expedition in late 1911, once more returning to New Zealand in 1912.

The blue and gold *Terra Nova* signing-on register, now kept at the Scott Polar Research Institute, Cambridge, England indicates Leese's home address was 37 Dimsdale Avenue, Porthill and 'Hanley' the place of registration of his birth, while his pay was 30/- a month.

This official document opens out revealing two facing pages ruled in columns. On the left hand side in the first column is the name of the person concerned (Scott is first, Wilson

Captain R.F. Scott writing his
journal in his quarters in
Antarctica during the *Terra
Nova* expedition.

To avoid entrapment in the
Polar ice, Scott sent *Terra
Nova* north to warmer waters
during the intense cold of the
Antarctic winter.
Leese, aboard *Terra Nova*
during this time, probably
spent three tours of duty in the
south.

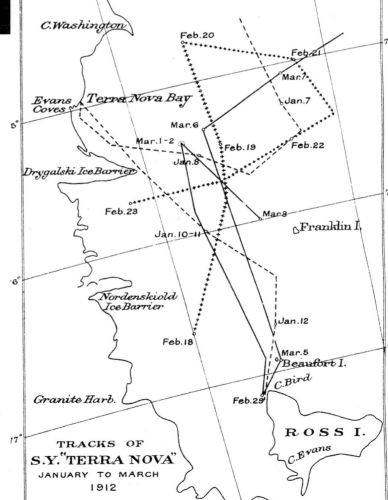

TRACKS OF
S.Y."TERRA NOVA"
JANUARY TO MARCH
1912

second, Bowers along with all the ship's company follow written in their own hand) with all their personal details.

Board of Trade rules in force at the time stating what was permitted to be taken on board ship plus other details concerning crew space etc have been crossed out. It cost Scott thousands of pounds to circumvent these regulations by registering *Terra Nova* as a yacht.

Additionally, in the collection held in Cambridge, there are 3 photographs taken by Herbert Ponting (the official ship's list details him as a 'camera artist'; Ponting hated the expression 'photographer') of AB Leese whilst on *Terra Nova*. One shows him (although the caption spells his name as 'Lees') and Tryggve Gran in the rigging of the ship searching out a 'lead' in the ice in December 1910. The other two show Leese in March 1912 in a group of three and four shipmates on board *Terra Nova* as it neared the coast of New Zealand. (This mis-spelling of Leese's name is not unique. It occurs in the Stoke on Trent registers of Birth, Marriages and Death held at London Road.)

Although it is not certain, crew members generally signed on for the whole voyage and to quote Mr Robert Headland of the Scott Polar Research Institute,

'It is probable that Leese remained to the last Antarctic season of Terra Nova - but I have no absolute confirmation.'

Terra Nova returned to the United Kingdom in summer 1913. Originally built in 1884 in Dundee, Scotland for the Arctic whale fishery, the vessel was reinforced below decks from stem to stern with 7 feet thick oak beams to take the strain of the pack ice. (Cf: Shackleton's Endurance which was crushed and sank in 1914 in Antarctica which gave rise to probably one of the greatest acts of seamanship and navigation ever, when a small party of her crew sailed 800 miles to effect a rescue.)

In 1903 *Terra Nova* sailed to the Antarctic along with the Morning to rescue Scott, then in Discovery, but in the event was not needed; Discovery returned under her own sail and steam. *Terra Nova* on its return in 1913 was sold to her previous owners, Messrs C.T. Bowring and Co. and was later engaged successfully, in seal fishing off Newfoundland for many years. Sadly, whilst returning from a voyage to Greenland, *Terra Nova* sprang a leak and sank on 13 September 1943, although happily, all hands were rescued by a cutter of the United States Coastguard.

During the 1930s, Joseph Leese was living in Meir when he received an invitation.

'Among those who have been invited to the reunion dinner of the Antarctic Club in London on January 17th (1930) is Mr Joseph Leese of the Meir Church Institute who is one of the survivors of the ill fated expedition of Captain Robert Falcon Scott to the South Pole. Mr Leese, who is a native of Burslem was formerly in the Navy and was lent to the expedition whilst on surveying work for the Navy. Along with his comrades he suffered terrible hardships until he was rescued. On his return to England he was decorated by the King with the King's Polar Medal and clasp for Antarctic Exploration, he being the only native of Staffordshire to be so decorated. Mr Leese is also the holder of the Royal Geographical Society's Bronze medal for discovery and exploration.' 4th January 1930

Joseph Leese later became a miner working at Florence Colliery, Normacot, Parkhouse in Chesterton, Stoke on Trent. Living in Meir he was a frequent visitor to Ewart

Key's newsagents shop in Weston Road. Alan, Ewart's son remembers Leese vividly as *'a small, wiry man.'*

Joseph Leese died at his home in Brookhouse Road, Meir, Stoke on Trent on 22 December 1948, aged 64, his death announced in the Times of London under the headline *'SCOTT EXPEDITION SURVIVOR'* with a reminder he was one of the last members the ill fated *Terra Nova* expedition to the South Pole.

In his years spent wandering the seas, he accumulated many odds and ends some of which were later auctioned at Christie's. The sale in April 2000 included an Antarctic Club reunion dinner menu from 1932 and his prestigious and rare Polar Medal and bar. But the strangest item of all was an old sea biscuit Leese owned from Shackleton's Nimrod expedition of 1907, which it was thought would fetch £1000. A Christie's spokesman said, *'The Antarctic is a very lively market at the moment. Much of this is due to huge publicity in the US celebrating Shackleton's epic journey from Antarctica. As a consequence, any items connected with the South Pole like Leese's tend to fetch a lot of money - particularly from the Americans.'*

PROFESSOR GEOFFREY BOULTON FRS, OBE, FRSE
Geologist, Academic, Policy Maker and Sportsman

Geoffrey Boulton was one of the Old Boys educated at Longton High School, then in Sandon Road and under its headmaster Mr M.V. Gregory. Tom Purcell of Longton High School and Commanding Officer of the RAF section of the Cadet Force was his mentor.

Geoffrey was admitted to the University of Birmingham, after being turned down by Bangor and Keele, to read Geology. He had many happy times at Birmingham, *'climbing and playing rugby for a local Welsh team who wanted a good centre and felt that someone with a granny called 'Davies' must be Welsh.'* He met his future wife Denise Bryers Lawns there.

'On graduating I joined the Geological Society but although it was a pleasant life, it was intellectually undemanding, very hierarchical and I could see a pleasant but vegetative life stretching in front of me until retirement. I applied for a temporary lectureship at Keele, failed to get it and was offered a job as a lowly paid demonstrator which I accepted, even though my salary was almost halved.'

His mapping of the Cheshire Plain for the British Geological Society, coincided with the construction of the M6 and revealed some fascinating sections in the glacial deposits of the Cheshire Plain. After spending an uncomfortable and freezing fortnight working on the sections, he was able to tell the folks at Keele *'my research is on glacial geology'!*

A year later he became part of a Cambridge Expedition to Spitsbergen to study *'real geological processes',* after which he took up a position as research Fellow at Birmingham University. *'I discovered in Spitsbergen the delights of glaciology which have over the years given me an opportunity to visit some of the world's finest mountain ranges and to climb them. It also gave me the chance to contribute to the development of a new science.'*

Following a sequence of experiments in Spitsbergen, Geoffrey was involved with the Americans in experiments in deep drilling in Antarctica.

The launch of the Centre for Geoscience Back row: Sir Muir Russell and Professor Geoffrey Boulton, former pupil of Longton High School, Sandon Road, Meir.
Front row: Sir Alwyn Williams and Sir Graham Davies.

Geoffrey Boulton is now Vice-Principal of Edinburgh University.

Keele University had many temporary buildings in the early 1960s. Now in the 21st century it has many new buildings, a full campus and a new medical school.

Professor Geoffrey Boulton FRS at the naming ceremony of the Dept of Earth Sciences and Geography, Keele University, with Prof. Ian Fairchild and Vice Chancellor Janet Finch.

During 1967 and working in NE Kenya he was engaged in looking for water in the desert, a task complicated by a war going on at the same time, which necessitated his being accompanied by a company of Kenya Rifles. The Foreign Office later decided he would need to become a soldier. He spent two enjoyable weeks at Farnborough, letting off *'thunderflashes and acquiring a commission as a lieutenant in the Royal Engineers.'*

Geoffrey Boulton was responsible, along with others, for the founding of the new School of Environmental Sciences at the University of East Anglia in 1968. *'It was immensely stimulating partly because of the variety of disciplines involved and the ideas that I met, partly because we had terrific students, and partly because of being in the vanguard of thinking the new thoughts about the environment that were beginning to emerge.'*

In parallel with ongoing research projects, he completed work on Baffin Island, the European Alps and more recently projects in Tibet and the northern flank of the Himalayas.

During the 1980s he devised a group of geophysical cruises in the Arctic which included *'being a member of the Swedish expedition that celebrated the centenary of Otto von Nordenskiold's first successful cruise through the NE passage in the Vega. We used the Stockholm Harbour icebreaker Ymer and now have two cats called Ymer and Vega!'*

In 1980, *'seduced by the thought of working abroad',* he was appointed to a chair in the University of Amsterdam and *'enjoyed the pleasure of working in that great city and the directness and robustness of the Dutch.'*

He became Regius Professor of Geology and Head of the Grant Institute at Edinburgh University in 1986. He was appointed Provost and Dean of Sciences and Engineering and then Vice-Principal of Edinburgh University.

During the 1980s and 1990s his work involved glaciological experiments in Iceland, which still continue today.

Professor Boulton was, until 2001, a member of the Royal Commission on Environmental Pollution. From its ranks came the ideas of a fuel duty escalator, congestion charging and concepts underpinning the Government's White Paper on Energy. His role as Science Adviser to the Scottish Government and Environmental Advisor to the Chinese Government ensure, even today, that he has a major influence on scientific thinking.

On May 9, 2001 Professor Boulton FRS attended the naming ceremony of the William Smith Building at the School of Earth Sciences and Geography, Keele University. The building commemorates two men bearing the same name; a clever choice that, at a stroke, eliminated any possible rancour between Geologists and Geographers.

The first William Smith 1546-1618, born in Warmingham, Cheshire, was regarded as the first recognisable geographer of the local region who developed the printed town plan in the country, while William 'Strata' Smith, 1769-1839, in his 1815 map, single-handedly provided the inspiration for all national Geological maps.

Speaking at the ceremony, Professor Boulton only briefly alluded to his time at Keele. However it would not have been lost on those listening that had he not moved on, the profile of that institution might have been that much greater.

STEPHEN MEAR: Businessman, Philanthropist and Sportsman

As well as the abdication crisis, 1936 saw the demise of one of Meir's most respected and wealthy citizens, Stephen Mear. But who was he? Living in Weston Road and reputedly a millionaire, he had inherited large commercial interests in timber from his father.

Stephen Mear JP. *Dorothy Mear collection.*

A director of the Potteries Electric Traction company and later the Potteries Motor Traction Company, Stephen Mear was, according to his relatives, *'a wonderful man of great character and very good company'*. He owned a green 1912 Daimler which sported large brass lamps at the front and a luggage rack at the rear. It was serviced at the PMT garage in Fenton.

As a keen sportsman and a member of the huntin', shootin' and fishin' fraternity, he was seen at many local meetings. On fishing trips to the Dane Valley, according to Dorothy Mear, *'Grandfather would roll up his trousers to the knees to tickle fish'*, and *'forgot his age and became a boy again. They always cooked and ate any fish they caught on the river bank before returning home.'*

His shooting trips often took him out to Brassington's in Ipstones and over to Cauldon Lowe. One jaunt was especially unforgettable. The car packed up en route to Oakamoor when *'flames were seen coming out of the engine. Workmen from Bolton's were passing and helped to put out the fire by throwing sand on the car!'*

But all these activities were curtailed as a result of a gun accident, when the breech of a shotgun he was using exploded, removing two of his fingers. Was this why he included on his headed notepaper 'National Scheme for Disabled Men'?

Stephen Mear's wife died on 7th January 1906, a tragedy affecting the congregation at Holy Trinity Church where she and her husband were regular worshippers:

'A churchwarden, Stephen Mear, and his wife have been prominent in Meir life, and the building of Holy Trinity church in the late 1890s and the Church Institute.' '

Their names appeared regularly in the Christian and social life of the parish:

'CONSECRATION OF THE MEIR CHURCH..... The organ has been presented to the church by MRS STEPHEN MEAR.'

And again at the foundation stone laying for the new Church Institute.

'Laying of the foundation stones of a Sunday School, Church Institute and parish room for educational and parochial purposes in connexion with the Holy Trinity church, the Meir took place on Thursday afternoon.'   15th May 1902 and:

'The clergy, choir and congregation proceeded to the site, the stones were laid as follows: South West corner by Mr W.R. Parker Jervis of Meaford Hall, The Henry Hill Memorial stone in the central bay by Miss Ethel Aynsley (representing Mr John Aynsley of Blythe Bridge); South-east corner stone by Mrs Warren of Belleview, Shrewsbury; The

Meir Social and Sports Club, showing the new extension built on the front of Beech House.

Stephen Mear's residence Weston Coyney House, in Weston Road, was one of four houses in this leafy part of town. With its ornate barge boards and gabled roofs it is an elegant example of the builder's craft. It had stables and a pigeon loft. The house no longer stands but the Meir Social & Sports Club was a neighbouring house of very similar design. These houses enjoyed a rear access to the Meir Golf Course.

Institute Library Corner by MRS STEPHEN MEAR OF WESTON COYNEY HOUSE.' and:

'The builder's contract is for £1,200 and the furnishing will bring the cost up to £1,600; to make up a further sum of £450 is required. Towards this, subscriptions have been received as follows: Rev J.G. Addenbrooke (vicar of Caverswall) £21; Mr W.E. Bowers £50; Mr John Aynsley, Mr J.G. Aynsley and Mr STEPHEN MEAR, £25 each.'

Dorothy Mear, a granddaughter of Stephen Mear lived at Weston Coyney House with her parents, Stephen and Ethel Mear until she was five years old. She told me:

'The Meir Workingmen's Club was originally known as Beech House. My father said many years ago the Mear brothers, Stephen, Alfred and James Thomas built four houses in Weston Road. The fourth one was bought by the Barlow family. I don't know if any member of the Barlow family lived there when I was born, however as a very small child I was frightened of the noisy dog next door. My mother used to say "It's only Bobby Barr - or did she say Barlow?" She often lifted me up to see him over the wall... a black Scottie dog. Eventually I was bought a little toy Scottie dog, called 'Bobby Barr' and I still have him!

I honestly don't know if my grandfather was a millionaire but the cost of his failed House of Lords appeal in a court case, £32 000, later reduced to £16 000, severely affected his personal fortune. My father never mentioned it. As well as the disastrous court case, the Depression in the 1920s had a devastating effect on the family, probably at the same period.

The council estate opposite the four houses, was built on land owned by grandfather and sold for much less than its actual worth, that is compulsory purchase. The family also owned Gordon Mill in London Road, Stoke, again compulsorily purchased by Stoke council for another low price. The 'Ethel Austin' store now occupies the site.'

Stephen Mear's house in the Meir, the largest of the four, stood in the leafier part of town, giving it an air of opulence and grace. With its winding path, ornate barge boards and delicate corbeling on the chimneys, Weston Coyney House was a tribute to the skill and expertise of Victorian craftsmen. It also boasted tennis courts, a billiard room and tucked away at the rear were stables, pig sties and later a pigeon loft. Before the City Council re-housed the inhabitants of Longton's slums to Meir's green fields, the views across Weston Road from the house to open countryside were unsurpassed.

Only one of the quartet, Beech House, survives in 2004, the home of the Meir Social and Sports Club, an inappropriate brick extension adding little of merit to a pleasing design. But the essence of the original remains for those who choose to take a moment to look.

With the passing of Stephen Mear, aged 81, hastened by his heavy fall against a tree whilst out walking on a windy day, the town lost a man of character and style. His house was demolished along with the other two and is now the site of a modern housing development. What would he have said?

STEPHEN MEAR,

TELEPHONE N°. 3659.

Longton, Staffordshire,

19

THE MEIR

Why was the town called THE Meir and not plain Meir? The query, raised by veteran Sentinel journalist John Abberley some years ago when reviewing my earlier book, *A Meir Half Century*, is intriguing.

The village was, by an account of Henry Bigges (reeve), in 1485 a 'marshy place', a mere or mire in fact. And so did 'crossing the mere' become part of the language? Imagine it said with a genuine Potteries accent - *'At geen cross th' mire?'*

Did 'THE' stick to Meir, like the mud to the boots of those travelling to the east and beyond? It cannot be proved one way or the other but during the next 350 years it is plausible, by word of mouth and by hand me down it evolved into what we have today, THE Meir.

And of course we do have The Marsh at Wolstanton, which probably came about for the same reason. What do you think, Abbers?

ABBERLEY
No solution to the riddle of the Meir

NO-ONE has ever been able to explain why Potteries people talk about "the Meir" instead of plain old Meir.

This conundrum seems to have defeated even Nicholas Cartlidge, author of a new book called A Meir Half-Century, though he does provide half a clue with his reproduction of an insurance note dated 1883, referring to the King's Arms pub at "the Mear".

And according to the author, a diversion sign put up during excavations for the new A50 told motorists they were in "Mere Road".

But a history book about the Meir? Has Meir got a history? The answer is provided in abundance by Mr Cartlidge's scholarly work. This is probably the most comprehensive book yet written about a district which, we learn, has a lot more to it than large council estates.

Antarctic

For instance, it may come as a surprise to learn that a native of Meir, Joseph Leese, journeyed to the Antarctic with Captain Scott. Amy Johnson flew from the old Meir Aerodrome. And Meir used to have its own golf links.

●A view of Meir crossroads in the 1920s, and, inset, historian Nicholas Cartlidge

APPENDIX 1

ECCLESIASTICAL RECORDS OF CLERGY AT CAVERSWALL AND HOLY TRINITY CHURCH, THE MEIR, STAFFORDSHIRE 1889-2004

John Gordon ADDENBROOKE Vicar of Caverswall

Born Walsall 20 December 1849. Admitted pensioner under Messrs Peile, Cartmell and Wright 5th July 1876. BA 1880; MA 1885. Ordained deacon (d) 1877. Priest (p) 1880, Lichfield.

CURATE of Holy Trinity, Chesterfield.	1879-1880
CURATE of Holy Trinity, Burton-on-Trent.	1880-1882
VICAR of St Luke, Wolverhampton.	1882-1889
VICAR of CAVERSWALL, Staffs.	1889-1902
Rural Dean of Cheadle, Staffs.	1901-1902
VICAR of St Mark's. Tutbury.	1902-1908
VICAR of St Wenn,Bodmin, Cornwall.	1908-1915
CURATE of Tiverton on Avon, Bath.	1918-1922

    Died July 3rd 1922 at 80 Bloomfield Avenue, Bath.

Herbert Metcalfe FOWLER   Vicar of Caverswall

Jesus College Cambridge. BA 1887: MA 1891: d.1888:p.1889 Hereford

CURATE of St James, Hereford.	1888-1897
VICAR of Donington.	1897-1902
VICAR of CAVERSWALL (inc the MEIR)	1902-1915
VICAR of Holy Trinity, Hereford.	1915-1922

Thomas Heywood MASTERS: Born Manchester April 9th 1865

Christ's College 1886: Inverness College and Polytechnik, Hanover. Matriculated Michaelmas 1886:BA 1889:MA 1893 d.1893 (Lichfield) p.1890

CURATE of Caverswall, Staffs	1889-1893
CURATE of St Mark's, Lakenham, Norfolk	1893-1895
CURATE of Coddenham, Suffolk.	1895-1896
RECTOR of N. Scarle, Lincs.	1896-1902
VICAR of E. Meon, Hants.	1902-1921
Served in the Great War	1914-1919
Chaplain mentioned TWICE in despatches:	
Acting Chaplain-General	1918
CBE	1919
VICAR of Petersfield and Sheet.	1921-1930
Went to India as part of the Church Mission of Help.	1922-1923
Hon. Canon of Portsmouth.	1928-1931
Chaplain to the King.	1921-1939
Provost of Portsmouth Cathedral.	1930-1938
Residentiary Canon.	1931-1938
Died September 1st 1939	

John Edward CAREY

Lichfield College 1886. d 1887: p 1888 Lich.

CURATE of Rushall, Staffs.	1887-1893
CURATE of CAVERSWALL, Staffs.	1894-1897
RECTOR of Otterham.	1898-1904
VICAR of Treverbyn, Penwithick, St.Austell	1904-1921

Charles ADDDENBROOKE

Brother of John Gordon. Born Walsall 27th March 1865. Admitted pensioner under Mr Cartmell 9th
Oct 1885 BA 1888: MA 1893 Deacon 1888,Priest Lichfield 1890

CURATE of Dawley Magna, Salop.	1888-1891
CURATE of St George's,Edgbaston,Birmingham	1891-1898
CURATE in charge,Holy Trinity, The Meir, Longton, North Staffs	1898-1903
VICAR of St Chad's, Smethwick.	1903-1906
VICAR of St Stephen's, Fairlie, New Zealand.	1906-1909
VICAR of Okato, Taranaki, New Zealand.	1909-1921
CURATE of N. Wairoa, New Zealand	1921-1922
VICAR of Warkworth, New Zealand.	1922-1927

Died in New Zealand in the 1940's

Edwin WHEELDON

St Bee's 1892 d.1893: p.1894 Liverpool.

CURATE of St Polycarp.	1893-1894
CURATE of Ravenhead, Lancs	1894-1896
VICAR OF Biddulph, Staffs.	1896-1904
VICAR of Caverswall (in charge, Holy Trinity, (The Meir)	1904-1905
RECTOR of Christ church, Biddulph Moor.	1905-1920
VICAR of Horton, Leek, Staffs.	1920-

William HERALD

Queen's College Cambridge BA 1889:MA 1905.d.1900:p.1901 Southwark

CURATE of New Basford	1900-1902
CURATE of Thornton	1902-1903
CURATE of Wordsley	1903-1906
CURATE of CAVERSWALL (inc Holy Trinity, the MEIR	1906/7
CURATE of Dresden, Longton, Staffs.	1907-1909
CURATE of St Pauls, Wolverhampton	1910-1912
VICAR of Northenden	1912-1920

Arthur A BROOKS

St Aidan 1892; d.1894 : p.1895   Liverpool

CURATE of St Thomas, Wigan	1894-1907
CURATE of Holy Trinity, The Meir, Caverswall	1907-1912
VICAR of Lapley and Wheaton Aston	1912

Ralph CREED-MEREDITH

MA 1912: d.1911 : p.1912   Dublin.

CURATE of St Andrews, Dublin.	1911-1912
CURATE in charge, CAVERSWALL. (c-in-c, Holy Trinity, MEIR)	1912-1914
CURATE in charge, St Barts, Armley	1914-1917
Gen. L. Diocese Lichfield	1917-1918
CURATE of St Pauls, Harbourne.	1919-1920

Robert Osborne WALKER

Univ Cambridge B.A. 1904: M.A 1908. d.1905 p.1907 York.

CURATE of Warthill, Yorkshire.	1905-1907
VICAR of Osbaldwick with Murton	1913-1914
CURATE of Caverswall (curate of Holy Trinity (The Meir)	1914-1916
VICAR of Edstaton.	1917-1920

Theophilus CALEB

Univ. of Allahabad:Chich.Theol.Coll 1905. d 1907 p 1908 Diocese of St Albans.

CURATE of Holy Trinity, Barking Rd and	1907-
St Michaels and All Angels, Watford.	1908-1911
VICAR of Royston, Herts	1911-1914
VICAR, All Saints, Stoke Newington	1914-1916
VICAR of CAVERSWALL (c-in-c, The Meir)	1916-1919
curate in charge, The Meir conv distr	1919-1923
VICAR of Norman's Heath	1924-1926
CURATE of Rossendale, Diocese Manchester	1926-

Harry Christie SHELDON

S.D.C.Lampeter: BA (1st Theol): d.1914 p.1916   Lichfield Diocese

CURATE of All Saints West Bromwich.	1914-1918
CURATE in charge, St Bartholomew & St Andrews Kings Hill, Wednesbury	1918-1923
CURATE in charge, Holy Trinity, THE MEIR conv.distr.	1923-1926
VICAR of Holy Trinity, MEIR*	1926-1936
VICAR of Silverdale, Staffs.	1936-1946

*1930 address 'Mayfield', Meir, Longton, Stoke On Trent, Staffs.

William R. BELL

University of Durham 1929; Lichfield Theological College 1928; d.1931: p. 1933

CURATE of St Pauls, Newcastle under Lyme	1931-1933
CURATE of St Pauls, Mount Pleasant, Stoke-on-Trent	1933-1936
*VICAR of Holy Trinity, MEIR, Staffs	1936-1946
*Chaplain, Royal Air Force Volunteer Reserve	1941-1946

Herbert Vivian WOODWARD

Curate, Holy Trinity, MEIR	1946
Parish priest, Holy Trinity, MEIR	1946-1960
Parish priest, St.Martin's, Wolverhanpton	1960-
Parish priest, John the Baptist, Stafford	

William Antony RICHARDS

b. 1928. Ex Coll Oxford BA 52, MA 56. St Steph. House Oxford 52, d 54, p 55

Curate, Fenton, Lich.	1954-1955
Curate, St Mary's, Kingswinford	1955-1960
Parish priest Holy Trinity, MEIR,	1960-1964
Rector Warmington with Shotteswell Cov.	1964-1975
Rural Dean of Dassett Magna	1970-1974
Org.Sec. C of E Children's Soc. Cov, Leic and Pet	1975-1981
Vicar, Bideford on Avon. Cov.	1981-1992
Permanently to office Cov and Worcester	1992

Frederick W OSBORN

Parish priest Holy Trinity, MEIR,	1964-1976
Bishop's Officer to the Homeless, Manchester	1976

Trevor John HARVEY

b 1943; Sheff Univ BA 1964; Kings Coll London MA 1997; Coll of Resurrection, Mirfield 1964, d 66, p 67;

Curate of St Mary's, Kingswinford, Lich	1966-1972
Vicar of Upper Gornal	1972-1977
Parish Priest of Holy Trinity, MEIR	1977-1986
Chaplain to St Georges School, Windsor	1986-1999
Minor Canon, Windsor	1986-1999
Chaplain Ellesmere College, Shropshire	1999-2003

Retired 2003

David Charles Frederick TUDOR

b. 1942. Sarum Theol. Coll 1970; d 73, p 74.

Curate St Peter's, Plymouth, EX	1973-1975
Curate Reddich, Manchester	1975-1978
Priest in charge Hamer	1976-1980
Vicar of Goldenhill, Lich	1980-1987
Parish Priest of Holy Trinity, MEIR	1987-1991
Chaplain Asst Nottingham City Hospital	1991-1994
Chaplain Central Sheff Univ Hospitals NHS trust	1994-1996
Vicar of St George's Nottingham with St John, S'Well	1996-

Gordon William WHITTY

b 1935, West Midlands Ministerial Training College d 82; p 83

NSM St Giles' Willenhall, Lich	1982-1984
NSM Christ Church, Coseley	1984-1985
Curate Christ Church, Coseley	1985-1987
Team Vicar Holy Evangelists, Hanley, Stoke on Trent	1987-1991
Priest in charge, Holy Trinity MEIR	1991-1998
Priest in charge Hanbury with Newborough and Rangemore	1998-1999

Vicar from 1999-

Mavis Mariam ALLBUTT

d 1998, p 99

Ordained Local Minister, Holy Trinity Meir, MEIR	1998-

John Stuart FOULDS

b 1964, Lanc Univ. BA 87; Southampton Univ BTh 91; Chich Theol Coll 1988, d 91, p92

Curate St Lawrence, Eastcote, LON	1991-1995
Curate Wembley Park	1995-1999
Priest in charge, Holy Trinity church, MEIR	1999-

PRIESTS AND CURATES AT CAVERSWALL
and HOLY TRINITY CHURCH, MEIR 1889-2004

John Gordon ADDENBROOKE	Vicar of Caverswall	1889-1902
Herbert Metcalfe FOWLER	Vicar of Caverswall	1902-1915
Thomas Heywood MASTERS	*Curate in charge, MEIR	1889 1893
Hugh NANNEY-SMITH	*Curate at Caverswall	1892-1894
John Edward CAREY	*Curate in charge, MEIR	1894-1897
Charles ADDENBROOKE	*Curate in charge, MEIR	1898-1903
Edwin WHEELDON	*Curate in charge, MEIR	1904-1905
William HERALD	Curate of Caverswall,inc MEIR	1906-1907
Arthur A BROOKS	Curate in charge,MEIR.	1907-1912
Ralph CREED-MEREDITH	Curate in charge, Caverswall,	
	and Holy Trinity, MEIR.	1912-1914
Robert WALKER	Curate at Caverswall	
	inc Holy Trinity, MEIR	1914-1916
Theophilus CALEB	Vicar of Caverswall inc curate in charge	
	of Holy Trinity, MEIR.	1916-1919
	and Curate in charge, Holy Trinity, MEIR.	1919-1923
Harry Christie SHELDON	Curate in charge, Holy Trinity, MEIR.	1923-1926
Harry Christie SHELDON	FIRST parish priest Holy Trinity, MEIR	1926-1936
William R BELL	Parish priest, Holy Trinity, MEIR	1936-1946
David A STEVENS	Curate, Holy Trinity, MEIR	1939-1942
Herbert V WOODWARD	Parish Priest Holy Trinity, MEIR.	1946-1960
William A RICHARDS	Parish Priest Holy Trinity, MEIR.	1960-1964
Frederick W OSBORN	Parish priest Holy Trinity, MEIR.	1964-1976
Trevor J HARVEY	Parish Priest Holy Trinity, MEIR.	1977-1986
David CF TUDOR	Parish Priest Holy Trinity, MEIR	1987-1991
Gordon W WHITTY	Priest in charge Holy Trinity, MEIR	1992-1998
Mavis M ALLBUTT	OLM, Holy Trinity, MEIR	1999-
John S FOULDS	Priest in charge, Holy Trinity MEIR	1999-

(* Curate at Caverswall inc curate at Holy Trinity, MEIR

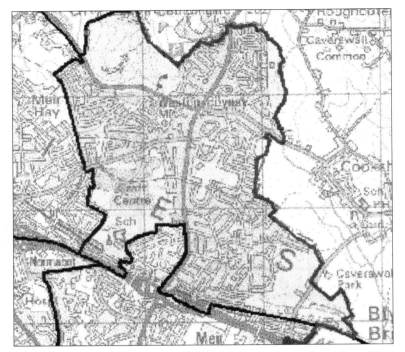

Weston and Meir North Ward, from the 2001 Census and reproduced from HMSO
under licence number CO2 W 0004158. The bold lines indicate the boundary.

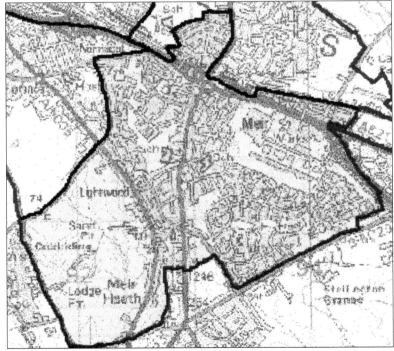

Meir Park & Sandon Ward, from the 2001 Census and reproduced from HMSO
under licence number CO2 W 000 4158. Note the odd-shaped piece at the top of
this map locates perfectly with a similar piece in the map above; between them
lies Uttoxeter Road.

APPENDIX 2

STATISTICAL APPRAISAL OF MEIR PARK AND SANDON, WESTON AND MEIR NORTH, STOKE ON TRENT AND ENGLAND AND WALES FROM CENSUS 2001

Depending a little on location, diet, exercise and good fortune, most people at the beginning of the 3rd millennium were living to an age seldom reached a century before. Social and industrial conditions, government public health legislation, improving health regimes, the discovery of key vaccines and drugs contributed enormously to overall human longevity.

Incredible as it may seem, boys and girls born in 1901 could only expect to live to 45 and 49 years of age respectively on average. A century later, that had been extended to 76 and 81 years, an increase of approximately 30 years, creating huge problems for social and medical services and pension fund managers everywhere.

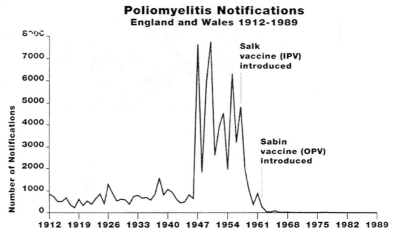

With old age comes extended nursing care such as that carried out at Longton Cottage Hospital, originally founded by the rector of Longton, Rev. Adam Clarke. The opening was by Rev Clarke's widow on 25th September 1890.

The medical staff at the hospital in 1912 were William Dawes MB, LL Burton FRCS, T.H. Richmond MB ChB and Alfred Parkes LRCP (Edin))

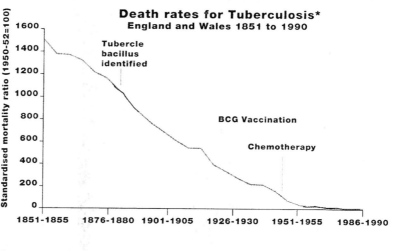

Nowadays Normacot House, a Day Care centre, is attached to the hospital attending to the needs of those, some from Meir, who have attained great old age.

The population of Meir in 2001 was 25,612 souls, a figure reached by combining the populations of the Meir Park and Sandon, and Weston and Meir North Wards (which made up almost all of Meir at the time of the 2001 census.) The tables provide a ready means of comparing these two Meir wards with Stoke-on-Trent, population 240,636 and on a wider

Longton Cottage Hospital.

stage, with the whole of England and Wales. Some of the figures from three sources are uncannily similar whilst others diverge wildly.

The emphasis placed on the potteries, coalmining and steelmaking, with their demise, has affected the population of Stoke on Trent greatly. This decrease has conversely occurred while the UK population between 1951 and 2001 increased by 17%, the USA by 80% and Australia by 133%. It will be a brave man who attempts to predict future needs in Meir, during the next 100 years.

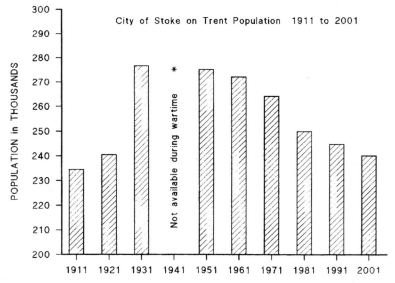

However with the Renew North Staffordshire campaign in March 2004 an attempt to address future needs has been started. In the next eighteen years it is hoped a £2.3 billion programme to upgrade the housing stock will demolish 14,500 old houses, construct 12,500 new houses and refurbish another 36,000. Meir is one of several areas in the City of Stoke-on-Trent in line for housing renewal, improved services and more green spaces. It deserves to succeed. However, whatever the future holds, one thing that will never change, like death and taxes, will be a queue of standing traffic at Broadway. Bet on it!

STATISTICS ABOUT MEIR NORTH AND WESTON

People Statistics

Resident Population and Age

The resident population of Weston and Meir North, as measured in the 2001 Census, was 12,281 of which 49 per cent were male and 51 per cent were female. The resident population of Stoke-on-Trent was 240,636, of which 49 per cent were male and 51 per cent were female.

Resident population (percentage)

	Weston and Meir North	Stoke-on-Trent	England and Wales
Under 16	19.9	19.9	20.2
16 to 19	5.0	5.4	4.9
20 to 29	11.0	13.5	12.6
30 to 59	40.3	40.1	41.5
60 to 74	15.9	13.4	13.3
75 and over	7.9	7.6	7.6
Average age	40.1	38.4	38.6

Source: 2001 Census, ONS

Marital Status

Resident population aged 16 and over (percentage)

	Weston and Meir North	Stoke-on-Trent	England and Wales
Single (never married)	25.2	30.2	30.1
Married or re-married	54.5	48.9	50.9
Separated	2.5	2.4	2.4
Divorced	8.1	8.8	8.2
Widowed	9.7	9.7	8.4

Ethnic Group

Resident population (percentage)

	Weston and Meir North	Stoke-on-Trent	England
White	99.0	94.8	90.9
of which White Irish	0.4	0.4	1.3
Mixed	0.4	0.9	1.3
Asian or Asian British	0.3	3.5	4.6
Indian	0.2	0.5	2.1
Pakistani	0.1	2.6	1.4
Bangladeshi	0.0	0.2	0.6
Other Asian	0.0	0.2	0.5
Black or Black British	0.1	0.4	2.1
Caribbean	0.1	0.3	1.1
African	0.0	0.1	1.0
Other Black	0.0	0.1	0.2
Chinese or Other Ethnic Group	0.2	0.4	0.9

Source: 2001 Census, ONS

Religion

Resident population (percentage)

	Weston and Meir North	Stoke-on-Trent	England and Wales
Christian	78.3	74.7	71.8
Buddhist	0.1	0.1	0.3
Hindu	0.0	0.2	1.1
Jewish	0.0	0.0	0.5
Muslim	0.2	3.2	3.0
Sikh	0.1	0.2	0.6
Other religions	0.2	0.2	0.3
No religion	13.6	13.4	14.8
Religion not stated	7.3	8.0	7.7

Source: 2001 Census, ONS

Health and provision of care

The 2001 Census asked people to describe their health, over the preceding 12 months as 'good', 'fairly good' or 'not good'.

Resident population (percentage)

	Weston and Meir North	Stoke-on-Trent	England and Wales
Good	61.3	63.0	68.6
Fairly good	24.9	24.1	22.2
Not good	13.8	12.8	9.2

Source: 2001 Census, ONS

It also asked questions about any limiting long-term illness, health problem or disability which limited peoples daily activities or the work they could do.

Resident population (percentage)

	Weston and Meir North	Stoke-on-Trent	England and Wales
With a limiting long-term illness	26.3	23.9	18.2

Source: 2001 Census, ONS

For the first time, the 2001 Census asked a question about any voluntary care provided to look after, or give any help or support to family members, friends, neighbours or others because of long term physical or mental ill-health or disability, or problems relating to old age.

Resident population (percentage)

	Weston and Meir North	Stoke-on-Trent	England and Wales
Provided unpaid care	12.8	11.2	10.0

Source: 2001 Census, ONS

There are two main benefits associated with health that are paid to people needing help with personal care. They are the 'Disability Living Allowance' and the 'Attendance Allowance'.

The Disability Living Allowance is a benefit paid to people under 65, who are disabled, and need help with personal care, and/or getting around. In August 2000, 15,945 people in Stoke-on-Trent received this benefit.

Source: Department for Work and Pensions, 2000

The Attendance Allowance is paid to people over the age of 65, who are so severely disabled, physically or mentally, that they need supervision or a great deal of help with personal care. In May 2000, 6,905 people in Stoke-on-Trent received this benefit.

Source: Department for Work and Pensions, 2000

Economic Activity

Resident population aged 16 to 74 (percentage)

	Weston and Meir North	Stoke-on-Trent	England and Wales
Employed	51.3	54.5	60.6
Unemployed	4.6	4.0	3.4
Economically active full-time students	1.8	2.7	2.6
Retired	17.5	14.0	13.6
Economically inactive students	3.2	5.1	4.7
Looking after home/family	6.4	6.3	6.5
Permanently sick or disabled	11.3	9.6	5.5
Other economically inactive	3.8	3.9	3.1

Source: 2001 Census, ONS

Within Weston and Meir North, 18 per cent of those unemployed were aged 50 and over, 8 per cent had never worked and 27 per cent were long term unemployed.

Source: 2001 Census, ONS

In August 2000, there were 3,930 Jobseeker Allowance claimants in Stoke-on-Trent of which 29 per cent had child dependants. The Job Seeker Allowance (JSA) is payable to people under pensionable age who are available for, and actively seeking, work of at least 40 hours a week. Figures produced here are those only for people claiming income-based JSA.

Source: Department for Work and Pensions, 2000

In August 2000, there were 21,270 Income Support claimants in Stoke-on-Trent, of which 3 per cent were aged under 20. Income support was introduced on April 11th 1988 and can be paid to a person who is aged 16 and over, is not working 16 hours or more a week, and has less money coming in than the law says they need to live on.

Source: Department for Work and Pensions, 2000

Students and Qualifications

Students and schoolchildren aged 16 to 74

	Weston and Meir North	Stoke-on-Trent	England and Wales
Total number of full-time students and schoolchildren aged 16 to 74	431	13,276	2,648,992
Percentage of total resident population	3.5	5.5	5.1
Total number aged 16 to 17	208	4,244	1,014,284
Total number aged 18 to 74	223	9,032	1,634,708

Note : Students and schoolchildren were counted at their term-time address.　　Source: 2001 Census, ONS

Resident population aged 16 to 74 (percentage)

	Weston and Meir North	Stoke-on-Trent	England and Wales
Had no qualifications	48.3	42.9	29.1
Qualified to degree level or higher	7.5	9.9	19.8

Source: 2001 Census, ONS

Housing and Households

In Weston and Meir North there were 5,161 households in 2001. 99 per cent of the resident population lived in households. The remainder of the population lived in communal establishments. The number of households in Stoke-on-Trent was 103,196.

	Weston and Meir North	Stoke-on-Trent	England and Wales
One person households	27.6	31.5	30.0
Pensioners living alone	14.1	15.4	14.4
Other All Pensioner households	12.0	8.6	9.4
Contained dependent children	29.1	29.5	29.5
Lone parent households with dependent children	8.0	7.7	6.5
Owner occupied	66.1	65.2	68.9
Rented from Council	24.4	19.5	13.2
Rented from Housing Association or Registered Social Landlord	1.5	5.0	6.0
Private rented or lived rent free	7.9	10.4	11.9
Without central heating	5.2	9.3	8.5
Without sole use of bath, shower or toilet	0.2	0.3	0.5
Have no car or van	31.5	34.6	26.8
Have 2 or more cars or vans	22.4	20.2	29.4
Average household size (number)	2.4	2.3	2.4
Average number of rooms per household	5.1	5.0	5.3

Source: 2001 Census, ONS

£'s and number of households (percentage)

	Stoke-on-Trent		England & Wales	
	Average price	Percentage of households living in this type of property	Average price	Percentage of households living in this type of property
Detached	89,699	13.2	178,806	22.8
Semi-detached	47,308	45.3	101,733	31.6
Terraced	27,790	32.2	89,499	26.0
Flat	34,366	9.2	120,185	19.2
All property types	46,685		119,436	

Sources: 2001 Census, ONS The Land Registry, 2001

Area Statistics

Levels Of Crime in Stoke-on-Trent

Notifiable offences recorded by the police. April 2000 to March 2001.

	Violence against the person	Sexual offences	Robbery	Burglary from a dwelling	Theft of a motor vehicle	Theft from a motor vehicle
Total number of offences rec'd, Stoke-on-Trent	5,591	292	341	3,176	1,857	3,367
Rate per 1,000 population, Stoke-on-Trent	22.3	1.2	1.4	12.7	7.4	13.4
Rate per 1,000 pop.Eng \Wales	11.4	0.7	1.8	7.6	6.4	11.9

Source: Home Office, 2001

STATISTICS ABOUT MEIR PARK AND SANDON

People Statistics

Resident Population and Age

The resident population of Meir Park and Sandon, as measured in the 2001 Census, was 13,331 of which 49 per cent were male and 51 per cent were female. The resident population of Stoke-on-Trent was 240,636, of which 49 per cent were male and 51 per cent were female.

Resident population (percentage)

	Meir Park and Sandon	Stoke-on-Trent	England and Wales
Under 16	23.0	19.9	20.2
16 to 19	5.3	5.4	4.9
20 to 29	10.9	13.5	12.6
30 to 59	44.4	40.1	41.5
60 to 74	11.5	13.4	13.3
75 and over	5.0	7.6	7.6
Average age	36.4	38.4	38.6

Source: 2001 Census, ONS

Marital Status

Resident population aged 16 and over (percentage)

	Meir Park and Sandon	Stoke-on-Trent	England and Wales
Single (never married)	25.5	30.2	30.1
Married or re-married	56.6	48.9	50.9
Separated	2.5	2.4	2.4
Divorced	8.4	8.8	8.2
Widowed	7.0	9.7	8.4

Ethnic Group

Resident population (percentage)

	Meir Park and Sandon	Stoke-on-Trent	England
White	97.7	94.8	90.9
of which White Irish	0.3	0.4	1.3
Mixed	0.6	0.9	1.3
Asian or Asian British	1.4	3.5	4.6
Indian	0.6	0.5	2.1
Pakistani	0.7	2.6	1.4
Bangladeshi	0.1	0.2	0.6
Other Asian	0.0	0.2	0.5
Black or Black British	0.1	0.4	2.1
Caribbean	0.1	0.3	1.1
African	0.1	0.1	1.0
Other Black	0.0	0.1	0.2
Chinese or Other Ethnic Group	0.2	0.4	0.9

Source: 2001 Census, ONS

Religion

Resident population (percentage)

	Meir Park and Sandon	Stoke-on-Trent	England and Wales
Christian	78.3	74.7	71.8
Buddhist	0.0	0.1	0.3
Hindu	0.3	0.2	1.1
Jewish	0.0	0.0	0.5
Muslim	1.0	3.2	3.0
Sikh	0.2	0.2	0.6
Other religions	0.2	0.2	0.3
No religion	13.2	13.4	14.8
Religion not stated	6.7	8.0	7.7

Source: 2001 Census, ONS

Health and provision of care

The 2001 Census asked people to describe their health, over the preceding 12 months as 'good', 'fairly good' or 'not good'.

Resident population (percentage)

	Meir Park and Sandon	Stoke-on-Trent	England and Wales
Good	67.6	63.0	68.6
Fairly good	21.8	24.1	22.2
Not good	10.7	12.8	9.2

Source: 2001 Census, ONS

It also asked questions about any limiting long-term illness, health problem or disability which limited peoples daily activities or the work they could do.

Resident population (percentage)

	Meir Park and Sandon	Stoke-on-Trent	England and Wales
With a limiting long-term illness	20.5	23.9	18.2

Source: 2001 Census, ONS

For the first time, the 2001 Census asked a question about any voluntary care provided to look after, or give any help or support to family members, friends, neighbours or others because of long term physical or mental ill-health or disability, or problems relating to old age.

Resident population (percentage)

	Meir Park and Sandon	Stoke-on-Trent	England and Wales
Provided unpaid care	11.3	11.2	10.0

Source: 2001 Census, ONS

There are two main benefits associated with health that are paid to people needing help with personal care. They are the 'Disability Living Allowance' and the 'Attendance Allowance'.

The Disability Living Allowance is a benefit paid to people under 65, who are disabled, and need help with personal care, and/or getting around. In August 2000, 15,945 people in Stoke-on-Trent received this benefit.

Source: Department for Work and Pensions, 2000

The Attendance Allowance is paid to people over the age of 65, who are so severely disabled, physically or mentally, that they need supervision or a great deal of help with personal care. In May 2000, 6,905 people in Stoke-on-Trent received this benefit.

Source: Department for Work and Pensions, 2000

Economic Activity

Resident population aged 16 to 74 (percentage)

	Meir Park and Sandon	Stoke-on-Trent	England and Wales
Employed	59.8	54.5	60.6
Unemployed	4.1	4.0	3.4
Economically active full-time students	2.4	2.7	2.6
Retired	12.0	14.0	13.6
Economically inactive students	3.3	5.1	4.7
Looking after home/family	5.8	6.3	6.5
Permanently sick or disabled	9.2	9.6	5.5
Other economically inactive	3.3	3.9	3.1

Source: 2001 Census, ONS

Within Meir Park and Sandon, 21 per cent of those unemployed were aged 50 and over, 8 per cent had never worked and 25 per cent were long term unemployed.

Source: 2001 Census, ONS

In August 2000, there were 3,930 Jobseeker Allowance claimants in Stoke-on-Trent of which 29 per cent had child dependants. The Job Seeker Allowance (JSA) is payable to people under pensionable age who are available for, and actively seeking, work of at least 40 hours a week. Figures produced here are those only for people claiming income-based JSA.

Source: Department for Work and Pensions, 2000

In August 2000, there were 21,270 Income Support claimants in Stoke-on-Trent, of which 3 per cent were aged under 20. Income support was introduced on April 11th 1988 and can be paid to a person who is aged 16 and over, is not working 16 hours or more a week, and has less money coming in than the law says they need to live on.

Source: Department for Work and Pensions, 2000

Students and Qualifications

Students and schoolchildren aged 16 to 74

	Meir Park and Sandon	Stoke-on-Trent	England and Wales
Total number of full-time students and schoolchildren aged 16 to 74	528	13,276	2,648,992
Percentage of total resident population	4.0	5.5	5.1
Total number aged 16 to 17	272	4,244	1,014,284
Total number aged 18 to 74	256	9,032	1,634,708

Note : Students and schoolchildren were counted at their term-time address.   Source: 2001 Census, ONS

Resident population aged 16 to 74 (percentage)

	Meir Park and Sandon	Stoke-on-Trent	England and Wales
Had no qualifications	35.7	42.9	29.1
Qualified to degree level or higher	13.1	9.9	19.8

Source: 2001 Census, ONS

Housing and Households

In Meir Park and Sandon there were 5,347 households in 2001. 100 per cent of the resident population lived in households. The remainder of the population lived in communal establishments. The number of households in Stoke-on-Trent was 103,196.

Number of households (percentage)

	Meir Park and Sandon	Stoke-on-Trent	England and Wales
One person households	24.3	31.5	30.0
Pensioners living alone	11.6	15.4	14.4
Other All Pensioner households	7.4	8.6	9.4
Contained dependent children	36.8	29.5	29.5
Lone parent households with dependent children	8.0	7.7	6.5
Owner occupied	70.8	65.2	68.9
Rented from Council	19.7	19.5	13.2
Rented from Housing Association or Registered Social Landlord	3.0	5.0	6.0
Private rented or lived rent free	6.6	10.4	11.9
Without central heating	3.8	9.3	8.5
Without sole use of bath, shower or toilet	0.2	0.3	0.5
Have no car or van	25.0	34.6	26.8
Have 2 or more cars or vans	32.7	20.2	29.4
Average household size (number)	2.5	2.3	2.4
Average number of rooms per household	5.4	5.0	5.3

Source: 2001 Census, ONS

£'s and number of households (percentage)

	Stoke-on-Trent		England & Wales	
	Average price	Percentage of households living in this type of property	Average price	Percentage of households living in this type of property
Detached	89,699	13.2	178,806	22.8
Semi-detached	47,308	45.3	101,733	31.6
Terraced	27,790	32.2	89,499	26.0
Flat	34,366	9.2	120,185	19.2
All property types	46,685		119,436	

Sources: 2001 Census, ONS The Land Registry, 2001

Area Statistics

Levels Of Crime in Stoke-on-Trent   Notifiable offences recorded by the police. April 2000 to March 2001.

	Violence against the person	Sexual offences	Robbery	Burglary from a dwelling	Theft of a motor vehicle	Theft from a motor vehicle
Total number of offences recorded, Stoke-on-Trent	5,591	292	341	3,176	1,857	3,367
Rate per 1,000 population, Stoke-on-Trent	22.3	1.2	1.4	12.7	7.4	13.4
Rate per 1,000 population, England and Wales	11.4	0.7	1.8	7.6	6.4	11.9

Source: Home Office, 2001

APPENDIX 3
THE DUKES OF SUTHERLAND and RECENT MEIR HISTORY

From the middle of the 16th century much of the land in and around Meir has been part of the Sutherland estate. Henry VIII (1509-1547), responsible for the dissolution of the monasteries, granted land belonging to Trentham Priory at Cocknage and Lightwood to the Duke of Sutherland. Sold to James Leveson, whose lineage can be traced to William I, a forbear of the Sutherland family, they became an inseparable part of the history of Meir Normacot and Longton.

The first George Granville Leveson Gower (1758-1833), an infamous reformer, succeeded his father as Marquess of Stafford in 1803. He married Elizabeth, Countess of Sutherland in 1785. Responsible for the notorious Highland Clearances around 1810, with James Lock his land agent, he oversaw great improvements to the Sutherland Estates. Many dispossessed crofters emigrated, some to the New World, some changing their surnames to 'Sutherland'. Locally a stone statue of the Duke gazes impassively down on motorists driving along the A34 from the Trentham Hills, but another in Scotland still evokes animosity today whenever his name enters the conversation.

George Granville Leveson Gower, the second Duke (1786-1861), continued improvements to the estates with his son George, and set out Dresden, a suburb in Stoke on Trent in the early 1860s, tugging the consciences of employers into giving better social conditions for their workers.

The third Duke of Sutherland, George Granville Leveson Gower (1828-1892), was responsible for laying out the grid pattern of housing and roads in Normacot. A benevolent man, he kept rents for his houses low and modest but any wayward and irresponsible behaviour by lessees forfeited their tenancy. He also gave land for establishing Queen's Park, Longton Park and Longton Cottage Hospital.

The fourth Duke, born 1851, was Liberal MP for Sutherland 1874-86, and married Millicent Fanny St Clair Erskine in 1884, by whom he had 4 children, Victoria, George Granville, Alistair St Clair, and Rosemary Millicent. A compassionate man he donated a generous supply of provisions to poor people throughout the bad winters around 1895:

The beautiful Millicent, Duchess of Sutherland - a Princess Diana like figure.

From *A Meir Half Century*:

At the beginning of 1895, the plight of many in the area had altered little and it is comforting to note that charity was about in broad measure.

'During the severe weather of the past week or two, 30 tons of coal have been distributed to 43 poor families and widows residing at Blythe Bridge and Forsbrook'.

'The continuance of the severe frost through another week has considerably added to the distress amongst the poor and the difficulty of the situation is being added to by the

scarcity of water on the factories through the freezing of the water pipes. Beef bread and coal has been distributed through the generosity of the Duke of Sutherland.'

And in early March, *'645 lbs of beef, 232 loaves of bread and 6 tons of coal were given away'*. This with the previous two distributions takes up the total amount of relief by the Duke to 2410 lbs of beef, 960 loaves and 51 tons of coal.'

Many hung on best as they could. By March 23, 1895 the Duke's 'inventory of kindness' was astronomic: *'The relief given by the Duke of Sutherland now amounts to 6570 lbs of beef, 2543 loaves and 115 tons of coal.'*

On his death at Dunrobin Castle on June 27, 1913, the demand on his estate from death duties meant a large part of his land and effects needed to be auctioned. The sale would have occurred shortly after his death but for the intervention of the Great War. It took place during the autumn of 1919 at the King's Hall in Stoke on Trent.

Everything about the auction was on a grand scale from enormous properties, gigantic plots of land, huge farms and much more. Even the expensive sale catalogues were large bound volumes, the complete opposite to 'pocket sized' and with coloured map.

For those who stopped to think, the sale signified far more than the disposal of land, a way of life was passing, its opulence and grandeur gone forever. The fourth Duke, in contrast to the first, was a great patron and beneficiary of the local population. Even after death, the Duke's trustees genuinely tried to accommodate the wishes of his former sitting tenants.

The pages and maps reproduced below are just an assortment from the immense range appearing in the sale catalogue. In amongst the farms and land appeared accommodation land cottages and houses, which fetched between £80 and £150, providing an opportunity for tenants to become owners relatively cheaply. Others though demanded a small personal fortune. A 52 acre spread at Cocknage, 'Windy Arbour Farm' cost Mr J.R. James, who was paying £80.16s. 8d annually as tenant, £2,400; a 3 acre plot with a frontage on Uttoxeter and Meir Roads at Normacot cost Mr J.S. Wild, living from 1918 onwards at The Beeches in Uttoxeter Road, £1 450; while John Wardle paid £750 for a sandpit in Star and Garter Road, Normacot extending to 3 and a half acres plus a plot of almost 7 acres close by.

As Meir was then an agricultural community, Meir Farm, Lot 467, attracted a great amount of interest with its 92 acres of land, a dwelling house, farm buildings and two cottages. The bidding, beginning at £4,000 raced to £ 5,300, the final bid from Mr Isaac Matthews from Milton, a prominent agriculturalist.

Meir House, one of the Meir's grand houses, had bidders drooling. Situated opposite to Holy Trinity Church it was once the residence of Charles Harvey (1779-1860), a banker and pottery manufacturer in Stafford Street, Longton. He founded Harvey's Bank in 1827 and in 1851 lived at 2 Longton Hall Lodge. His son William Kenright Harvey succeeded him following his death in 1860 but in 1866, the bank failed, making many small family businesses insolvent. William Harvey hot footed it to the United States.

Until his death in 1892, Meir House was the home of Mr William Webberley, a Justice of the Peace, who *'also took an active part in the erection of the Meir church, contributing liberally to the funds.'* He instituted the Webberley Dole, a fund set up to help out those *'unfortunates'* in the local community long before the Welfare State came into being.

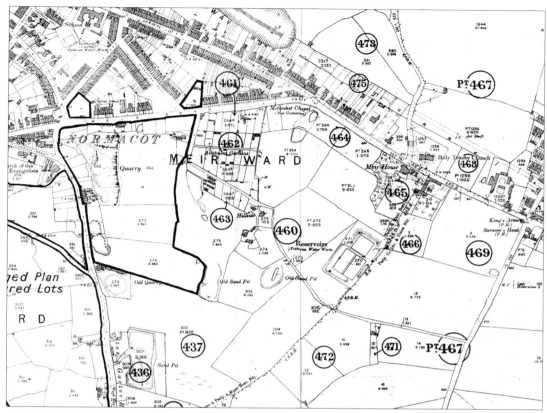

A section of the map showing numbered lots which corresponded to the sale catalogue of the Sutherland Estate in 1919.

With extensive grounds, shrubberies and more besides, Meir House in 1919 occupied an unenviable position overlooking the main Uttoxeter Road from behind a huge 6 feet high stone block wall. It was from here, the procession to consecrate Holy Trinity church began almost twenty years earlier.

The description of the whole house from an auction document in 1919 at the break up of the Duke of Sutherland's estate.

It must be said in contrast to the nefarious first Duke, the fourth was a great patron and beneficiary of the local population. Land for the building of Holy Trinity Church was one amongst dozens of gifts.

Even today after nearly a hundred years, many of the houses and buildings in Meir in 2004 can still trace an association with the former Sutherland estate, dozens of legal documents lying in dusty old vaults annotating it in deeds and *'rights of way'*. In Normacot and Dresden too, name connections with the Sutherland estate abound; the Dunrobin Hotel, St Clair Street and Sutherland Road in Longton are all examples.

But perhaps locally, one building, erected on a *'generous parcel of land'* in Longton, the Sutherland Institute, Longton Library, is the most high profile reminder of the Sutherland dynasty. Over 100 years old and one of the few redeeming architectural gems on the featureless new A50, it remains a constant reminder of the Sutherland family.

LOT 467.

The compact and very desirable

FARM

known as

" THE MEIR FARM,"

situate at the Meir, immediately on the outskirts of Longton and having special attractions or occupation by a Dairyman or Milk Seller.   The Farm possesses

Excellent Building Frontages,

situate on that part thereof fronting to the Leek and Stone Roads.

The Premises consist of

Dwelling House, Farm Buildings, Two Cottages, and 92 Acres of Land.

THE FARM HOUSE—Brick-built and Tiled—is situate on the Uttoxeter Road.   It contains :
On the Ground Floor : Entrance Lobby, Two Sitting Rooms, Kitchen, Scullery, Pantry, Dairy.

On the First Floor : Landing, Three Bedrooms, Box Room.

On the Second Floor : Large Attic Bedroom.

E.C.

Good Garden.

The Potteries Water is laid on to the Premises.

THE FARM BUILDINGS are of an extensive and substantial type ; they contain Cow House with tying for 16, Cow House with tying for 16 and having feeding passages : Milk House and Mixing House with Granary over, Waggon Horse Stable with standing for 4, Hackney Stable with standing for 2, Two Loose Boxes. Trap House, Blacksmith's Shop.

Fold Yard with feeding and lying Sheds, Potato House, Two Poultry Houses and Chaff House, the whole with Threshing Floor over, Four Bay Implement Shed, Two Pig Sties and Three Duck Pens.

The land belonging to the Farm is all of good class, and in excellent state of cultivation.

The Arable land is of open texture, and well suited for the growth of either corn or roots.

The Pasture land is sound, and the herbage is abundant and of good quality.

No. 1 Cottage in the occupation of Mr. Samuel Wright, contains Living Room, Scullery, Pantry, Two Bedrooms.

E.C.

No. 2 Cottage in the occupation of Mr. James Lovatt, contains Sitting Room, Kitchen, Pantry Store Closet, Landing and Three Bedrooms.

E.C.

The Potteries Water is laid on to both of the Cottages.

Off Meir Road, Normacot.

LOT 464.

Notice to quit has been given, which will expire with 25th March 1920.

THE TIMBER on the land has been measured up and valued at controlled prices at £14.

SCHEDULE.

Borough of Stoke-on-Trent.						AREA.	AREA.
NO. ON PLAN.	DESCRIPTION.					ACRES.	A. R. P.
Pt. 264	Pasture	..	..	..	..	..	
Pt. 265	,.	..	..	..	..	3.002	3 0 0

Meir House, Normacot.

LOT 465.

The extensive and conveniently arranged

PRIVATE RESIDENCE

known as

" MEIR HOUSE,"

together with

Pleasure Grounds, Shrubberies, Kitchen Garden, Out-Offices, Out-Buildings, and Croft of Pasture Land connected therewith,

the whole directly overlooking and possessing frontage throughout the whole of its Northerly Boundary to the Uttoxeter Road.

THE HOUSE—Brick-built and Slated—is situate in the centre of a nicely laid out pleasure ground. It is approached from the Uttoxeter Road by carriage entrance.

The principal rooms have a Southerly aspect and possess a very pleasant outlook over the adjacent area of open country.

THE HOUSE contains on the Ground Floor : Entrance Hall, Drawing Room, Dining Room, Breakfast Room, Writing Room, Kitchen, Scullery, Larder, Store Room, Wash House and Store Closet.

On the Chamber Floor : Landing, Corridor, Six Bedrooms, Dressing Room, Bath Room, W.C., Two Box Rooms, Housemaid's Closet.

Front and Back Staircases.

Good Cellar.

Coal House and W.C.

Greenhouse, Potting Shed and Stoke Hole.

THE OUTBUILDINGS consist of Cow House with tying for 14 and having feeding passage, Carriage Horse Stable with standing for two, Two Loose Boxes, Saddle Room, Coach House, all with Lofting over, Stable with standing for three, and Two Loose Boxes all with Lofting over. Hay Bay, 2-Bay Cart Shed, Workshop and Range of three Pig Sties.

Meir Farm as seen in a catalogue of the sale of the Sutherland Estate in 1919.

Hillside Cottage as pictured in the sale catalogue of the Sutherland Estate.